LEARNING OUTSIDE THE LINE

Innovative Homeschool Solutions

A Guide to Homeschooling
By Melanie Summers BA, Elem. Ed.; MA, C&I

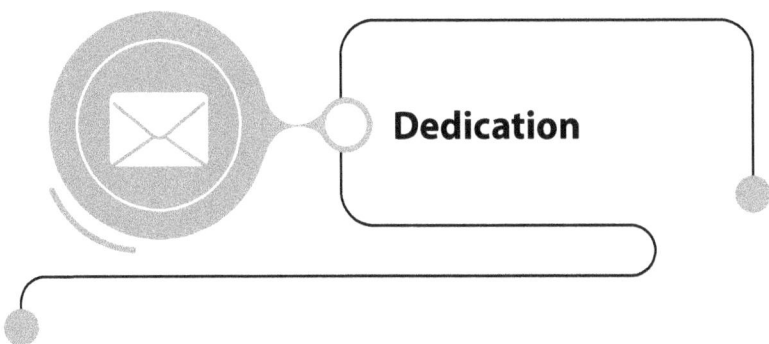

Dedication

There are many people to whom I am dedicating this book.

First, I want to recognize all the teachers who graced my life from elementary school through college and graduate school. You taught me reading, writing, and arithmetic and challenged me to be a thinker. Special thanks go to Miss Dietrich, my second-grade teacher; Mrs. Mary Smith–my junior high school Reading teacher, who later became my mentor; and Miss Phyliss Lamm, my high school English teacher. Most of these people have passed on; I honor them as they helped mold me into who I am today.

Next, I dedicate this book to every student who walked through my door. I may have taught you how to read, write, and calculate math, but you helped me to grow into a better teacher year by year. You challenged me to reach beyond a textbook to find ways to stimulate your minds and your hearts. You helped me to grow, and I am most grateful.

I must also acknowledge all parents and guardians who trusted me to educate their children. You trusted me to keep your precious gifts safe and to give them love and compassion.

My husband, Rick, who puts up with my late-night writing binges, gives me different perspectives on how, what, and why I do what I do and lets me fly without complaint. He brags about leftovers on days when I don't have time to cook something new, doesn't mind my endless back-to-back Zoom calls, and always kisses me goodnight when he goes to bed, but I'm still typing away on yet another project.

Finally, I dedicate this book to all my mentors who have lifted me up, encouraged me, listened to me, responded in ways to help me improve, and figuratively slapped my fingers on occasion. You have all inspired me and influenced my life's work. Thank you, Jay Noland, Jo Dee Baer, Scott Harris, Dame Doria Cordova, Rex Sikes, Manny Lopez, and Les Brown. I listen to you still.

Without the love and support from all of you, I would not have written this book. You have my humble gratitude.

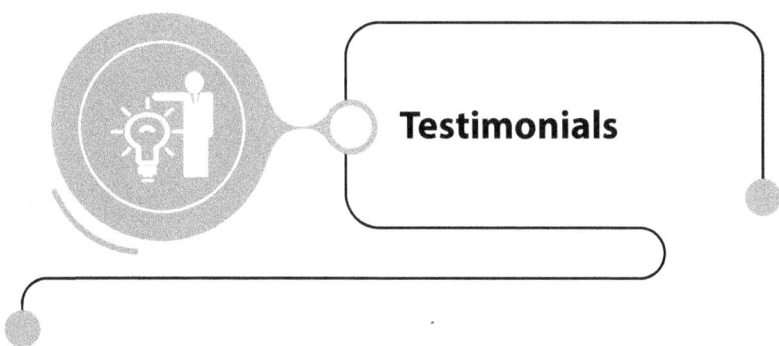

Testimonials

I am in awe of Melanie Summer's dedication to homeschooling and her relentless pursuit of excellence in education. Melanie shares a treasure trove of wisdom, practical advice, and innovative approaches to homeschooling through her book, *Learning Outside the Line*. As an author, Melanie effortlessly weaves personal experiences, expert research, and heartfelt encouragement, making her book an indispensable guide for homeschooling families. Prepare to be inspired and motivated by Melanie's remarkable journey and unwavering commitment to nurturing young minds.

—**Robert Mehler**,
Senior Vice President, MYB Publishing

Melanie Summers lays it all on the line in her upcoming book, *Learning Outside the Line*. I have known Melanie since 4th grade, and she definitely walks the talk in this exceptional treatise on homeschooling and personalized education. She brings her extensive teaching experience, demanding excellence in a thoughtful, forthright, and loving approach. She recognizes the innate potential in all whose lives she has touched. Melanie Summers has taken experiences that some may call setbacks and used them as a refining fire, giving her the maturity and motivation to assist all parents and guardians in creating a no-nonsense, pragmatic, caring, personalized learning approach. *Learning Outside the Line* won't leave you on the sidelines; the game becomes much clearer using it as your playbook. Ensure your child is the winner they were born to be.

—**Greg Goodfellow**, M.A. Reading;
Retired Reading Specialist, Tyler County Schools, WV.

In *Learning Outside the Line*, Melanie Summers doesn't just lift the veil on homeschooling; she shatters every preconception. I have always been awe-struck by Melanie's unwavering commitment to education. As an expert in subconscious thought, I can tell you that Melanie's approach will radically alter your child's educational paradigm. She doesn't merely teach; she ignites a passion for learning that transforms homes into vibrant centers of intellectual and emotional growth.

—**Adam Mendoza**, Educator

Throughout her illustrious forty-two-year career in education, Melanie Summers has exemplified what it means to be a dedicated and passionate educator. Her book, *Learning Outside the Line*, is a testament to her depth of knowledge and commitment to equipping homeschooling families with practical and effective tools. Melanie's unwavering work ethic, her stead-fastness in honoring her word, and the impeccable character she brings to every endeavor are truly inspiring. As a homeschool coach and consultant, she continues illuminating paths for countless families, guiding them with expertise and compassion. I wholeheartedly endorse Melanie Summers as a beacon of excellence in the world of education.

—**Dan Gilman**, TV/ Radio Producer/ Designer Director

When you read this book, you'll feel like you've embarked on a wonderful journey with a trusted guide who has traversed the landscape of education for over four decades. Melanie intertwines compelling anecdotes, groundbreaking theories, and pragmatic solutions, creating a tapestry of wisdom that will decorate the walls of your family's educational setting for years to come. Her insights empower you to break free from conventional methodologies and embrace a learning environment as unique as your child's.

—**Dr. Peggy Woods**, CEO of Write Now Publishing Co.

Melanie Summers is a consummate professional in all she's done in her educational career and an exceptional human being to her core. Melanie pours herself into whatever she endeavors to do, takes instruction immediately, and executes with the perfect combination of heart, mind, and soul. Her book has exactly that same kind of impactful outpouring. It will do wonders for those privileged to read it and implement its educational wisdom for the next generation.

—**Dr. Jo Dee Baer**, PhD.,
Certified Health Coach and Holistic Nutritionist

Melanie Summers has an unparalleled passion for education and a genuine commitment to empowering young minds through homeschooling. She brings a wealth of experience and knowledge to the table, making her book a must-read for anyone considering or already on the homeschooling journey. Melanie's expertise shines through, and her ability to inspire and guide parents and students alike is truly commendable. Get ready to embark on a transformative educational adventure with her book, *Learning Outside the Line*. Throughout this book, Melanie shares a treasure trove of wisdom, practical advice, and innovative approaches to homeschooling. As an author, Melanie uses personal experiences, expert research, and heartfelt encouragement to make her book an indispensable guide for homeschooling families; her genuine desire to see every child succeed is truly inspiring.

—**Scott Harri**s, President, MYB Publishing

Melanie is an exceptional teacher whose passion for education is contagious. Melanie goes the extra mile as she tailors her lessons to students with educational needs. Her innovative teaching methods keep students engaged and wanting more. She is a role model for all and a true advocate for education. I fully endorse Melanie's book, *Learning Outside the Line*.

—**Capt. Joie Bier**, USA, Retired

Melanie is an exceptional, intuitive educator. I strongly urge you to get her book and see what she has to say. Truly eye-opening.

—**Dave Morgan**, MA Educator

Testimonials of Melanie as a teacher:

As a parent of a homeschooled boy, I have been fortunate enough to witness Mrs. Summers' remarkable impact on my child's education; I am truly impressed by her dedication and teaching prowess. Over the past two years, her nurturing guidance has resulted in my son's accelerated learning journey. Through her patient and engaging approach, my son learned to read within an astonishingly short period and developed a genuine affinity for mathematics. Mrs. Summers' ability to tailor her teaching to my son's learning style has fostered an environment where he thrives. Her commitment to his growth, both academically and personally, is evident in every interaction. I am deeply grateful for the positive influence she continues to be in my child's life.

—**Lina Noland**, Co-Founder, MYB Publishing

Our homeschooling journey would not have been the same without Melanie. She has been a true partner in our children's education, offering unwavering support, insightful advice, and a wealth of educational resources. Melanie's dedication to our children's growth and development has been evident in the personalized learning experiences she has crafted for them. She has been a teacher, mentor, and friend, and we are so grateful to have her on this incredible journey with us.

—**Amber House**, Parent

Melanie Summers is an incredible educator, motivator, writer, and friend. She inspires people of all ages to learn and develop their skills in their own ways. She finds ways to help even the most struggling students become successful. Keeping learning fun and engaging while maintaining an incredibly structured environment is one of her many strengths. She continues to inspire me and others to this day.

—**Symantha Mendoza**, Site Director,
Learning Foundation of Performing Arts

Our experience with Melanie led to my daughter's education and nursing career success. Melanie, never quits on your child. I recommend her with no reservations.

—**Rebecca Summers**, Parent

As a former colleague of Melanie's, I witnessed firsthand her student's growth and enthusiasm for learning. Her methods were engaging and fun. She always put the students first. I had a lot of fun working with her. It only makes sense that she continues spreading her wisdom by teaching homeschooling to the world.

—**Adam Mendoza**, Educator

Melanie has been in my life for over 25 years, beginning when she was my 3rd-grade teacher. That year was my most memorable year of learning. I recall her giving all my classmates (and me) individual education, which was positive and challenging in the best ways. I was learning math several grades ahead because of her teaching style, and I still remember how she made me feel—excited to learn. Her dedication to children and teaching is like none other. I highly recommend Melanie as a mentor, teacher, and friend.

—**Meredith Carroll**, RN

I have had the pleasure of collaborating with Mrs. Summers as a colleague and friend for several years. We have worked on numerous education-related projects, and I am continuously impressed by her expertise in education. She is an excellent educator and strives to improve and share her knowledge with her colleagues. Mrs. Summers is a committed educator who strives for perfection. As a new teacher, I was blessed to have her as a mentor. I can say that I am a better educator and person by knowing her.

—**Rosemary Crawford**, 5th and 6th grade retired educator.

I have known Melanie Summers for several years. I worked with her at Short Line School, and she was an inspiration to her students and other teachers. She started many new programs and supported those programs already in existence. She was a hard worker and a great team leader. If you want someone who works hard, supports co-workers, inspires those around her, and is very creative, Melanie Summers is someone you want on your side

—**Connie Dakan**, Educator

I have known Melanie Summers for 30 years and have nothing but positive things to say. I first became acquainted with Melanie when I was placed in her classroom as a parent volunteer. At that time, she was teaching 8th grade. I wasn't sure what to expect when I entered her classroom that day, and I guess she picked up on my apprehension because she immediately made me feel like I had been there for years. When I think back to that day, it puts a smile on my face because little did I know then that the days ahead were going to be a turning point for me. Melanie and I became the best of friends. I couldn't wait for my next day (and the many days that followed). As her parent volunteer, I witnessed firsthand her compassion for teaching her students. She always wanted each of her students to excel beyond their imaginations, and she did her utmost to ensure that happened. I was so glad and very fortunate that each of my children had her as a teacher. Any student should be proud to have her as a teacher. Any parent should proudly say, "Melanie Summers is my child's teacher."

—**Cindy Glasscock**, Admin. Director Folsom Fire Department

Melanie Summers' *Learning Outside the Line* is a game-changer. Drawing from decades of teaching experience, she transcends traditional boundaries, offering an innovative roadmap for homeschooling success. Her passionate approach to child-centered learning is both inspiring and practical. As an expert in subconscious thought, I believe this book can shift your perspective and empower you as a parent-educator. Melanie isn't just telling a story. She's providing a transformative curriculum for life.

—**Jay Noland**, MYB Publishing, CEO

Melanie and I got to know each other by co-authoring the book *Ignite Your Wisdom*. After reading Melanie's story of her formative years in the Wisdom book, it became apparent that she survived many childhood challenges, which developed the foundation for becoming a very empathetic human being, teacher, principal, and mentor to anyone she meets. Melanie has a huge, compassionate heart. She has gone above and beyond as an educator and principal to act and lead in the children's best interests under her care and guidance through a long, dedicated career. Her vision and enthusiasm for improving the lives of children, parents, and coaching clients are communicated through her book and unique platform, *Learning Outside the Line*. I highly recommend Melanie to parents homeschooling their children and wellness coaching clients committed to transforming their health.

—**Loree J. Kim**, Ph.D., Founder, Flex IP Counsel, PLLC

Contents

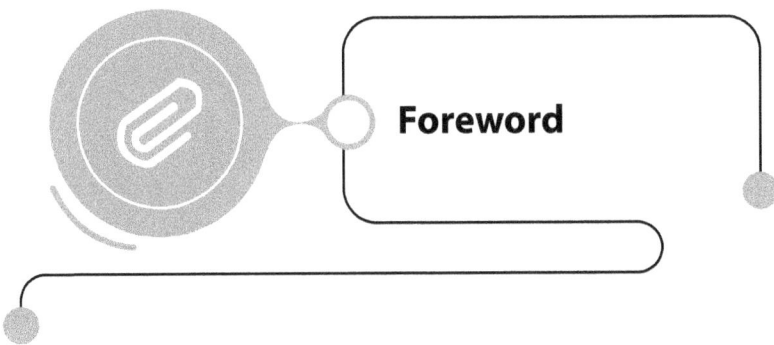

Foreword

We are tasked to love, protect, teach, and guide our children. We love on them as infants and hold their soft, puffy hands when we teach them to walk, blow, and catch kisses while admiring their smiling faces, dancing, and singing the Alphabet Song to them. Yet when they are of school age, we casually visit child's classroom on 'Meet the Teacher' day, trace our fingers over their names on their new desks in their classroom, hope for the best, and cry when we leave them in the care of a well-meaning teacher and 28 little strangers that we pray are nice to our precious child.

Over the year, we are amazed at their mental development, cheer at their drawings of objects, and jump for joy when they can legibly write their names. Yet, we cringe when they learn choice words, aggressive behaviors, and lessons that do not match the morals of our households. We then spend years, tears, and frustrations undoing social damage, re-teaching a lesson my child's particular learning style may not have captured, and hoping the bullies leave our child alone. It is like sending our children out to combat on a daily basis. It can be scary, and thankfully, we now have options to help protect and teach our children in a safe and controlled environment that will propel them toward success.

Learning Outside the Line; Innovative Homeschool Solutions, by Melanie Summers, is a wonderful resource designed to answer every question and concern from a caring, proactive, and responsible parent looking to educate their child or children in a positive space and academically rich method and curriculum.

This powerful book will give you the confidence, insight, and motivation to do something bold and different for your child to guarantee their confidence, happiness, and daily accomplishments. As parents, if our children are thriving, joyous, and brilliant, all is well in this life.

As the daughter of Les Brown, a world-renowned motivational speaker, youth minister, and author of a few bestselling children's books, it grieves me when I mentor and coach youth who are dealing with life-long scars from school, either from their peers or their teachers. And let me repeat, school, ideally, should be one of the safest and most sacred places our children should be able to trust, but it has let them down.

Author Melanie Summers is a trusted expert, not because of her many degrees and qualifications in this field but because she is a passionate mother who wants the best for her children, grandchildren, and peers. She is changing and disrupting the educational system with love, kindness, and compassion for this and many generations to come.

Serena Brown Travis
Author/Speaker/Trainer/Minister
www.serenabrowntravis.com

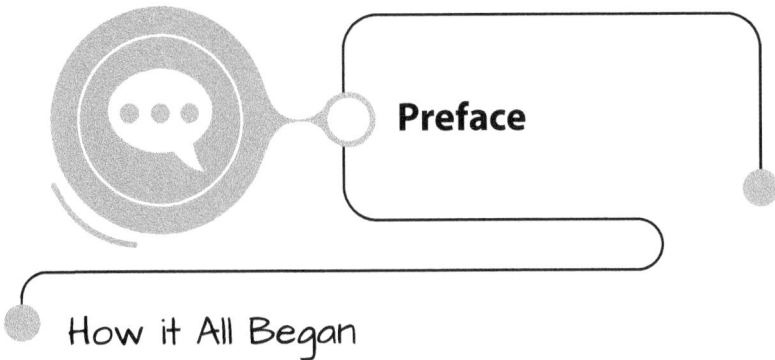

Preface

How it All Began

Welcome to an innovative book about how to educate your child at home. The most important years of learning are between birth and seven years old. Even Aristotle said way back when, "Give me a child until he is seven, and I will show you the man." In those formative years, your child is molded by what surrounds them, and the most influential people in their lives are their parents. I will go as far as to say education begins while your child is in the womb because there is research that points to the developing fetus becoming familiar with the sound of their mother's voice. Other research points to a fetus having developed the basic structures for hearing, taste, touch, and smell by the end of the first trimester. That's pretty thought-provoking!

Education is not only learning that two plus two equals four, but it's learning how to navigate through life. In *Learning Outside the Line,* I show you not just the mechanics of homeschooling, but I take you on a journey with your child so that every day is an *adventure.* Think of my book as this: every second, of every day, is a chance to learn something new.

I wrote this book, *Learning Outside the Line,* to address the most common questions parents have asked me regarding homeschooling principles. I titled it *Learning Outside the Line* because I believe that education should never be static—that every child responds to engaging activities and lessons that challenge their minds to reach for *more.* My approach to homeschooling is not just motivating children to think outside the box, but inspiring parents to think creatively in their activities and instruction, also—encouraging exploration in their own minds so they can communicate with their child in new areas of interests that will improve their cognitive intelligence, while taking active responsibility in engaging them, so their child can become all that they are meant to be.

Learning Outside the Line allows students the freedom to become thinkers and doers and encourages their *parents* to be more for them. This book helps parents find and source materials, books, and websites—everything they will need to be successful teachers. You see, homeschooling is not just a way to educate children but a pathway to discovery, allowing both the student and the parent to think about education from a new perspective.

Parents will find that inner teacher inside of them and discover they have what they need to be their child's teacher. After all, *who helped their child to become interested in a toy so they learned to crawl toward it? Who taught their child how to hold a spoon in order to eat their favorite food? And, who held their child's hands as they learned to take their first step? Do you remember the pleasure and joy in those 'first' childhood adventures and the smile on your child's face?* You can continue to experience those feelings as your child matures!

I know you will find joy and wonder as you assist your child in *Learning Outside the Line,* because you, too, will be learning alongside them! Education includes activity, conversation, thought, and the thrill of discovering the unknown. Your child will experience curiosity in the world around them, leading down paths that open doors to their future. They will think for themselves, question the *norm*, and realize they can not only *Learn Outside the Line* but *Live Outside the Line* also. There is where greatness lives—a place where inventions are constructed, self-confidence is fostered, and dreams are imagined and materialized.

This book is intended to assist as many parents as possible in the 'ins and outs' of how to make homeschooling joyous and meaningful to everyone in the family, and at the end of the day, to not only find contentment and purpose but become aware of the laws and education regulations that most people never think about.

Most importantly, you will watch your children flourish in ways that you would miss if you did *not* homeschool them. You will see them become more confident in who they are as they gain skills in communicating in the written word, speaking their truth, and developing their own unique character and interests. From my own personal experience, there is no greater joy than watching children 'becoming' who they are meant to be.

This book *will* assist you in all the ways you need, allowing your child to grow and experience life on a level that permits them to explore the world in ways that would not be possible in any other fashion than a homeschool setting. It is my pledge to support you in what to expect on your journey as you teach your children from home. Homeschooling is a wonderful opportunity for both you and your child to grow productively together, and this book provides the information and support you need to make it happy, enjoyable, and fun for everyone.

Introduction

A Supportive Guide to Homeschooling

Not long ago, I was having lunch with a friend who was a teacher in the public school system. While catching up on what each other was doing, I mentioned that I was writing a book about innovative teaching solutions and concepts designed to support unique learning styles in students who were being homeschooled. Her eyes widened, and she said, "Melanie! I want your book!" It immediately occurred to me that I had something that not just parents would want, but that teachers and school districts could use to train their faculties. Epiphany! I was creating a valuable resource to continue what I love most—teaching and serving children while helping the most important people in a student's life: other teachers, educators, and their parents.

What was needed became abundantly clear: a book with usable tools and action steps to help everyone involved in a child's homeschooling experience. As I thought about what was most important to include in such a book, I began writing about what factors went into becoming a successful teacher: *What did I do that no one else did? What practical things did I insist my students do that helped them learn faster and retain information? What did I allow my students to do that other teachers did not? What was my personal philosophy? How did I manage behavior issues? How did I keep students engaged?*

All of those questions led me to realize that many parents were unaware of the complexities and nuances of homeschooling, and if I could ascertain the steps I took during my forty-two-year-long career, I could help them.

Yet, pondering those questions opened a new set of questions that led to the unasked questions that a parent will not even know to ask but are essential if they intend to homeschool their child, especially throughout high school! A parent might not know how to ensure their child has a high school transcript. *What are the requirements of their state or country to homeschool their child? How do they build a portfolio to prove their child has the skills and knowledge to enter college? How do they ensure their child gets quality materials and time to learn?* Quickly, it became apparent if a parent wanted to begin homeschooling, I needed to help them answer all these questions and more.

That inspired not just any book about childhood education but a book that addressed the issues facing both students and parents in today's current landscape. That meant veering *'outside' the lines* of convention and writing something that would both serve and support the needs of homeschooling families.

I believe you are reading this book because you are not looking for just any teacher for your children but, because *you* are ready to be your child's teacher. You see the value in providing personalized teaching and the benefits of learning from home. You also recognize the needs and demands that come with that responsibility, and you want to do your best. There might be occasions when you will need someone like me to tutor or explain some math concepts you have forgotten, or grammar rules to help your child's writing processes. Additionally, you likely want solid action steps that can be implemented right now to make your child's journey easier—that you can teach. Ideally, you are looking for tools that will support you in teaching your child *outside the lines* of convention, and they are all right here, in this book.

The suggestions throughout these pages will save you time and effort, eliminate the headaches, and undoubtedly accelerate your children's learning and life endeavors. It is full of what you need to know to embark on a homeschooling model that will enhance your child's homeschooling experience. It gives you strategies and tips on what's best to do and what to avoid. It also outlines the many learning styles and differences children have in the way they take in information. It is packed full of game-changing suggestions that will make teaching your child an enjoyable endeavor.

As your homeschooling coach, I want to help you set up a system that will be successful, all while supporting you through the educational process. With knowledge from me and determination from you, your child will have the best education that cannot be found anywhere else but in your home.

The great news is that everything you need to love your homeschooling experience is in the coming pages. I encourage you to be willing to try new things, implement the suggestions, and go outside the line of customary thinking. Expand your imagination and foster your innovation skills. This is going to be both fun and informative at the same time. Let each chapter guide you in a new way and since we are all students and continue to learn, educate yourself in all the ways that you can be a better leader, teacher, and educator in your child's life. This will be a wonderful time for you, your child, and your entire family.

Let's get started.

How this Book Will Inspire Learning

Making the Leap to Homeschooling

I realize that deciding to homeschool your children is a big decision for everyone in your family—it requires a giant leap of faith and a willingness to accept your life will become restructured to fit your child's needs. If your child must learn to navigate schooling at home, so must you. However, I am confident you already *have* the skills you need to take on this challenge. Sure, it may be a bit scary the first day you begin the journey of educating your child, and it may be more daunting if you have more than one child to work with, *but you don't have to go it alone!* You have me. You will learn about various organizations, different places to find materials, and innovative ideas to support you. Most importantly, you will discover magic as you take your children and yourself *outside the line* of traditional thinking and begin to explore the world by looking at each day with excitement and wonder. You have already landed safely on the other side of that line after taking that huge leap when you picked up this book.

Everything you are about to learn will provide ways to ignite your creativity to support your unique teaching style. Maybe you're someone who is considering homeschooling, but you don't know where to begin or what you need to get started. Possibly, you have great teaching skills but need help with devising a system and adding structure to your child's day. Wherever you are in the process, this book lays it all out for you. Perhaps you have been homeschooling your family for a while but never knew how to record your child's progress efficiently and effectively. Maybe you didn't know about rules and regulations and laws that could become problematic if you didn't think to check on them. What I will share here gives you information on where to find all the materials you will ever need without spending a fortune, and how to use those resources in a way that will support you.

This book is your secret sauce on how to implement effective homeschooling techniques, as well as ideas for enhancing the teaching you are already doing. Begin each chapter with the attitude of discovering something new and valuable; then, read over the content, taking notes and highlighting information you find beneficial. I have included many exercises for you to both ponder and implement. Use what I have shared to make homeschooling an exciting time in your life, *and*, most importantly, your child's life!

This book is not meant to be a 'one size fits all' approach to homeschooling but a guide to help pave your way as you navigate the various paths of homeschooling. In chapters one through six, I introduce you to one of my mentors and the concepts of learning styles, Dr. Howard Gardner. Here, you will discover the ins and outs of *how* each of your children thinks, their interests, and why their learning is unique to them. You may also discover in this section the way *you* learn. Knowing that information and your learning style will undoubtedly assist you in how you teach your children. I know that when you understand this content and the power of learning styles, you will have many 'ah-ha' moments, just like I did in the mid-1980s when I first discovered how effective it was!

In chapters seven through fourteen, I take you through a deep dive into each of the multiple intelligences and provide a detailed look into the ways of teaching that interest each learning style. I provide lesson ideas for elementary, middle school, and high school students for language arts, math, science, and social studies so that you can see how to plan lessons to suit each of the multiple intelligences. You may see similar ideas in each chapter, but the presentations are different to suit different styles. I also show you how to plan lessons around a central theme so you get maximum results. You may not implement the entire chapter, especially if you only have young children, but it's nice to know that you can always go back and read the next section as your child grows and matures.

In chapters fifteen through twenty-two, I will discuss the many aspects to consider and to be aware of as you navigate homeschooling regulations—such as where to find your state's policies for homeschooling, where to find research on homeschooling nationally and globally, how to document your child's progress, how to make a high school transcript, how to jumpstart into higher education, and how to navigate other peoples' opinions and feedback.

Finally, my book ends with over one-hundred-and-thirty website suggestions, all vetted by me as some of the best places to find free or low-cost materials to use in your homeschooling adventures. All of these chapters combined will give you the confidence you need to lead your child toward their path of greatness. I am excited knowing the tools I provide will give you everything you require to make that journey enjoyable and possible.

Someday, someone will ask your future adult child, "*Who were your favorite teachers?*" Think of the satisfaction you'll feel when they answer, "*My mom and dad. They loved me enough to homeschool me.*"

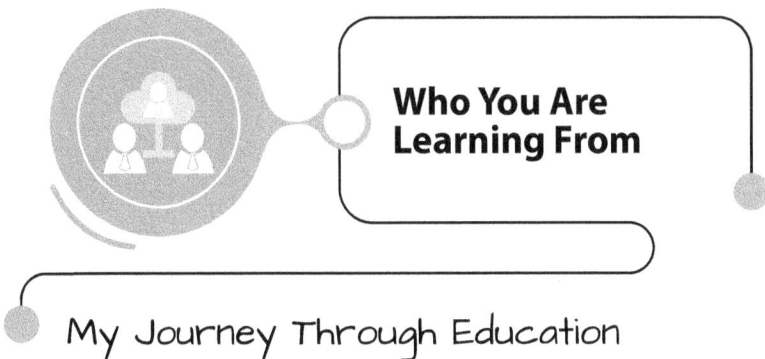

Who You Are Learning From

My Journey Through Education

Since we are about to embark on the important task of teaching your children, I wanted to take a moment to share with you exactly *who* you will be learning from. I believe that knowing my background in education and my intention in writing this book will be valuable information to you as we go forward. Since I ask you to do your due diligence in everything you teach your child, I wanted to take a moment to fill you in on how teaching became the most important cornerstone in my life.

I am not the product of being homeschooled. I attended public school in the United States to grade twelve. In the 1950s, pre-K and kindergarten were not offered in public schools. If your family could afford it, they could pay for kindergarten. Mine couldn't afford it, so I didn't go. Back in my day, our teachers focused on 'teaching, reading, writing, and arithmetic.' They also were responsible for providing weekly art projects and maintaining their own libraries in each classroom. If we were lucky, our classroom teacher would play a musical instrument, and thus, we would have a weekly music session. Our thirty-minute recess counted as physical education. Back when I was a child, if you were not in class on a school day, you were either sick or there was a family emergency. No parent would allow their children to skip school for any reason except illness or a death in the family. Parents certainly did not consider educating their children at home, either. If you didn't do well in school, chances were you became a 'dropout' because no programs were available for children with special needs.

At a young age, I decided to be just like my second-grade teacher, so after graduating from high school in 1973, I went to college to become an elementary teacher. I graduated from *Fairmont State College* (now Fairmont State University) in 1976 with a BA in Elementary Education and a Specialization in Early Childhood. Within a few weeks, I started setting up my first classroom. I had big ideas of how I would be the perfect educator. Over the years, I acquired certifications in several other areas of study: Inclusion, Math, Reading Specialist, and finally, MA in Curriculum and Instruction. In addition, I was a member of different educational societies, attended numerous conventions and seminars each year, and eventually became a lead teacher to guide the teachers in third through sixth grade in what was required on a weekly basis. We discussed everything from the standards in various curriculums that would be tested each spring, to students' behaviors, to uncompleted homework.

My first job was in my hometown; the school was built the year before. 'Open classrooms' was the newest trend in schools. Let me explain: Imagine building your brand-new house and deciding to only put walls around the bathrooms and the walls that define the outside of your new home. There are no inside walls—only poles from the floor to the ceiling—after all, you wouldn't want the roof to fall on your head while you were eating dinner! Now imagine organizing the furniture in your house so that it does not interfere with the flow of 'space.' You can actually see the 'area' where each family member sleeps, the 'area' where you cook and eat, and the 'area' where you do your laundry.

Take that picture you now have in your mind and imagine trying to take a nap, and everyone is home. Or maybe you have an infant who is cranky because it's time for its two o'clock morning feeding! *Can you see how one person trying to study for a test would be disturbed by another person watching a movie?* Perhaps someone is sick and has a headache, but someone else is practicing a musical instrument, maybe drums! *Oi Vey!*

Now, imagine this 'open' visual in a school. I could see the fifth-grade 'areas' from my third-grade class area! *Can you think of the problems this trend might create?* Kids were moving around, talking to one another in groups, answering questions, and playing games all around, as well as multiple other teachers and their classes from other grade levels. There was nothing to block out the noise or movement from all over the building, which caused distractions galore for every child in the school. The only thing we could do was force children to be as quiet as little mice–which is a horrible way to ensure our students were learning to their potential because children learn best when they can engage with their peers—talking, doing hands-on activities, and moving around! I quickly learned I either did not know how to teach, or the 'Open Classroom' concept wasn't working! I felt sorry for my first class—they were guinea pigs. Bless their hearts, they did their best.

As an educator, I had countless opportunities to build on my skillset to become a better teacher every year. I retired after teaching for over forty years, and guess what? I still look for opportunities to expand my skill set. However, as a parent, I know the feeling of one day being presented with this small little bundle of joy and expected to be an overnight parenting expert. Some of us read books beforehand. Others call their mothers. *Many do both.* Before you know it, that bundle of joy is three years old, and you feel pressured to enroll them in preschool. What? Three years old? You just finished potty training, and now you're supposed to push this baby out the door into someone else's arms whom you don't know and have never met before. *Why would anyone do that?* If you're reading this book, you might say, "Not me!"

I have been asked why I have become an advocate of homeschooling after teaching for forty-two years in public schools. Frankly, I didn't consider coming out of retirement to launch my homeschooling platform until the Covid-19 pandemic hit in 2020. Suddenly, schools were closed, everyone was quarantined, and children went weeks without formal instruction. When school districts finally figured out what they would do to tackle school and learning, the only way to accomplish this was through virtual classrooms. Needless to say, there were more problems than anyone could imagine; some children are not as responsible as others, many learn differently, and most need an extra push to be motivated; therefore, their level of understanding and mastery was not as it would have been with face-to-face learning. My phone began ringing off the hook from past students and parents who knew my skills: they needed help. Then, as schools began to open up again and kids returned to the classroom, other issues began to emerge.

It became abundantly clear that children were struggling with material in their grade level, and they *still are*, according to several teacher friends. Other parents were unwilling to send their children back to school, fearing Covid-19 outbreaks and the ever-changing strains of this virus forcing them to stay home. After a few weeks, my phone finally stopped ringing; then the second wave began.

As the Covid-19 issues persisted, I started making plans to teach online, but soon realized I was planning on building *another* online platform that mirrored the online model that had not been highly successful for children thus far. Then I had an epiphany. *Why not ask parents what they want and need?*

After surveying and interviewing many parents, it became clear that parents who homeschool their children or are interested in the concept of homeschooling desire clear, concise 'how-to' information. They need tools to help ensure their children are not losing out on learning. They want their children to embrace learning as the adventure it can be and become excited for each new day. Homeschooling parents want their children to be able to follow their dreams and visions of their futures unencumbered by middle-of-the-road percentiles or bell curve averages.

In the spirit of transparency, I acknowledge that my formal education has been in the United States. All of my experiences have been in American schools. Even though each state I taught in had differences in certain set-ups and guidelines, the basic rules of public education were relatively the same. It is interesting, though, to find out from my discussions with other people from outside of the United States that many of the concerns of American parents are shared by a worldwide community—parents everywhere want *more* for their children than the norm provides. They want their children to learn *Outside The Line*. They desire their children to reach beyond the average, ask questions, and seek answers; they want their children to find what makes them tick and feel purpose in pursuing their goals and dreams; they want their children to learn without feeling they have to fit in a standard mold to become just like everyone else.

That being said, the US is also known as the world's melting pot because one can find multiple cultures from around the world in our schools. For instance, one year, I taught very near Washington, D.C. Many of the students were children of ambassadors and other diplomats. The community also hosted a college associated with West Virginia University, so since many of the professors of the college were from other countries, those children often came from cultures outside of the United States, too. That was an interesting year because I feel I learned more about what other cultures expected than any other year of my career. The students taught the teacher! That information is important to know if you're reading this book and wonder if I can relate to you if you are a parent from outside of the United States.

The spirit of learning and teaching is universal. We are all intelligent and curious beings, and we want our children to grow into the people they were meant to become. *Do you remember a time when your child zeroed in on something that caught their attention? Did they reach for that thing? Was that the moment that caused your child to pull themselves up using the coffee table for balance and take that first walking step? Do you remember how excited you were?* You may have even recorded that event in your baby's journal so they could read about all their firsts as they grew.

'Firsts' should be as important when a child is thirteen as when they are learning to walk. People who have chosen to homeschool their children from the very beginning never have to lose the excitement over their children's 'firsts.' People who decide for one reason or the other to pull their children from traditional education can begin to witness 'firsts' again! Families who homeschool recognize there are challenges to overcome and decisions to make for the good of everyone. Others will not always agree with your decisions. Perhaps your parents voice opinions that are contrary to your decisions, or your sister or brother, an aunt or uncle, or even your best friends may challenge your choice. Everything I have been through and experiences I have learned will support you in trusting your convictions to support your child in this way.

Looking back over my forty-plus years of classroom teaching, I discovered the best teachers were the ones at home who continued to pave the way for their children to be excited about learning and gain knowledge to prepare them for their future.

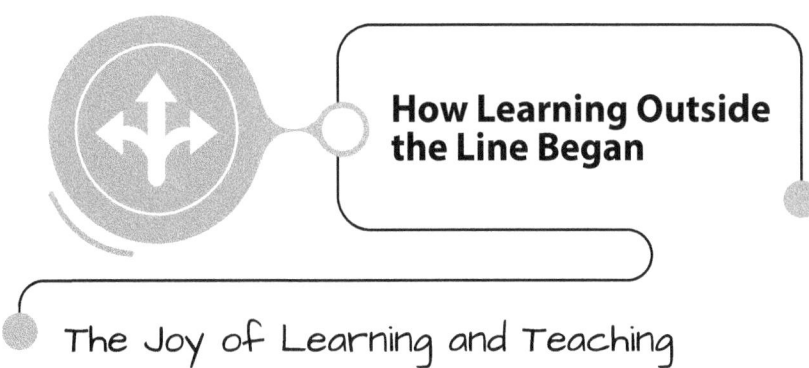

How Learning Outside the Line Began

The Joy of Learning and Teaching

I believe every person has been endowed at birth by our Creator with at least one gift. James tells us in Chapter 1:17, *"Every good gift and every perfect gift is from above, coming down from the Father of Lights, with whom there is no change, nor shadow of turning."* and in Romans 12:6-8, *"Now having different gifts, according to the favor which was given to us, let us use them accordingly: prophecy, according to the proportion of belief; if serving, in the serving; or he who is teaching, in the teaching; or he who encourages, in the encouragement; or he who is sharing, in sincerity; he who is leading, in diligence; he who shows compassion, joyously."* I believe my Creator endowed me with several of the above. Let me explain.

As a child, I grew up on a farm overlooking the Ohio River outside of a sleepy little town, Sistersville, West Virginia. It wasn't a huge farm, like the sweeping ranches of the West, but it wasn't small, either—about one hundred acres. There were few children near to play with, so I played with my dolls and my imaginary friend, Jockey. We had tea parties under the colossal maple trees in the front yard or strolled on the sidewalk in our front yard with my baby buggy and parasol, but most often, I lined my dolls and Jockey up in front of my play-size blackboard and played school. That was my favorite game because I dreamed of becoming a teacher someday.

Later, when I started school, I was a good student and loved learning. My second-grade teacher—Miss Dietrich—was my favorite teacher of all time! She was gentle and kind, and made sure every child in her class was acknowledged.

She never raised her voice, but if she just looked at you without saying a word—no expression upon her face—you knew you were doing something she wasn't pleased with. I remember the day she had that expression on her face for the entire class—except me.

It was springtime, and she was introducing a new math concept—fractions. She wrote ½ and ¼ on the chalkboard and said, *"These are fractions, and one of them represents more than the other. How many of you think ½ is bigger than ¼?"* My hand went up, but no one else's. *"How many of you think ¼ is bigger than ½?"* Everyone's hand went up except mine. That's when the class began laughing at me and saying mean things. Miss Dietrich would have none of that! She gave the class 'the look.' When it was quiet in the room again, Miss Dietrich asked me, *"Melanie, why did you choose ½ instead of ¼ like everyone else?"* It only took me a few seconds to reply. *"I help my mother bake, and she lets me measure things into the bowls. Sometimes, a recipe needs ½ cup of something but only ¼ cup of something else. One-half is more in the measuring cup than ¼ is. Also, my mother goes to the grocery store once per week. She always buys each of the kids in our family a candy bar. When my older brother and sister are away from home, my little sister and I get their share. That means instead of getting one candy bar for four kids, the two of us get two. We get more."* Miss Dietrich looked stunned. She looked around at the class and said, *"Melanie is correct, and I believe you owe her an apology."* Then she looked at me and smiled, *"Melanie, you will make a great teacher someday."* I beamed from ear to ear. That was the moment I *knew* I would become a teacher, just like Miss Dietrich.

I pursued my ambition of teaching through high school and after graduation. Unfortunately, some family issues made my father decide that my younger sister and I would *not* be allowed to go to college. I was crushed because that meant I would have to figure out how to become a teacher all on my own. I discussed my dilemma at 4-H camp a few weeks later with Mrs. Thomas, the Extension Officer of Tyler County. When she heard about my situation, she promised that I *would* be in college in the fall. She got to work making phone calls and enlisting other resources and finally confronted my father. Guess who was enrolled at Fairmont State College, now Fairmont State University, with Pell Grants and low-cost school loans for college within two weeks? That would be me, and I never let down any of my former teachers or Mrs. Thomas, the Extension Officer. Instead, I did a four-year degree in Elementary Education and a specialization in Early Childhood in only three years. I graduated Magna Cum Laude in the top percent of my class.

As the years passed, I became certified in many different areas of expertise—Math, Inclusion, Reading, and Language Arts, peer mentoring, and much more. I have taught in Virginia, West Virginia, Tennessee, and Arizona. I earned my MA in Curriculum and Instruction and served as lead teacher in the last school I worked in, eventually retiring in 2017 after forty-two years of service to children and families. At that time, I couldn't tell you how many lunch bills I paid, how many pairs of shoes I bought for needy kids, and how many school supplies I provided so no child went without. What I can tell you is I was not just any teacher—I was the teacher that every parent wanted their child to have. My individual state testing scores at the end of the year always exceeded the seventy-fifth percentile when the expectations and norm were in the forty-ninth percentile.

I like to refer to the next stage of my life as 'After Retirement.' I won't lie. I became bored and gained a lot of weight from sitting around and not doing much. In fact, within six months, I had gained so much weight I weighed *nearly two hundred pounds*. That's when I decided I needed something in my life other than boredom and food. I went back to school, became certified as a health and wellness coach, and proceeded to lose eighty pounds! As an extra benefit to my new standards of cooking and exercising, my husband lost over one hundred pounds! By my sixty-fifth birthday in 2019, my small home business was taking off as a health and wellness coach, and I was doing sixty-five military-style push-ups at the gym during my daily workouts!

Then, my world and the rest of the world came to a shattering stop. The Covid-19 pandemic hit, gyms closed, schools closed, and everyone was quarantined. If you left your house, you had to wear a mask and stay at least six feet apart, and your *only* choice of where to go was either the grocery store or the hospital. Although things felt bleak, I used my skills to encourage my clients to stay positive, provided simple recipes that were nutritious, delicious, and calorie-conscious, and suggested at-home exercises using their own body weight and items around the house to help keep their bodies in shape.

A few months later, amidst the pandemic, I sat at the kitchen table looking for a healthy recipe to cook that evening. I was somewhat startled because I heard a voice in my head that said, *"They still need you."* I didn't know what it meant then, so I carried on with making dinner, letting the thought marinate in my mind. As I stood to check for ingredients, my phone rang.

"Hello," I said, burrowing through the freezer looking for chicken breasts.

"Mrs. Summers? This is Jasmine from school. Do you remember me?"

"Why, yes!" I stood quickly, banging my head on the open door, forgetting for a moment I was bent over in an upside-down V halfway inside the freezer. "What can I do for you?" I asked, rubbing my head.

"I was wondering if you could help me out. I'm having some problems in math, and you were always able to explain things in a way I understood. We can't go to school because we're quarantined, and we're going online to see what we need to be doing in our subjects while the school tries to figure out how we will do school sitting at home."

"Are you having any other troubles? What about your other subjects?" I inquired.

"I'm okay because the other stuff is basically reading, except science. I'm not sure about some of the chemistry stuff. But my brother is having a lot of trouble with everything. He's sort of overwhelmed with all the stuff he has to do. Do you think you could help us both somehow?"

"Of course I can!" I answered with enthusiasm. "Let's schedule a time to connect online next week, and I will help you both."

As I hung up the phone, a small smile found my lips. The voice in my head a few minutes earlier had prepared me for that call. *They still need you* made perfect sense. And just like that, my *new* career in *homeschooling* had begun.

As the days stretched on, I realized I had missed teaching and that I had obviously impacted the lives of the students I had taught before. I began to feel like I had a higher purpose that still needed to be fulfilled. I felt chills every time I remembered that 'voice' I had heard, *"They still need you."* I felt the excitement I had so many times before as I stood in my classroom, surrounded by the children who had given me purpose and fulfillment my whole life.

It didn't take long for the word to spread to call Mrs. Summers for help. Parents either called me from a stored phone number or looked me up on social media and messaged me for help. I found myself assisting former students of mine who couldn't understand the complex ideas in various subjects, how to get organized at home, or how to complete their assignments with more clarity. I also supported parents with facilitating their children at home and assisting with proper study habits. Both the parents and students were overwhelmed because they were now working *and* studying from home. Each needed help in their own way to navigate the challenges of learning in a home environment.

I snapped into gear and started doing what I did best—teaching—only on a more defined and personal level. After being retired for nearly four years from a forty-two-year career, my passion for teaching—and that voice I heard in my head—was calling me to return in new and different ways.

The next year, schools began to open up, but when the children went to school, they found out they had to wear masks all day, their desks were six feet apart, and they attended either half days or every other day so that all the kids had at least some formal schooling in the classroom. After talking with some of my past colleagues, I discovered that by the end of that year, it became apparent that public school children were about two years behind. Many students still hadn't caught up to the learning they missed, leaving teachers scrambling to compensate.

I began researching and digging on the internet to learn some facts about homeschooled children. One website I found was www.NHERI.org—the National Home Education Research Institute—where I discovered some startling information. According to their research, kids who were homeschooled before the Pandemic were not behind because those children's education had never stopped. Homeschooled children were never dependent on any school institution for their instructions or education, so their learning had not been interrupted; it simply continued.

Parents who had decided from the beginning of the Pandemic to teach their children did not have to rely on school districts to devise a solution to educate their children. They understood it would take up to three months or more to design a platform to use, create lessons that could be accessed on that platform, and schedule classes so that various grade levels had specific times to meet online for instructions. Many parents did not want their children to miss essential learning time due to a 'wait and see' approach to education. Studies suggest these children were farther along in their studies than those who waited for school districts to find a way around quarantined children and learning.

Later, statistics indicated that when schools finally opened for onsite instruction, parents who continued to teach their children full-time from home instead of opting for only half days of onsite school instruction found their kids were maintaining their learning and continued to progress at a relatively fast pace.

What was most interesting about the study was that kids who were home-schooled before the Pandemic were not behind because their education had never stopped. Those homeschooled children were not dependent on any school institution for their learning or education. Therefore, they could continue homeschooling and, in some cases, advance their learning while benefiting from a home-based system.

Parents who decided *not to* send their children back to school when children were allowed to return to onsite schooling, or those who continued to teach their children full-time from home instead of opting for a modified curriculum, were not falling behind. Instead, some parents found their children excelling in a home-based system from the very beginning of the Pandemic and preferred to teach their children from home going forward. At the same time, parents wanted to ensure they were not just doing 'enough' but were moving forward above and beyond what their peers in public education were achieving. In order to do this, they wanted to make sure they, the parents, were fully aware of what they needed in their home, what subjects they may need to address themselves, and how they could elevate every experience in and out of the home to make education meaningful, exciting, and relevant to the child and family.

When it became abundantly apparent that children and parents needed tools, skills, and strategies to navigate the challenges brought on by the changing system, I came out of retirement to launch my own business, *Innovative Homeschool Solutions™*. After forty-two years of teaching, I have become a homeschooling coach, a profession that, although little known about pre-Covid-19, is becoming more popular and necessary. Since research varies from government educational statistics and independent analysis, as well as from one country to another globally, it is estimated that between documented homeschooled children—those living in places that require various information and approval for one to homeschool children—and undocumented homeschooled children—those who live where there is no required documentation whatsoever to homeschool children—homeschooled children have risen in numbers in leaps and bounds. Obtaining a global number of homeschooled children is impossible, but I imagine the trend is comparable to North America. In the United States, at the beginning of 2020, between documented and undocumented homeschooled children, an estimated two million seven hundred thousand children were homeschooled. Today, that number has risen to approximately fifteen million homeschooled kids.

Parents are finding value and satisfaction in homeschooling their children. They love the idea that they spend more time with their family unit, they value going on family excursions whenever they choose, and they appreciate that their children can accelerate in their education or even slow down when needed to master concepts. However, parents still need guidance on how to teach certain concepts, coordinate multiple children so each one gets their needs attended to, incorporate adventures into learning time, build a high-school resume, navigate state-wide regulations for homeschooling, as well as a myriad of other "how-to's" that would yield educational success. That's where I felt I could use my experience and expertise to support both parents and students. I also wanted to make homeschooling accessible and instill the idea of *learning outside the lines.*

For me, *learning outside the line* is a way to show parents that they can educate their children at home with a more holistic approach to learning, engaging their child's emotional, social, ethical, and academic needs to foster optimum learning and personal growth. I want *outside the line* to mean there are ways to engage your child's higher learning with thought-provoking discussions, engaging their creative abilities by designing projects, experiencing what they are learning with real-life, hands-on opportunities, and giving them the freedom to disagree by learning the art of debate.

My goal in introducing you to the *outside the line* ideas is that you begin to get out of a mindset of traditional schooling—sitting for long periods of time, completing worksheet after worksheet—and into the mindset of something better. It should be refreshing to know that you are gifting your children the means to explore outside the boundaries of traditional schooling. You can feel enthusiastic knowing that every minute of every day can be an exciting adventure and learning opportunity for you and your whole family, from baking cookies to learning to ice skate, to visiting the Seven Wonders of the World! *And best of all?* Your child will be excited to get up every day knowing there is adventure in the air, and they will be part of that adventure as they engage in truly *Learning Outside the Line.*

Section 1

Homeschooling
With Positivity

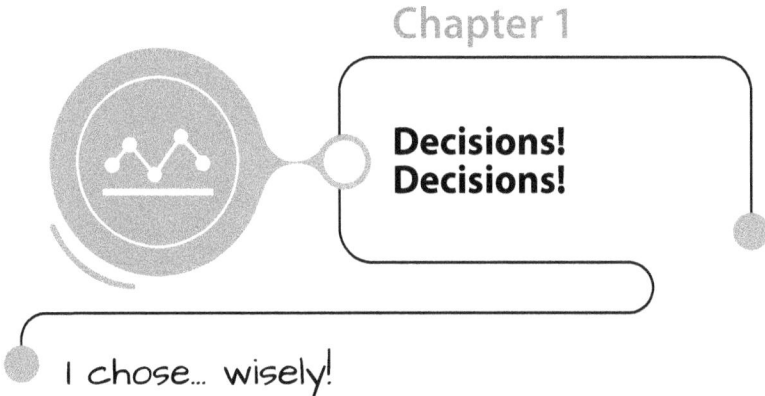

Chapter 1

**Decisions!
Decisions!**

I chose... wisely!

*"Time is free but priceless. You can't own it, but you can use it.
You can't keep it, but you can spend it. Once you've lost it,
you can never get it back."*
— HARVEY MACKAY

Not long ago, I was asked, "How many children are homeschooled in the United States?" An exceptionally good question. In researching an answer to this, I found that according to the United States Census Bureau, around one million children were homeschooled in 2019. They went on to state, "Empirical evidence shows that homeschooling doubled in the United States during the pandemic lockdowns. The growth occurred from the 2019-2020 institutional school year to the 2020-2021 year, to perhaps as many as five million school-age children." To give you more perspective, in 2020, around two million documented students were being homeschooled in the U.S. According to www.nheri.org—The National Home Education Research Institute—upward of five million children were being homeschooled in the U.S. in the school year 2021-2022. That number has increased to fifteen million children as of 2023.

It is estimated that these numbers could be double, or more, due to the fact that there are families who live in areas that do not require documentation for homeschooling. In other words, if you live in one of the twenty-two states that do not require documentation, all a parent has to do to homeschool their child is show up at school and withdraw their kids. Or, they never have to enroll their children in a school to begin with, and never go through any formal registration process.

The 2020 statistics do not include every student in America who began homeschooling because of the Covid-19 pandemic, only those who were already part of the homeschooling movement. However, since schools have reopened, parents now have the choice to place their children back in school, but many have not. The question remains: *why have those numbers doubled or even tripled each year since the beginning of the pandemic, even though schools have reopened?*

Since the onset of the pandemic in 2020, the United States has been one of the many countries where homeschooling is growing in popularity. Research shows that Canada, the United Kingdom, Australia, New Zealand, Germany, France, South Africa, Brazil, and India have joined the ranks of parents who now know that educating their children at home greatly benefits their child's educational progress (www.nheri.com).

During my research on homeschooling, I spoke to many parents who shared their views on the numerous benefits of homeschooling, and I have taken the time to list many of them here. Take a moment to read through the list to see which one of these reasons resonates with you.

Benefits of Homeschooling

The top factors that contribute to the success of homeschooling are as follows:

- **Flexibility**—Parents like the ability to customize their children's educational programs to their child's talents and interests. They preferred not to have to fit into a rigid schedule or curriculum that may not suit their children's needs.
- **Personalized Attention**—Parents like giving each child one-on-one attention and individualized instruction. They appreciate that their children can progress at their own pace and get extra help where needed.
- **Values and Beliefs**—Parents loved that they could instill their own values and beliefs in their children's education without influence from outside opinions. This was particularly important to parents with specific religious and cultural beliefs.
- **Safety and Health Concerns**—Parents believe they can provide a safer and healthier learning environment, especially if their children have

particular health and safety concerns. Some children require specific modifications for these needs, while others have emotional situations that traditional schools cannot meet.

- **Academic Excellence**—Some parents I spoke to believe their children gain a higher quality education at home, with access to resources and opportunities they could not get in traditional school settings. They love that their children can see and experience their surroundings by actually going places—not just reading about places. They are not 'stuck' in a classroom for hours, memorizing facts that are great for playing Trivia™ but otherwise not of general use.
- **Bullying and Socialization Concerns**—Homeschooling parents are aware of the amount of bullying and negative social experiences children are inundated with in public schools. They make extra efforts to equip their children with good humanity beliefs and ensure that they have social interaction with quality programs, such as scouting, 4-H, volunteer programs, and playdates with like-minded people.
- **Unique Family Circumstances**—Homeschooling is practical for those families that travel extensively, live in remote areas, or have children involved in activities, such as being a child actor or athlete where homeschooling is necessary.

If you are a homeschooling family already, you may agree and value the benefits I have listed above. If you are ready to homeschool, review the list and consider which ones are most important for you and your family. When you focus on the benefits and the positive outcomes homeschooling will add to your family, you will find your decision has already been made. All that's left is for you to implement the process.

Indicate your top three factors for homeschooling:

1) _____

_____

2) _____

_____

3) _____

_____

Valuable Lessons

Of all the parents I interviewed, the most common and consistent feedback was that most parents felt their children *were* learning at school but were *not* learning some of the important lessons and skills in life. That prompted a huge exodus of public-educated children into the home environment. It also brought to light the top concerns that parents have when it comes to homeschooling versus institutional learning.

Allow me to share some of the key factors prompting this movement toward homeschooling. Trade education, such as home economics, retail, construction, automobile mechanics, photography, foreign languages, art, music, band, choir, and even sports are often considered less important than other areas of public education. As a homeschooling family, you can explore these topics if your child is interested and teach them the valuable lessons that will support them later in life.

I remember hearing this story from my husband:

Many years ago, when his daughter was in high school, she wanted a car after receiving her driver's license. Instead of taking her to the car dealership to find a nice, new, perfectly running vehicle, he took her to a used car lot and found a car that needed a lot of work 'under the hood.' It was an inexpensive and affordable option for his daughter since she had to chip in to help purchase the car. Together, they rebuilt the engine, replaced needed parts, and adjusted the brakes, timing, and air conditioning so that when the project was completed, she had a safe, usable automobile to get her back and forth from her after-school job, school, cheerleading practice, and the many things teenagers like to do.

My husband made sure his daughter had practical information and learned skills she could use in the future. Several years later, she was stranded on the side of the road with a flat tire. Instead of calling for help, she opened the trunk of her car, got out the spare tire, lug wrench, and hand jack, and, like a pro, changed her own tire.

This is the essence of homeschooling—combining the essential intellectual core subject matter of math, language arts, science, and social studies with life lessons and family values—to guide and develop the *whole* child.

I personally recall when those 'life-skill' classes were removed from the curriculum at the school where I spent most of my career teaching. It was a sad day when home economics, photography, Spanish, choir, and some sports were removed from the curriculum. I taught in a rural farming community. Most of the children needed to learn how to cook, sew, and do laundry correctly. Many of these children might have received scholarships to colleges for their athletic abilities if they had had a way to show their abilities with different sports.

You, as a homeschooling parent, can ascertain your child's gifts and find a way to allow them to excel in whatever they love. At the same time, you can also teach them to respect other's needs and interests in a loving environment. You empower your child for the future while instilling confidence and skills to take charge of their lives when they reach the age of independence. The great Les Brown says, "Children are forty percent of the world's population, but one hundred percent of our future." I agree, but I will add, "Children are one hundred percent of their own future and that of generations to come." As a homeschooling parent, you will provide the guidance, support, and tools your child needs as your child grows into adulthood.

Interesting Statistics

According to the Learning Policy Institute, there was a shortage of one hundred thousand teachers in 2018. That number increased to one hundred and ten thousand in 2019. The problem was exacerbated in 2020 with the onset of Covid-19, with teachers leaving the profession over health concerns or burnout. The RAND Corporation is a nonprofit organization that focuses on improving policy and decision-making in health, education, national security, international affairs, law and business, and the environment through research and analysis. They reported that up to one in four teachers either considered or did leave the profession due to Covid-19. In 2021, the National Education Association (NEA) reported that the teacher shortage in the U.S. was of significant concern, while some states were experiencing critical shortages in specific subject areas. They also reported that the pandemic had continued to impact teacher retention rates. This data remains consistent, and according to Chalkbeat, a nonprofit news organization that covers education, teacher turnover is the highest it's been in the last five years. This issue has also been reported to have affected schools in Canada, Europe, Asia, and Australia.

However, homeschooling parents are not concerned with those statistics. Their children never have to worry about not having a teacher because their children happen to live with their teachers. That would be you and your spouse.

Cost of Homeschooling

According to www.worldpopulationreview.com, school districts in the United States spend, on average per student per year, around 12,600 USD. That cost varies from country to country. Mexico spends approximately 3000 USD a year per student, while Luxembourg spends almost 26,000 USD per year. This is based on school facility expenditures, personnel salaries, supplies for learning, transportation, technology, and utilities.

The average cost per child, per year, to educate a homeschooled child ranges between 700 and 1200 USD. These costs were based on curriculum, learning supplies, field trips, technology, and extracurricular activities. However, I found it interesting that the average family who does not homeschool spends anywhere from 1500 to 7000 USD per child on public education. These expenses include everything from food, uniforms, and transportation to equipment rental, field trips, and tutoring.

In talking to a school administrator recently, I was told that they get a lot of money from state and federal funding and local taxation. He complained to me because he knew I was a homeschool consultant and coach, and he thought he could shame me into thinking I was complicit in robbing the school systems of the money they needed to run their budgets. Try to picture the look on my face when he said that! Then, try to picture the look on *his* face when I pointed out that homeschooling families still had to pay taxes from which schools get those funds. Also, homeschooling families were not responsible for fixing their school budgets or cutting spending costs. Needless to say, he stopped complaining once he learned the actual stats.

Knowing Your Reasons

My goal is to convey all the wonderful reasons why people homeschool their families and give you pertinent information that validates that homeschooling provides both vital and positive benefits. Hopefully, in this chapter I have succeeded in affirming your stance on homeschooling and empowered your rationale that you *are* doing the right thing for your children and family. Take a moment to reflect on the reasons you feel homeschooling is the best choice. Hone in on the values, qualities, and outcomes that will serve you and your family. Knowing why homeschooling is the choice for you and your family will help you develop your own teaching style, build confidence in what you are doing, and build a family rapport second to none!

List your reasons here:

_____

_____

_____

_____

_____

_____

_____

_____

_____

_____

Well done for evaluating the benefits of homeschooling and tapping into the power within you that *you* already have. It's there, just waiting to be used, and that's part of the work in being a great homeschooling parent—making the effort to understand how you as a teacher and education provider will navigate this wonderful adventure, getting to know your child on a deeper level, being able to hold meaningful discussions with them, and helping them to become the great person they are meant to be.

In the next chapter, we will explore the emotional needs of your children when homeschooling and I will give you suggestions that will help you navigate this path with ease, allowing your children to adapt to their new norm—*education at home.*

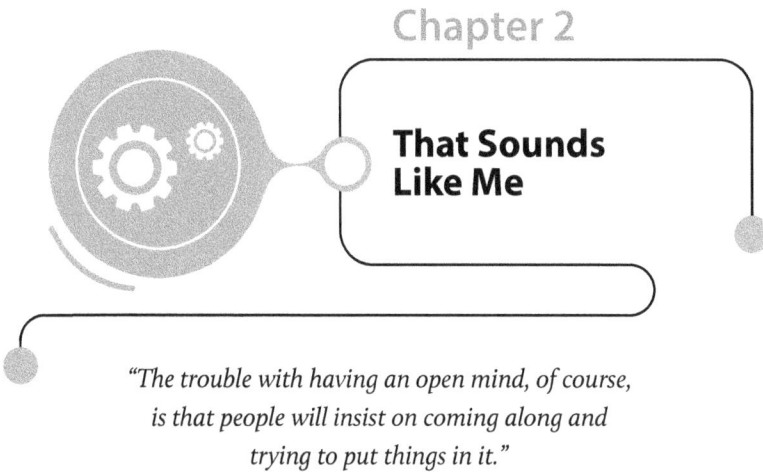

Chapter 2

That Sounds Like Me

"The trouble with having an open mind, of course, is that people will insist on coming along and trying to put things in it."
— TERRY PRATCHETT, DIGGERS

Since this is a book about homeschooling, I have to ask... *Why are you choosing to homeschool your children? Why do you like the option of homeschooling? Why is homeschooling important to you? Why do you feel homeschooling is the better option?* These questions are important to consider right out of the gate. *Why homeschooling? Why this decision? Why now?*

Knowing the reasons behind your *why* and being clear on your homeschooling choice will make the endeavor to teach your children at home successful or subsequently unsuccessful. If you are still pondering the decision or not clear on your *why*, then the information I have compiled here will give you the clarity you need to form an educated choice. I want you to know exactly *why* you are making this decision and *how* best to support yourself in this incredible opportunity to teach your child. I also want you to have *all* the facts and tools you need to succeed and make it a lasting experience.

To make sure I help you thoroughly define your reasons, I interviewed several homeschooling parents and asked them the same exact questions I have just asked you. Some of the answers I received differed from what I expected, while others I had heard many times before. There were brief answers and detailed answers—some specific to personal core values, some concerned disagreement in school regulations, while others were more about incidents that had happened at school that upset their child. I received many answers that firmly told me the positive aspects they encountered as homeschooling families, and I want to pass on their encouragement to you to persevere in the undertaking of being a homeschooling parent.

I remember the first answers I received concerned the policies of school districts and the legislative requirements for homeschooling—later on, I received more comments that included specific incidents of teacher conflicts, such as losing their patience with children, not understanding the emotional maturity of their students, or not being able to ascertain the individual style or learning process each child learns from. Parents shared the mental and emotional impacts their children were facing while in the care of public schools. Many had challenging issues at school that negatively affected their child's well-being and emotional state of mind. Some wanted more time with their kids to watch them grow. Others loved learning, teaching, exploring, and nurturing the direction of their child's inherent inclinations. Many parents spoke about their child's hobbies, abilities, and goals, wanting that to be fostered rather than adhering to a standard curriculum. Overall, I heard that parents were invested in *how* their children learned and exactly *what* they were learning.

Parent Sharing

If you are feeling alone in your decision to homeschool, let me share some responses to a survey I sent to homeschooling families. The parents I questioned gave responses that influenced their decisions to homeschool their family, and then later on in the survey, they shared their personal developments because of the decision to homeschool. You may relate to a few of them and connect with others who have faced similar experiences in your schooling journey.

Personal Well-Being

Each of the following examples shares how the emotional needs of a child were not being met at school. After making the decision to homeschool, the needs of the child were being met with kindness and understanding at home and the child began to flourish.

Example 1: Providing Emotional Stability

"My child was constantly bullied in school. He is shy, smart, and a wallflower in group activities. He was called many unkind names! When we asked for a parent conference and spoke about these issues, we were told that unless the bullies were caught red-handed, there was nothing they could do because there was only my son's word against theirs. When it got so bad my son developed an ulcer at the age of nine, we took him out of school. Now that he is homeschooled, my son isn't bullied and disrespected by other kids. He doesn't wake up sick to his stomach. He no longer has to take medicine for an ulcer. He is no longer shy—he engages in conversations with others all the time now. In fact, within a few months, he was thriving. We find group activities outside of the home, and it's truly a joy to see how he interacts with other children he is meeting. He's even exchanged contact information with other kids so they can plan to 'connect' outside of homeschool or arranged activities. The best part of homeschooling is we have found out that he has outpaced his previous class and is doing things in homeschool they will not be taught until next year."

 ## Example 2: A Making Change Enjoyable

"My husband was in the military. We moved around a lot, depending on where he was stationed. It made more sense to homeschool our children. We never had to worry about our kids having to get used to a new school in the middle of the year, 'fitting in' issues, catching up with the new class, receiving tutoring, trying to figure out schedules, and all the other things we would have had to deal with if our kids jumped from school to school. I homeschooled from the very beginning. We avoided 'all that.' As a result, our kids graduated from college earlier than if they were in public schooling. One is working on her master's, one on her doctorate, and the youngest just graduated from college and wants to pursue a career in the military, just like Dad."

These two parents shared why they felt their decision to homeschool was the best choice for their children, families, and themselves! Each made it abundantly clear that they believed the decision to homeschool was the most appropriate decision for their family because homeschooling eliminated the negative elements of public school that their children were experiencing. Instead of having to endure unpleasant situations that lead to, in some cases, traumatic episodes in their children's lives, their children now thrive. They have the time and opportunity to focus on what they are learning instead of their emotional challenges.

Emotional Intelligence

Personal dynamics found at public schools and curriculum demands were another big reason parents gave as to *why* they homeschooled their children. Parents want their children to learn math, science, writing skills, grammar, geography, and social studies. However, they also want assurance that their children are progressing at optimum levels of understanding—not being rushed if they do not grasp the concept, and certainly not held back because others in the class cannot keep up with their children's understanding of the subject matter.

Current curriculums require that the average child/student maintain a certain Grade Point Average (GPA) in order to graduate. Schools also require a minimum grade average per subject to pass that class for credit. Suppose the child does not have that minimum average. In that case, the child either has to attend summer school—usually at the parent's expense—or retake that class the following year, putting them in jeopardy of not graduating with their peers. Many parents I spoke to were concerned with the arbitrary school rules that did not address the needs of every student. They wanted the emotional needs of their children to be addressed, as well as the academic growth of their child.

 Example 3: Unjust Penalties

"My child was very ill and missed a week of school. The school policy allowed two days to complete homework that was missed while he was sick, but he had six teachers who all gave homework as well as the assignments during class for a total of seventeen assignments. However, since he missed the assignments, as well as the instructions as to how to complete them, he didn't know how to answer the

overwhelming amount of work. That didn't include the NEW assignments when he got back to school. He asked the teachers to help him, but they wouldn't stay after school, nor did they want to meet with him at lunch to help him. Since he didn't complete many assignments, he received zero's on the work he didn't complete, affecting his final grade. When I went to the principal, I was told my son had been given the same time as anyone else.

Once we began homeschooling, none of our children had to deal with stringent rules and regulations about make-up work anymore. They no longer have to be stressed to get everything done. I can teach my kids at an accelerated pace, so they are already ahead of the game if they get sick. My kids don't sit in a subject for forty-five minutes doing mundane work if they spend forty-five minutes on a subject, it's certainly not about reading a chapter in some textbook and answering fifty questions to 'prove' they understood it. They may have to read something, but then we have a meaningful discussion about it instead of answering a bunch of questions no one will grade. There is NO make-up work. There's only moving on to the next thing. There is no chance to be overwhelmed. If something is not understood, we stop and find a way to make it meaningful; then we move on."

 ## Example 4: Recognizing Individuality

"Seeing my eleven-year-old in tears every day after school due to relentless bullying, primarily centered around her learning disability and weight, was the final straw. My child was identified with reading (dyslexia) and writing (dysgraphia) learning disabilities. She is overweight by twenty-five pounds, so she is at a disadvantage in classes such as physical education. She wanted to try out for the JV volleyball team but quickly changed her mind due to unkind remarks about her weight. I couldn't stand to see my child go through such emotional trauma any longer, so we decided to homeschool."

"Six months into our homeschool journey and I can't believe the transformation in my child. Not only has her progress been remarkable, but her emotional well-being and self-confidence have also flourished. Without the constant bullying, my child has become more outgoing, and her self-esteem is soaring. It's incredible to witness her newfound love for learning. All it took was patience and attention to her particular needs. Without the constant noise and confusion of the schoolroom and

extra time to focus on her dyslexia and dysgraphia, her reading and writing abilities have improved. Since she is not limited by only a few extra-curricular activities at school, her passion for exploring new interests is heart-warming. Physically, the whole family has embraced a healthier lifestyle in support of her weight loss, and we're all enjoying cooking nutritious meals together. She has lost 18 pounds, and her pediatrician is delighted! Homeschooling has truly been a blessing, allowing my child to blossom into a happy, well-rounded individual."

These parents wanted their children to feel better about themselves and learn in a way that served their emotional needs. Unfortunately, public school teachers do not have the time for allowing children to balance their emotional needs as teachers are only focused on curriculum, and have many children in each class to oversee. Schools are held accountable for mastering the standards of learning they are required to teach per grade level only, not how the student was *feeling* while in school.

Social Influence

The second section I addressed in my survey was around the social issues prevalent in schools. Although current trends are debatable, many parents are not happy with public education requiring topics to be covered that they believe should be discussed at home—topics such as whether children should be allowed to pursue gender reassignment or have a same-sex marriage. More controversial conversations, such as predators on the internet or child trafficking in classes as early as kindergarten age, often seem too harsh for young, impressionable minds. In some school districts, teachers are not allowed to communicate with parents about issues that children may express at school, such as depression or ostracization. Parents also faced issues where social or political opinions were discussed that had no relevance to public education. They struggled over religious beliefs that did not align with their particular theological doctrines or moral preference for societal rights. There were many sensitive issues and topics open for interpretation that were being shared and not always adhering to the traditional subjects such as math and science, which were less polarized.

Conversely, other parents were concerned that the teachers were moving too fast so that children couldn't socially master important skills. Many parents also believe that the curriculum is controlled by bureaucratic agendas that do not support intellectual progress and by social media that is less educational but globally trending. Parents who have no problem with those trends are generally less concerned about what is being taught in schools; however, those who do not agree with current trends are unhappy with what their child is being exposed to in public schools.

Lack of Individualism

Many children are placed in classes because it is easier and more convenient to make schedules for the entire school population than cater to each individual child. Therefore, children are unhappy when some of the classes they desire are not on their daily schedule. For example, when a child has chosen to take Spanish as a second language choice, but finds they were assigned to French class, it can be very upsetting, especially if the child has a reason to be able to converse in Spanish. Parents have begun to take matters into their own hands and consider the option of homeschooling so there will be no question as to what their child studies or if their child's interests are being met. Parents want their children to be *happy* in their learning while *excelling* in what they are learning, and have discovered that homeschooling is a better choice for their family's needs.

I would be remiss if I didn't mention one very important component of public education that most parents do not understand: *What is an IEP (Individual Education Plan)?* Let me explain. Children do not learn at the same speed. Some learn very quickly and seem to be able to soar in everything they do; others struggle to grasp basic concepts, working hard to maintain an average grade in all subjects. Children who are highly successful academically and need very little extra help are usually referred by a teacher to be tested by a school professional. They are placed into 'gifted and talented' classes if they meet specified requirements where they are instructed at higher levels of understanding.

In contrast, children who are not highly successful academically and need more assistance and extra tools for learning are also referred by a teacher to be tested by a school professional. Yet, if it is found that the child is in great need of help, they will be placed in 'special education,' where they will receive individualized services and accommodations that address their specific needs.

Both of the spectrums of *identified children*—gifted and talented students, along with educationally struggling students—have individual goals and measurements in a written legal document called an Individualized Education Plan. This individualized education plan comes with a range of specific actions upheld in school law geared only to students within these categories. However, the teacher is responsible for every child in the classroom, not just identified IEP students. The teacher must legally prove each child on an IEP has been taught every day, and every lesson, according to what is written in these documents.

The majority of students in any school are regular education students. Because they do not have an IEP, they do not get special services or accommodations. 'Regular education' parents can become upset with the teachers and the school because *their* child does not have a legal document protecting *their* child from 'the rules,' such as homework policies, tardies, missed days of instruction, and behavior policies, to name a few. Below are a few other comments I received on my survey concerning parents' dissatisfaction with these type of policies:

 ## Example 5: Enjoying Certain Subjects

"My child understands math skills very quickly. He got in trouble because the teacher was still teaching the skill, and my son had already completed the worksheet with 100% accuracy. He then tended to become distracted and complete another class's homework or talk to peers during class. He should have been in a more advanced class, but the school would not place him in a different class."

Since we have begun homeschooling our son, he has been able to accelerate in Math. After only four months, he is already two years beyond what he was doing in traditional school. He still needs a slower pace in other subjects, but he is happy he gets to excel in his favorite subject.

 ## Example 6: Conforming to Issues

"My child had to take classes for electives she did not sign up for. Electives are usually put in the curriculum so teachers can go to planning. My child did not get

any of her requests, so she was enrolled in two different classes she didn't like. She wanted to take Spanish but was assigned French. She wanted to take Art because she is particularly good at it, but was assigned to Computer Science. I wouldn't have cared so much if these electives didn't affect her GPA. It was hard to get her to focus on subjects that weren't important or as important as Math or Science."

When we began to homeschool our daughter, we enrolled her in a Spanish course offered by a community group. She loves it and has advanced so much that she gets to help first-time enrollees! We also have her taking private art lessons, and she is doing well and finding her talents. She is happy that her other courses are improving so that she can get to her 'favorite' classes sooner.

Physical Importance

The third area addressed in my survey was centered around the loss of learning and family time. Depending on where one lives, weather can often disrupt learning and school attendance. For instance, in northern areas of the U.S., winter snowstorms often close schools for one or more days. In midwestern states, heavy rain and tornadoes frequently occur, and states that border oceans deal with the threat of hurricanes interrupting school. Often, utilities are down, so conveniences such as electricity are not available for children to continue to go to school. No one can prevent these natural catastrophes, but sometimes they cause schools to be closed for several days in a row and sometimes several times per school year.

Parents who homeschool their children never need to be concerned with the school being 'closed' because learning can continue, even without the modern conveniences of lights or power. As one mom told me, *"Abraham Lincoln became a lawyer by studying by the fireplace in a log cabin!"*

Another issue that causes learning loss is transportation. It is unsafe to travel in inclement weather by car, public transportation, or school bus. On a normal daily schedule, those children who travel to school on city transportation or a school bus often experience a travel time of thirty minutes or more to get to school. When they get to school, they often have to wait thirty minutes or more for homeroom to start. Homeroom is the classroom where every student is required to report at the start of every school day, and the session lasts around ten to fifteen minutes. Then there are class changes, settling into the next class, and sitting through a class that is often interrupted by announcements, fire drills, or misbehavior of other students. At the end of the school day, some children often spend time in after-school care while waiting for their parents to collect them; up to thirty minutes or more to return home. All of these conditions attached to public education add up to hours of lost time that could be spent with the family or dedicated to in-home education and further advancing their progress.

When children arrive home after school, dinner needs to be fixed and served, and everyone has to prepare for the next day—homework, pet needs, laundry, and kitchen cleanup, as well as any other chores or activities that need attention in the family's evening routine. The following examples share these concerns.

 ## Example 7: Travel Stresses

"I found that everyone was already stressed out by the time we got ready for school and work. Take out lunch/recess—another forty minutes. Then it took fifteen minutes to get on the bus and a thirty minute drive home. My child lost three-and-a-half to four hours daily, five days a week, and they could never get that time back, so you do the math. It just made sense to homeschool.

The time my kids gained by being homeschooled was the time my kids were able to accelerate their coursework. The stress was greatly reduced and limited to family issues or sibling rivalry, handled immediately with love and fairness."

 ## Example 8: Having a Stand-out Child

"Our children have specific learning needs. The school doesn't tailor the instruction of our children's specific needs and abilities, even though they wrote an IEP and are supposed to follow it. That's what we understood when we agreed to testing them.

Now that we are using the homeschooling model, our children are not labeled as kids who are SPED—SPecial EDucation students. They're just our kids, and we've been able to help them achieve where the schools could not. We find their strengths and accentuate their gifts, not make any challenges the focus."

Family Values

The final topic in my survey was 'family values.' My research reflected the notion that what is important to some families is not as important to others. I have heard it said time and again, by many people, including close friends and colleagues: to remain friends with everyone, you must never speak about politics, religion, or sexual orientation. However, the whole trajectory of public education has changed, especially in the last eight to ten years. Some parents made the following statements in regard to the importance and maintenance of family values, cultural beliefs, and traditional, or historical preservation.

 Example 9: Keeping Our Values

"Our family has certain religious observances that school policy does not allow. We celebrate New Moon Day and Sabbath based on the moon, not the Gregorian calendar, which places Sabbath on every Saturday. We also observe the festivals the Creator gives that require certain observances others do not celebrate, nor do we celebrate any other common holidays, like Christmas. Most school districts only allow children to miss a certain amount of school each semester apart from the school calendar for things like emergencies or illness. School policy and the school calendar do not make it easy for our children to attend public school because, according to our beliefs, the Sabbath is rarely on Saturday, we do not celebrate the holidays laid out in the school calendar, and some festivals require us to be away from home for several days at a time. Therefore, they miss too many days according to school policy."

"As a homeschooling parent, it is easier to homeschool than explain why our children are not in school due to our cultural preferences. Our children are learning and achieving just as much as public education students. However, we are not harassed or judged for keeping our faith. We are free to practice our beliefs as we see fit and teach our children what we see as valuable."

Example 10: Learning What Matters

"I agree that everyone is different and has the right to be whoever they are born to be and to follow their ideals and beliefs. However, I don't want my child involved in political discussions because too many disagreements occur—too many opinions transpire into topics that are often opinions and not always facts. Some of the things my child was learning were against our morals, family values, and contrary to our spiritual beliefs."

"Once we began homeschooling and teaching the things we valued most, my child became much happier at home, knowing my husband and I were guiding her learning. She does not feel uncomfortable at home because we do not teach her things she isn't ready to receive or engage in, including uncomfortable conversations beyond her years. She is blossoming in academics and forming her own interests."

From all the parents I spoke to, I can say that almost *every* homeschooling parent agreed that teaching their children is their top priority. Even if both parents have careers, they arrange their schedules to ensure one or *both* of them are at home daily and share teaching responsibilities around their careers. They want their children to be successful and believe they can accommodate them better in their home, rather than in a classroom of sometimes up to forty other children.

Homeschooling parents also shared that they enjoy providing positive social interactions for their children. They ensure their kids have social interactions with other children of their age groups, to learn from and expand on social skills. There are a wide variety of ways to expand not only the child's, but also the parents' circles of influence. For example, at an extra-curricular meeting such as a chess club, or a community sports organization, or even while they are performing volunteer work at an animal shelter. Church or other spiritual venues, activities sponsored by homeschooling groups, and a number of other communal or community settings are all great social interactions. Because of the relationships formed within homeschooled families, parents believe that their children know they can come to them if they have issues with one or more friends; they also believe their children are trustworthy and hold to family teachings when unattended.

Homeschooling Builds Connections

If you are thinking about homeschooling or are *already* homeschooling your children, it's not a stretch to think you want *more* for your child, and you are willing to figure out a way to homeschool your children effectively, regardless of the sacrifices you might have to make. *You* will show them the world of innovative education and then let them determine what they want to explore first!

Homeschooling encourages you to become creative and more focused on your schedule. You will pour into your children in ways that make you proud of your children *and* yourself! You will know you are the driving force in your child's learning and that they are successful because of *you*, the parents. *You* show them the world and then let them determine what they want to explore first!

Everyone has different *'why's'* for homeschooling their children. If any of the above resonate with you, then you are not alone. *What are your motives for exploring the option of homeschooling? Which of the above examples do you agree with, at least partially?*

Make a list of all the reasons *why* you want to incorporate home education options for your child. Keep this list at the top of each lesson plan or re-read it at the beginning of your day to support your efforts going forward.

My Why for Homeschooling:

_____

_____

_____

_____

_____

_____

Henry Ford once said, "Whether you think you can or you think you can't—you're right." If you *think* you have the ability to teach your children, then I would agree with you; because *you think you can, you will.* If you have doubts about your ability and *think* you are not qualified enough to teach your children, then I would also agree with you because if *you think you can't, you won't.* Statistically, I believe most people think they can't. Realistically, I believe most people can, but you have to believe it to make it happen.

In the world of education, homeschooling emerges as a dynamic and personalized journey where parents become the guiding stars in their children's academic universe. Whether motivated by a desire for academic excellence, a commitment to instilling values, *or* the sheer joy of witnessing their child's self-discovery—homeschooling parents embark on a path that is as diverse and rewarding as the students themselves.

The flexibility to blend work and education, the power to curate a curriculum that matches their child's unique learning style, *and* the assurance of social interaction opportunities illustrate the unique palette from which homeschooling families paint their educational philosophies. It's a journey that requires *creativity*, *dedication*, and a *sprinkle* of imagination.

As you dive into discovering the wisdom and unique homeschooling methods that I share with you in this book, remember that there's no one-size-fits-all approach. Your motives, methods, and aspirations are valid and personal to you and your child. Whether you're carving out a new adventure or fine-tuning an existing one, rest assured that your commitment to your child's growth and success shines as bright as the sun in their educational universe.

Embrace the exciting blend of educator and parent that you are, and keep those *why's* close to your heart, for they will be your guiding stars on this educational odyssey. May your journey be as entertaining as it is professional, as you embark or continue with your child on the wonderful adventure of homeschooling!

Chapter 3

Things Parents Can Do to Support Their Child's Wellbeing

*"Don't let the sadness of your past and the fear of the future
ruin your happiness today. Stay positive because
today could be the best day of your life."*
—Linnea Sinclaire

In the previous chapter, we explored samples of why other parent's have decided to homeschool their children. I imagine that some of those reasons resonated with you and supported your decisions. They shared *why* they made the decision, and the progress after the decision, but they didn't explain *how* they went about homeschooling.

This chapter is dedicated to all those who want to homeschool, are already homeschooling families, or have recently become homeschooling families, as I offer useful 'how-to-homeschool' tips which I call *Mellie's Miracle Methods and Moments*. These are fundamental psychological tools that will aid you in developing your child's intellectual and emotional brain, and will help to dispel any negative energy that may be stored in their subconsciousness from incidences in their past. I call them *Mellie's Miracle Methods and Moments* because these tips will support you and your child in finding your magical moments while *learning outside the line*.

Mellie's Miracle Methods and Moments have been gleaned from over four decades of personally working with children, continuing education in child psychology where I acquired my Master's Degree in Curriculum and Instruction, and by reading dozens of 'how-to' self-help books. These books were from notable child psychologists, such as Tina Payne Bryson and Daniel J.

Siegel's *'The Whole-Brain Child; 12 Revolutionary Strategies to Nurture Your Child's Developing Mind.'* I have developed these strategies to support your homeschooling journey, I have also used them on my own children when they were in need of a boost to aid their own learning processes, so, I know they work!

Let's take a look at some of the common issues affecting kids today and then use *Mellie's Miracle Methods and Moments* as strategies to help them further. I'm sure you will bookmark this page and refer back to them as a handy reference to apply to your child's needs. I want to make sure you have the tools you and your child need to flourish and succeed.

Methods to Combating Bullying and Create Emotional Positivity

Do you remember the first time you held your child after giving birth? I do. I remember the weariness of childbirth, but also how the memory of the ordeal vanished with an overwhelming feeling of awe, wonder, and unconditional love. I remember counting each finger and each toe, and when my baby cried, my heart broke, and I quickly tried to comfort him by offering him the opportunity to feed.

I remember calling the entire family the first time he smiled, and later, I *almost* planned a party so everyone could watch him roll over once he discovered he could reposition himself. I cheered, my husband cheered, and the grandparents dropped everything to drive over to watch my son roll over. We ordered pizza and celebrated.

As time went on, there were more firsts, each one a milestone to record into his baby's book. There was the first time he rolled his body like a rolling pin to get something he saw and wanted. Wow! Smart guy! Soon he was crawling, and then his first step, Before I knew it, his first birthday had arrived. The next few years were filled with all kinds of firsts and soon enough it was the big first—his first day of school. Nothing could have prepared me for that, and somehow, I didn't want to celebrate it. I did, though—it was the right thing to do when he looked up at me with that look of, *'I don't want to go in there. Do I have to?'* I gave him a hug and told him how smart he was and how proud I was of him and that I couldn't wait for him to tell me all the fun he experienced that day.

When I picked him up after school, I could tell he was tired, but he was smiling. He started to pull things out of his backpack while we drove home as he described each treasure. This routine continued: I picked him up from his school, we jumped in the car, and as I drove home he explained each and every item in his backpack. It appeared he was going to be okay... until he wasn't.

When I picked him up that day, he didn't talk my ear off. He didn't take anything from his backpack to show me what he had done in school. He looked sad and upset, so I asked him if he felt alright. *Did he have a tummy ache? Did his head hurt?* He said no to all my questions, so I asked him what was troubling him. He said, "Mommy, am I dumb?" I said, "Of course not! Who said you were?" He told me a name. I asked if he had called him that before, and he said, "Yes." I asked him if this other child had called him *other* names, and I was shocked at the things he had been calling my son, some with foul language. I asked him why he was just now telling me about this other child, and my son said, "This time he made other kids say mean things to me."

The next morning, I mentioned this conversation to his teacher, and she assured me she would pay close attention and get to the bottom of it. I knew the routine, though: Teachers spend a few minutes to discuss and reassure the parents that they take their concerns seriously and will do what they can to correct misbehaviors. Needless to say, the problem did not get solved at school, and I finally decided it was up to me to make sure my child was feeling emotionally secure. It never occurred to me to homeschool my child because *I was a teacher!* I understood how hard it was to notice emotional bullying. However, in today's world, I get why parents throw up their hands and say, *"That's it! I'm homeschooling my child."* In today's world, I can see how many things are affecting both kids and parents alike.

Due to the fact I *was* a teacher, I was prepared to help my child deal with the emotional trauma of bullying. I believe it is a good idea to share some of these ideas with you when you begin to experience the emotional challenges that come with attending public school. Many kids face bullying and have lingering thoughts and subconscious programming due to those events. To support your child and overcome issues of bullying, I have some *Miracle Methods* to counteract the experience and foster new feelings and boundaries that will support your child's emotional health.

 ## Mellie's Miracle Methods and Moments

Ways of Countering Bullying and Distress

- **First thing in the morning**, have your child name five affirmations. Affirmations sound like this: *I am smart. I am curious. I am kind. I am brave. I am handsome (or beautiful).* Have your child look you in the eyes as they say these statements, then you repeat them back like this: Yes, you *are* smart. Yes, you *are* curious. Yes, you *are* kind. Yes, you *are* brave. Yes, you *are* handsome (beautiful).
- **Inspire your child to try new things,** such as cooking, karate, volunteering at the animal shelter, or taking a foreign language. Be supportive and find ways to ensure your child gets to do things they think about or want to try.
- **Encourage your child to role-play** where he or she becomes the 'conflict-resolution' enactor. Your child gets to handle these situational incidents in a calm and assertive way without aggression. This way, your child takes a situation that is not so kind and acts out the way he or she thinks is a good way to combat bullying situations.
- **Find ways to allow your child to interact** with a new group of children who do not know them to create new and more positive friendships and interactions. Support your child in fostering positive relationships with them.
- **Motivate empathy and compassion.** Allow your child to help other children whenever possible. Don't assume your child knows exactly how to do this. Be the role model so your child can copy your expectations.
- **Allow your child to explore physical activities,** such as martial arts or a community sports team that will build social skills around athletics, not intelligence.
- **No matter how small, celebrate** your child's achievements and efforts.
- **If you allow your child to interact online with others,** monitor those interactions and place a time limit on online interactions!!
- **Promote problem-solving skills,** adaptability, and resilience in the face of change and challenge. You don't always have to sit down in a face-to-face discussion. Encourage discussion while taking a walk with your child or sitting outside of an ice cream shop enjoying a treat together.

- **Create a scrapbook** with your child. Place photos, awards, special memories, places visited, etc. in it to remind them of pleasant and enjoyable interactions.
- **Talk about those days when bad memories crop up.** Acknowledge those memories, but emphasize those memories are in the past. Ask, *"If you could redo that situation, is there anything you would do differently?"* Then, act out the 'how I would do this differently.'

These activities will keep your child busy making new friends and memories that focus on the awesome person he or she *is* while allowing them to gain confidence and self-esteem.

 ## Mellie's Miracle Methods and Moments

Combating Social Influence with Family Values

People are social creatures by nature. We choose our friends based on the commonality of interests, beliefs, customs, and values. Children are the same way, so when our children attend group gatherings designed for them, we tend to gravitate to those people whom our children are developing friendships with based on authentic commonalities. Psychologists say this is normal behavior because it allows for shared experiences, familiar interests, comfort, and emotional support. These connections can be mutually beneficial, helping both parents and children feel more connected and supported within their social networks.

I intentionally created a fun environment in my home where my children would be comfortable enough to invite their friends to visit and have sleepovers. By the time my kids were in high school, they were involved in all sorts of activities, from clubs outside of school, to sports teams, to playing in the band—It was never a surprise to come home after work to find half the football team in our basement. My husband and I had intentionally stocked a refrigerator full of soft drinks and bottled water, cabinets full of snacks and candy, bought a full-size pool table, and arcade games. We even installed a sound system so they could listen to their favorite music. Outside, their father built a backstop to play baseball and a half-court for basketball.

I made it a point to have enough food around to fix dinner for all of them. After dinner, before they could go back downstairs and 'play,' they had to get their homework out and ask me if they needed help. When news got around to all the other parents, I started getting donations of money and food. *Why?* Because the other parents knew us and trusted us, and if their child was at our home, they knew they were supervised and taken care of. What was most important to me was I knew where *my* kids were and what they were doing.

When my children were growing up, we lived in a small-town environment. You might not think there were negative social influences in a tight-knit rural community, but that wasn't the case. There were drugs, alcohol, cigarettes, raging hormones, and clandestine parties when parents were out of town—the same concerns back then as now. I realize there are more powerful drugs with nastier effects nowadays—more addictive and life-threatening. Parties have become raves. In many cases, society appears to be less strict. The older your children become, the more peer influence drives their actions and responses. In order for your children to be prepared for the negative influences they will encounter, you have to prepare them for those things that may not align with your values. You have to make sure they have the social and emotional tools they need to walk away from those influences that do not support their positive growth.

You can begin by making your home inviting and a place where your children's friends are welcome. All kids need social interactions and friends, even those that are in a homeschooling environment. Here are some wonderful ways to make sure your children know you support them, you are invested in their needs, thoughts, friends, and what motivates them. It's also a fantastic way to inspire communication and family interactions.

 ## Mellie's Miracle Methods and Moments

Influencing Kids Without Them Even Knowing
- **Designate an area of your home** that is to become 'the kids' zone. Have a discussion with your children to make sure they understand it is a place where they can relax and invite friends over to visit. Brainstorm

how they would like to decorate it and what they would like to have in it. Then, make a list of the things that can be done now to make it better and a list of what you can do as money is saved to accomplish their wish list. Realize that there will be items brainstormed that probably aren't doable, but when brainstorming, all ideas get listed to validate the idea, and as discussion ensues afterward, the things less likely to be added will naturally weed themselves out.

- **Find out what's 'in'** when it comes to your children's generation—clothing styles, word usage (kids don't say things like, "that's peachy," anymore), the latest music trends, popular movies, popular snacks—all the things your child and their peers like and talk about. This is important because your kids *want* you to be the 'cool' parents. Of course, you have a hidden agenda, and that's to keep a watchful eye on your children and have a safe space for them and their friends. Both of these first two suggestions subconsciously allow freedom for them to establish positive friendships and accumulate trusting peer relationships.

- **Try to plan at least one family meal** a day where everyone sets their cell phones aside, where you can strengthen family discussions and discover what's going on in your child's life. When I was a child, my family always said grace before dinner, our sit-down family shared meal. We discussed what was happening in school, what chores needed to be completed on the coming weekend, and what was happening that we wanted to participate in, like band trips, movies, birthday parties, holiday plans, etc. Those are topics that families can still share in, as well as all the new and improved gadgets and social trends—fashion, music, concerts, etc. Spend quality time together that gives you the opportunity to model behaviors you approve of—volunteer together, watch a movie together, read together, and engage in fun activities and hobbies, such as a painting class, a fitness class at the gym, or putting a puzzle together. Think of the fun you can have taking a foreign language class and conversing at home as you both attain new skills.

- **Encourage your child to become a critical thinker** so they can make judgments when they are away that are within your family values and social acceptance. This will encourage their independence as they mature, but at the same time set boundaries on their decisions.

- **Model a healthy lifestyle** and practice what you preach. Eat healthily with limited options of 'junk food.' If someone has a restrictive diet, then the family should support that person by not eating 'no-no foods' in front of them. Take walks or bicycle together. If you don't want your children to do something, then be the example and not do it yourself.

Keeping your children safe and able to make sound decisions when they are not around you is the greatest gift you can give your children. Our children are our treasures, but unlike gems and heirlooms, they can't be locked up to ensure safety. They are making decisions and constantly in motion, not sitting gathering dust. Treat them like the rare gifts they are, and you will have an extreme sense of accomplishment when, later in life, you see your children acting in similar ways with their children, your grandchildren. I know this to be true because I witness it all the time now that my sons are grown and have their own families.

Promoting Individualism

I grew up in the 1960s, a time in history when family values were the most important lessons a child could learn. In my house, and everyone else I knew, there was a tried and true realism—there were two ways to do things: the wrong way and 'Father's Way.' There are many times in recent years that my siblings and friends have laughed over shenanigans and such when 'Father's Way' was challenged, and someone reaped the 'consequences' of that challenge.

Later, when I was raising my own children, I sometimes considered 'Father's Way' in dealing with them, but often re-evaluated it in search of a *new way*. I realized that 'Father's Way' did not allow for my siblings' or me to develop a sense of individualism until we were out on our own. That may have been the norm when I was a child, but as society changed and new theories developed, it became more and more the responsibility of the parents to promote their children's individuality, not trap them in a box and seal the top closed.

Promoting individualism in children is important as it helps them develop a strong sense of self, allows them to make independent decisions, and resist negative peer pressure. This can be especially valuable in public arenas where children encounter challenges to their family values and experience bullying or emotional conflict. Promoting individualism is a lifelong process that involves nurturing your child's self-esteem, independence, and ability to make informed decisions while respecting their individuality. By doing so, parents can help their children navigate the challenges of public situations while staying true to their family values and sense of self.

It is incredibly important to recognize your child's opinions because you can know when they are subconsciously speaking their thoughts while mimicking family values, as well as when they are mimicking their peers or social influences. It is not constructive, nor supportive to negate their thoughts and opinions. It's more empowering to have an open discussion, honest conversation or even an intelligent debate with you to keep the communication flowing. This is generally the *norm* among homeschooling parents, where open thought and constructive conversations are encouraged and welcomed.

 ## Mellie's Miracle Methods and Moments

Individualism 101
Maintain open and non-judgmental communication with your child. Encourage them to express their thoughts, feelings, and concerns. Be an active listener and validate their emotions.

- **Allow your child to make age-appropriate decisions and choices,** like what they want to wear that day, or the type of sandwich they want for lunch. As they get older, their opportunity to make individual decisions will mature. For instance, making the decision to do their schoolwork in a timely manner (or not) can get them a reward or a consequence. When they have the opportunity to make decisions, they learn to take responsibility for their actions and develop a sense of autonomy.
- **Encouraging your child to explore their interests and passions** allows them to pursue hobbies, sports, arts, or other activities that align with their innate talents and passions.
- **Help your child develop critical thinking skills** by discussing various perspectives, asking open-ended questions, and encouraging them to analyze information critically. Teach them to think for themselves rather than conform to others' views.

- **Instead of telling your children** what they should do in different situations, teach them problem-solving skills. Involve your child in discussions about challenges or dilemmas they may face. Guide them in finding solutions and evaluating the consequences of different choices.
- **Teach your child to respect and appreciate diversity** and differences in others. Emphasize that it's okay for people to have varying beliefs, backgrounds, and perspectives. Since people grow up in different cultures, with different spiritual beliefs, and religions, talking about differences is a way to educate them about the various customs and cultures around the world.
- **Children learn by observing their parents.** Be a role model for individualism by making your own decisions, pursuing your interests, and standing up for your values.
- **Teach your child resilience** skills to help them cope with challenges and setbacks. This includes strategies for managing stress, building self-esteem, and emotional intelligence. Resilience skills include regulating emotions, developing positive thinking habits, being adaptive, defining a unique sense of purpose, and learning to reframe thoughts to lead toward an independent and constructive mindset.

Adapting to Your Environment

Many homeschooling parents indicated that it was difficult to navigate public school hours when they had to travel for work, or when they wanted to enjoy family vacations, or even when dealing with family emergencies—due to the schedules and restrictions. Many parents have lifestyles outside the traditional nine-to-five work day and struggle with the confines of a rigid routine.

I wanted to take this opportunity to highlight the daily dance families go through of getting ready for school, getting to school, and then getting home and attending to everything needing to be done at home once school is over. Often parents and children do not function optimally within the heavy confines of time strictures. Be assured homeschooling can alleviate these concerns, giving you valuable extra time *to not only promote family values, personal well-being, emotional health, individuality, and social life, but also foster individualism within your family unit. What if you have to move for a job, the military, or any other circumstances that require a change in scenery? What if your child struggles with being up early or thrives learning after dark? What if you appreciate traveling and visiting family in other countries to maintain family relationships?* Let me share some ideas that can be adapted to wherever you find yourself living, no matter the circumstances!

 ## Mellie's Miracle Methods and Moments

Changes in Latitude and Longitude

- **Inform your family** as soon as possible about the change in environment that is coming in their future. Be open and honest about why you are moving or about the reasons you are choosing to homeschool versus continuing in public education.
- **Involve everyone** in the process of adapting to new, uncharted territory. Ask your children for their opinions, talk about their concerns, and keep them in the loop, informing them of changes and new information as it develops.
- **Research the surrounding area** to find places to explore. In a group discussion, list the places in order of preference that your children find interesting and plan to go on an adventure as soon as possible. Remember that what one family member loves may be something another might not think they will enjoy. In that case, assure each family member they will go to their place of interest also.
- **Foster individual time** In the event that one of your children is feeling alone or left out, take them on a walk and talk to them, or visit a special place. Allow your children to set up their new study area and/or their bedroom.
- **Stay positive and patient** even if things appear to be chaotic at the moment. Those moments will pass, like a sudden summer storm that ends with blue skies. Try a deep breathing exercise: Inhale slowly to the count of five. Hold this breath for another slow count of five, then slowly exhale to a final count of five. Do this three times.

- **Stay connected** to friends and family by having weekly phone visits, group email threads or group chats. Encourage your children to invite old friends over to visit, as well as family members.
- **Be confident in your decisions** as confidence instills trust. When your children trust that you are doing everything in your power to educate them they try harder. They are prepared to take on challenges, even if they have never seen the new material you are presenting. The cycle will continue because then your children will be confident, too.

The many *Mellie's Miracle Methods and Moments* I have shared are designed to help you navigate through many scenarios that pop up along your homeschooling journey. Use them when you need a quick remedy for unanticipated events that show up on any given day. As you learn more tricks of the trade, write them down, recording new ideas to add to what is here. In doing these practices you will notice more smiles, extra enthusiasm in completing assignments, and your home environment *will* become a place of harmony. It will take time and practice to acquire new practices when you are balancing what you know with the various personalities in a full-time homeschooling habitat. Yet, soon enough, you will become such a pro as a homeschooling parent, you will know you have made the best possible decisions for your family as you thrive and enjoy their education *learning outside the line.*

You are the fearless leader of your family whether you are feeling fearless all the time or not. There will be times when you question yourself, even second-guess yourself. If you're like most people, those are things we do unconsciously all the time. Sometimes we are our worst judge and jury, but I say, "Be gentle on yourself. You owe it to your family." We wouldn't be human if we didn't think of better ways to do things, smarter ways to navigate situations *the next time,* and more effective ways to organize and *truly enjoy life.*

Chapter 4

Understanding My Child's Gifts and Talents

"Anything worth teaching can be presented in many different ways. These multiple ways can make use of our multiple intelligences."
—HOWARD GARDNER

Years ago, while taking a college course, I was introduced to an award-winning American developmental psychologist, Howard Gardner, a Harvard University graduate. He proposed that children didn't learn in only one, *general* way but learned in a combination of eight different ways called *The Theory of Multiple Intelligences*. He also proposed that intelligence was not stagnant but increased throughout one's life. He introduced this theory in his 1983 book, *Frames of Mind: The Theory of Multiple Intelligences.*

Before I delve into this theory, let me explain what I was taught in college. I learned that in any given classroom, there were three levels of learners: The 'top' level was those students who were the 'smart ones.' The 'middle' level was the 'average' students and comprised the bulk of the classroom—approximately three-fifths of the students. The bottom level was the children who would 'struggle' no matter the subject. More often than not, these students were placed on an Individual Education Plan, an IEP. All my professors directed us to teach all of our lessons to the middle group because they represented the bulk of the classroom population; the top level would learn no matter what, but the bottom level would always labor to learn. Those students, often labeled special-education students, required extra time and resources to learn. Teaching to the middle would ensure that the needs of the majority of the children were met because it would address the needs of the upper-level students, also.

I was additionally taught in college that a person's intelligence was determined at birth, and nothing could be done to change it. Now that I think back to my college education to become a teacher, I think some classes should have been renamed Cookie Cutter 101, Baseline 102, Teaching to Averages 201, Blinders On 202—You get the drift! Every education course I took insisted the 'top, middle, bottom' was factual and, just like intelligence, could not be changed. When I began my teaching career, I followed along with that mindset, writing my lesson plans for the middle group of children. However, something always bothered me about that attitude—*the bottom level couldn't learn?* That couldn't be right! When I heard about Howard Gardner's *Theory of Multiple Intelligences*, I sat up and took notice.

Gardner's theory challenged that the more one learned, the higher one's intelligence rose. I had already taught for a few years, and I knew some kids learned faster when they were interested in what I was teaching. However, if I moved to a subject that wasn't so interesting to them, they wouldn't do as well. I wondered, *How could this child make A's in math but barely achieve a C in spelling?* Gardner answered my question: people have different styles of learning. It finally made sense. If that child was a Magical Mathematician but was not a Vivacious Verbalist, they would excel in one subject and struggle in the other. Based on their learning style, they would learn in their own way. Knowing that children learn differently and retain information uniquely, I realized that teaching the middle intelligence spectrum did not address each child's needs. *No more Cookie Cutters!*

This opened Pandora's box of the different *types* of learners, and tapping into *how* a child learns was the key to unlocking their learning potential. I then discovered that Gardner constructed a list of statements that helped identify one's learning styles. Strengths and inherent preferences were highlighted by assigning a numerical value of one to five to a series of statements. From there, a learning style was revealed, and how one best receives information and processes new concepts was put into categories. I am not a fan of categories or labeling anyone, but Gardner's eight categories became a goldmine of opportunity for me as a teacher to understand how each of my students could learn to their greatest capacity.

Using Multiple Intelligences at Home

I took Gardner's learning style questionnaire and discovered I was a *mathe-matical-logical* learner but weak as a *bodily-kinesthetic* learner. In other words, I was not very athletic or physically coordinated, so anything physical did not appeal to me. Finally! There was a reason I had two left feet! Reading about sports heroes or athletics would not be a way to reach me, but it gave me a geometry problem to solve, and I was on it! However, I was almost as equally strong as a *visual-spatial* and *interpersonal learner.* This means I love art and designing things, so hands-on projects are never a chore. It also meant I love working with people in groups and making friends easily. It also explained why Miss Kerr nicknamed me 'Chatty Cathy' as a child due to how much I loved to socialize! It occurred to me that I may have just discovered the secret sauce of teaching. I asked, *"How can this be useful to my teaching and all my students?"*

After discovering the *Theory of Multiple Intelligences*, I decided I should try addressing each one of the learning styles with my students! I had everything to gain and nothing to lose! But first, I redefined the statements on the questionnaire to fit my students because children of different ages understand questions differently, and diverse cultural differences in families can lead to misunderstandings because of word usage. I also wanted every child to understand the wording and answer the questions appropriately. Children from diverse cultural environments speak in different vernaculars. Kids with different sociographics and demographics have preferences instilled in them through environmental necessities. I modeled my new questionnaire off of the original questionnaire, but added new references so that children from diverse backgrounds could understand the statements more clearly. When I tallied the scores, I found out how my students learned in relativity to the theory of multiple intelligences. Immediately, I realized I had hit the jackpot of how to teach efficiently and effectively.

If you adapt what you teach your child to how they learn best, your job as their teacher will become much easier. You'll be teaching your children *how* they process and retain information versus a middle-of-the-road approach. It will also help you if you have more than one child, each with different learning styles. In that case, you can now accentuate their learning modalities, making communication easy and strengthening their ability to succeed by knowing which style they learn from. In teaching to their strengths and preferences, they will be more interested and successful in *how* they think. That is a H-U-G-E bonus for them and you!

I hope this revelation interests you in knowing *"What are these styles of learning?"* and *"Which style is my child?"* Once you discover this information, I assure you that learning will be easier and more enjoyable. When you know how your child processes information you can begin to tailor lessons to their unique learning attributes. You will be maximizing their learning with less time involvement, allowing them to process information quickly so they can move on to the next level of learning or another subject that needs to be addressed; all of a sudden, your child will be interested in what you are teaching, participating in their learning, enthusiastically diving into their lessons, and appreciating you for teaching them in the ways they love to learn.

Innovative Intelligences Start with YOU

You are the key to your child's success and the catalyst for how well they receive new information. How you support them in learning, according to their style, will help define their future. As you begin to understand these styles, you will see how these innovative techniques yield outstanding results.

The next chapter describes all the Innovative Intelligences I have created for homeschooling children and explains how each style likes to learn. I wanted both you and your child to have fun with each style and recognize that they are all terrific. No one is better than the other; each has wonderful attributes and amazing qualities. I have given them all positive names and empowering references. If we give out any labels, we want them to be uplifting and encouraging, and to reflect the many gifts each child possesses. I made sure to not only give you the amazing qualities of each learner, but to also give you examples of what your child might aspire to become in the future, based on those attributes.

Since you, too, are an avid learner, I suggest you take the time to read over each style and see the many different ways of learning that have been identified. As you read the different styles, you will see resemblances of yourself and your child in the explanations.

Remember—every single person *is* all eight Innovative Intelligences, but some are more than others. Since each learning type has unique characteristics, you will soon uncover the 'secret sauce' that will empower you to teach your child better and empower them to learn in a better, more productive way. When you focus on *how* your child learns, instead of only *what* they need to learn, all the puzzle pieces you thought were missing, sometimes frustrating to you and your child, will fall into place.

The puzzle pieces were always there, but now you know how to fit them into place with joy and ease. Keep that in mind as you discover new ways to teach your child in ways that will keep them interested and engaged. For instance, if you find out your child is a Conscious Creative learner, then you know it is imperative to use rhymes, rhythms, tones, music, and mnemonic devices in their everyday learning and assignments. On the other hand, if you find out your child is a Vivacious Verbilist, you know your child excels in anything that has to do with Language Arts, whether it is the written, spoken, or listening word. This child needs books to read—both fiction and non-fiction—newspapers to peruse, to debate issues near and dear to their heart, and the ability to write journals, letters, responses, and debates.

Different age groups will require different tactics to get them excited to learn. Since it would not be practical to give the learning questionnaire to young children, it is up to you to put on your detective hat and play Sherlock Holmes™.

With small children ages one to three, you can observe what toys they like to play with. *Do they like the musical ones that play sounds and tunes, or do they like the toys where they have to figure out how to stack the donuts from largest to smallest? Do they like to roll the ball back and forth and try to catch it, or do they like a toddler computer that plays stories and has the alphabet matching lower case letters to upper case letters?* The toys they gravitate toward will help you see their innate inclination. Be aware of what you see as their favorite pastimes, such as playing with an imaginary friend or wanting to spend time with the family pet outdoors. Everything they do is a viewfinder into their learning style.

The same is true with toddlers ages three to six. *Would they rather play in the sandbox with various trucks and other vehicles, or do they like to dig to find hidden treasures you have hidden? Do they like to sing along with their favorite learning show on TV, or do they insist you read the same book repeatedly?* These little 'tells' are sure signs of interest, and if you are observant, you will pick up on these indicators and structure play time that is *actually* learning time. For instance, hide plastic letters in the sandbox and see if your child can find them all and line them up in order. For the child who wants you to read the same book over and over again, point to the words as you read. Show them the word *'the'* and let them read it every time you come to that word in the story. The next time you read that book, show them another sight word. Make sure you let them find those same words in other books you read to them.

Older children will display similar likes and dislikes as they mature, continuing to excel best in how they think according to what *'floats their boat!'*

Completing the questionaire reaffirms what you already know and provides insight into other learning patterns and their strengths, which gives you further insight into other ways to arrange your lessons to get maximum results with minimum effort and work. Although the questionnaire doesn't outline their weaknesses, assume that their weakest score on this questionnaire indicates those are not a favorite way for them to learn, nor do those call to their interests and intellect.

Your child might see this questionnaire as a test and not want to participate. They might not take it as seriously as you want them to. I suggest you talk it up first as something magnificent or an experiment you'd like them to help you with. Offer an incentive for doing their best. I had my students make a picture of which intelligence they were most strong in. I let them pick a colored piece of cardstock that they liked. In the center, they wrote their name as fancy as they wanted. In the top left, they *wrote* the type of intelligence they were. In the top right, they drew a picture of themself in a way that reflected that intelligence, such as them reading a book under a tree with birds and butterflies flitting overhead. Along the bottom left, they wrote their secondary intelligence, and in any open space, they drew a picture of what those intelligences looked like. For example, the *Exceptional Ecologist* might draw things that help the environment or animals on the endangered species list. We framed their pictures in other cardstock and hung them on their desk for a few weeks. Then I moved them to the *"Wall of Fame"* in my room, where, at a glance, I knew which children would pair best with others when planning my lessons. You can do something similar, but make it a family fun time when everyone is working on their own profile!

The key to any kind of assessment or evaluation of this nature is to let your child know that there is no *right* or *wrong* and every answer is the perfect answer. Ensuring total acceptance and fostering their self-confidence will yield the best results and have your children answering with genuine conviction. That will give you a real reflection of how they like to learn best.

As you move into Chapter Five, you will see I have outlined the basic 'tells' of each of the eight Innovative Intelligences, followed by the questionnaire to determine your child's strongest learning intelligence and any others that are as strong or nearly as strong. If you would rather have a full-sized copy of the PDF, it's free to download on my website, www.innovativehomeschoolsolutions.com; print a copy for everyone!

Once everyone takes the test, compare your results to the descriptions in the next chapter and get excited to learn, *"That's me! That's my spouse! That is 100% my child!"* Get prepared to be blown away because you are going to have a game-changing teaching tool that no one has ever told you about! Once you understand that each person has a distinctive way of learning, and that is *the* key that unlocks their successes, you will know exactly how to approach your child's education.

Chapter 5

Innovative Intelligences Makes it Easy

"The biggest mistake of past centuries in teaching is to treat all students as if they were variants of the same individual and thus to feel justified in teaching them all the same subjects the same way."
—HOWARD GARDNER

I was amazed at the results when I began implementing Innovative Intelligences into my classroom. After allowing each child to answer the questionnaire according to how true each statement was compared to their likes and dislikes, I immediately realized a few truths. *First*, children learn on different levels of *interest. Second*, teaching a lesson in one way allowed for only a few children to understand the lesson completely. *Third*, some of the children who were considered 'average' or 'below-average' were not learning as quickly as they could because they could not relate to my one-dimensional lessons. *Finally*, I needed to sculpt my lessons away from a 'one size fits all' approach to teaching to a more diversified learning experience that incorporates the different intelligences in one lesson.

A few realizations occurred once I began to streamline my lessons for everyone in the class. *First*, my kids were more eager to learn; therefore, behavior issues nearly vanished. *Second*, papers were turned in with more correct answers than wrong answers. *Third*, I became more creative in my teaching tactics. *Finally*, test scores rose to the point where no one was struggling.

Before defining Innovative Intelligences, I always wondered why something I taught quite successfully one year bombed the next year. I realized classes have personalities, just like individual people. What worked in one class wouldn't work the same way the next year because the personality of the class was not the same. After addressing the personalities of each student, I discovered I was accurate in my deduction, that the classes' personality was based on the students' interests. I noticed the preceding class may have had a high frequency of Magical Mathematician learners in it, but the new class had a high frequency of Conscious Creative learners. Things I used successfully for the class with a high frequency of MM learners would *not* work well in a high-frequency of CC learners.

Imagine if *you* found the secret sauce that elevated your child from where they are now to awakening their exceptionality. *Wouldn't you want to use that sauce liberally? Wouldn't you like to know if what you did successfully for one child will work with another?* You can be more effective in teaching your children if their questionnaires show them to be different types of learners. This will save you a lot of time and potentially a lot of frustration because your teaching techniques won't miss—they will be right on the mark!

The Eight Innovative Outside the Line Intelligences

The following is *my* adaptation of Gardner's Theory of Multiple Intelligences and each personality type. I have modified them to be more conducive to home-schooling parents and positive terminology that kids will resonate with. I called them Innovative Intelligences because I believe that each child is innovative in the way they learn since they are a combination and culmination of the many styles interchangeably. No two students are truly the same and that makes them both innovative and intelligent in the way they process all information and see the world around them. We want children to be innovative and grow their intelligence, and these eight styles build a well-rounded approach to learning the many things the world has to offer.

As you read over each style, highlight different descriptions that sound like members of your family, indicating which person applies to which description. Remember that learning styles can overlap, and everyone has a little bit of each style in them. After administering my questionnaire, you may soon discover why your child seems to have predominantly one intelligence but also several secondary intelligences. Recognizing each style will allow you to choose what you want to teach, when to teach that material, and most importantly, *how* to teach it. Paying attention to the various nuances of each innovative style will give you insight into your child's mind so that they can focus more clearly on the information presented to them and retain it for future use. Bookmark this page so you can reference it to compare what you have observed about your child over time to the type of learner your child is so you can adapt your lessons concisely to your child, focusing on their interests and needs.

 ## The Exceptional Ecologist (EE)

The Exceptional Ecologist, or EE for short, can recognize and categorize various aspects of the natural world, such as plants, animals, and geography. They love the outdoors and activities such as hiking, camping, and gardening. The EE can understand and appreciate nature and how it works to create our world. They love identifying different types of plants, animals, and rocks. They have a good sense of observation. They enjoy anything from studying dinosaurs to camping, rock climbing, and searching for fossils. Most archeologists are EEs, as well as outdoor survivalists who teach others how to live off the land. Other possible EEs are botanists, biologists, geologists, ecologists, astronomers, and environmentalists. Exceptional Ecologists love anything in nature and learn well outdoors or by reading about nature studies. If you are the parent of an EE, let them study and learn outside as often as possible, and make sure you take them to zoos, aquariums, and places where they can study the environment. If you go on vacation to the beach, you will probably find your Exceptional Ecologist looking for seashells, digging for sea animals hiding in the sand, or observing how the birds act before they jump into the ocean! Don't be surprised if your EE learner becomes involved in environmental issues such as climate control, ocean pollution, or animals and plants on the endangered species list.

 ## The Magical Mathematician (MM)

The Magical Mathematician can reason, think logically, and solve problems mathematically. They question everything because they really want to know the answers to what is happening around them. They will ask difficult questions and search for logical answers to their inquiries. If asked if they want to learn to play chess or go outside to play tag, they will choose chess. The Magical Mathematician will get excited about and play for hours with a Rubik's Cube™ but get bored with a skateboard—unless they are searching for a way to improve it. MMs analyze cause-and-effect relationships, like learning about and using numbers, especially in problem-solving activities, and can decipher abstract visual information in charts, graphs, and maps. Suppose you are the parent of an MM; you might find them designing something like architectural projects, working on the next roller coaster design, crunching numbers at a bank, or being a statistician for a research and development company. MMs focus on careers that involve problem-solving, critical thinking, and logical reasoning. Careers that attract the MMs might include doctors, lawyers, mathematicians, scientists, computer programmers, accountants, engineers, statisticians, researchers, microbiologists, or eventually working for NASA.

 The Vivacious Verbalist (VV)

The Vivacious Verbalist can use language effectively and express oneself through writing and/or speaking. They excel in using language effectively and learning and recalling information just by what they hear. They have superior skills in speaking, understanding many ways of communication, writing, and putting their thoughts on paper. The VV learner will sign up to attend lectures, especially if there are group discussions and collaboration opportunities. They have no problem inserting information from memory. They can work in any learning environment involving written, spoken, or listening activities, conveying their thoughts concisely and sequentially in speeches, while debating, or in writing. English courses are their first love, but they will do well in math with word problems versus simple math equations. VV learners are often skilled at learning new languages, telling stories, and understanding complex texts. They thrive on listening to stories and getting to know others through interviews but will need you to explain or clarify written directions in detail. If your child is a VV, they may become a journalist, a teacher, an author, an editor, a copywriter, a translator, a public relations specialist, or someone who interviews others, such as a talk show host—or even become an actor!

The Conscious Creative (CC)

The Conscious Creative can understand and appreciate music and create musical compositions. They are basically the opposite of the Vivacious Verbalist learner. They not only have the ability to understand and produce music, but they are also skilled at recognizing and producing different sounds, rhythms, and melodies. They learn better with pictures and images rather than with verbal information. CCs do well with hands-on activities, especially if they can express themselves by showing their work through what they construct or put together. They are the children whose room is a wreck; they falter at note-taking skills and get annoyed at step-by-step directions. The Conscious Creative learner will challenge 'the correct answer' by thinking 'outside the box.' Of course, the CC learner will listen to music. At the same time, as they do their homework, they pretend to be playing drums in a rock band or tap out the rhythm of songs on the arms of a chair or with pencils while sitting at the table. They are good at poetry and will write poems and then put them to music, meaning they make amazing songwriters. They like all kinds of music and will be comfortable at the opera or attending a Broadway musical. They love dancing, singing, and creating art. Your CC learner may become a creative arts teacher—in music, art, or even woodworking—a musician, a singer, a composer, a sound technician, or a music therapist. They will dream of becoming the next pop singer or organizing a band. They may become a dancer or an actor in a musical. Their favorite genres of reading or movies are science fiction, time travel, or fantasy.

The Super Spatialist (SS)

They can think and reason about objects in three-dimensional space, such as visualizing a building's design or mentally rotating an object. They are fast at thinking in terms of space and visual imagery. People with high spatial intelligence are often skilled at visualizing objects and scenes in their minds, understanding maps and diagrams, and manipulating images. Super

Spatialists synthesize information quickly, so don't expect them to follow step-by-step instructions because they understand the entire concept in record time. They are the ones who are working on their homework and doing it correctly after the first fifteen minutes of instruction while everyone else is still on step two! They are the children you give assignments to and then get out of their way. They look for patterns and use them to build the next step. They can read facial and body language easily, so it's hard to fool them. They are the child who learns to spell by writing in the air; they draw from memory and relate what they know to other areas of study. The SS learner can weave a picture in their mind, such as a memory of somewhere they have been, into the written word so that the reader also believes they have been there. Expect the SS learner to do well with technology, communications, criminal justice, and law. Some examples of careers the SS learner would gravitate toward include artists, architects, graphic designers, cartographers, photographers, interior designers, video game designers, and commercial or military pilots.

 The Phenomenal Physicalist (PP)

The Phenomenal Physicalist learner can control body movements and handle objects skillfully, as in sports, dance, or surgery. They do well with anything that uses the body, have fantastic hand-eye coordination, and have excellent muscle memory. They excel in sports where they perform because of muscle memory: dance and any other activity that requires physical activity or manual dexterity, such as surgery, playing musical instruments, and acting; arts and crafts, such as someone who creates designer objects of interest— jewelry designs, clothing designers, three-dimensional wall art; anything that involves artistic movements, such as ballet or ballroom dancing, even professional sports. They love hands-on activities but find it difficult to retain information using only audible or visual forms of learning. PP learners like to explore, discover, and do things independently as long as it's hands-on! If your child is a PP learner, they may become an actor, an entrepreneur, an athlete, an inventor, a dancer, a carpenter, a chef, a mechanic, a massage therapist, or even a brain surgeon.

 ## The Amazing Adaptist (AA)

The Amazing Adaptist can understand and interact effectively with others and recognize and respond appropriately to their emotional states. They thrive on other people and are curious about how others see the world. They understand and interact with other people very well. AAs understand the emotions, motivations, and intentions of others and can effectively communicate and work with others. They will engage in conversations to get other people's viewpoints on a topic of interest. They are adept at gaging other people and how they think, feel, and interact with others. They are empathetic by nature. They naturally understand how others see the world differently; no one has to teach them that. That makes them good negotiators, peacekeepers, and mediators. They are excellent leaders who can quickly organize groups to achieve common goals. They are particularly good at both verbal and nonverbal communication. If you have an interpersonal learner, expect them to be outgoing. They will strike up a conversation with others everywhere they go because they like people in general. On the other hand, because they seem to read people so well, they might manipulate others to get their way or get others to agree with them to get the outcome they want. Your Amazing Adaptist might become a social worker, a counselor, a talk show host, a teacher, a human resource professional, a manager, a salesperson, a psychologist, an event planner, an entrepreneur, or even a campaign organizer.

 ## The Impressive Independent (II)

The Impressive Independent learners are the complete opposite of Amazing Adaptist learners. They can understand one's emotions, motivations, and inner self and reflect on one's thoughts and feelings. IIs are independent learners and prefer to be by themselves in quiet places. They understand themselves and their thoughts and feelings. They are in tune with their emotions and motivations and can effectively manage their behaviors and goals. They prefer their own space and do *not* like to learn in a group or spend time at functions that involve crowds. If given the choice of reading in their room or attending a professional football game, they will choose to read a book alone. They are goal-oriented, they tend to be shy, and they are perfectionists. The II child may know the answer to every question you ask but will think the answer, not speak the answer. They are quite content just knowing they know the correct answer. II's don't have to broadcast it. The II learner can be challenging, especially for large families—they would rather be an only child. If you have an II child, you cannot make them be outgoing and command control of a group. Impressive Independent learners will choose a career where they can be their own boss or work independently. You might find your Impressive Independent child grows up as a psychologist, a spiritual advisor, a counselor, an entrepreneur, or a self-help author.

The Eight Innovative Intelligences and YOU

I hope that in reading the different styles, you identified with one yourself and saw glimmers of your child in one or more of them. I am sure some resonated with you immediately, and others thoroughly described your child or someone you know to a tee. That is the beauty of this system: it identifies the strengths and interests of each individual.

You now have the 'secret sauce' that allows you to immediately present ideas and information in a way that grabs your child's attention, focus, and imagination. You no longer need to guess at how your child learns or how to present information. Knowing how your child's mind works allows you to 'cut to the chase' on what and how to present information, then allow your child to run with it and go beyond the boundaries of what they can learn. Your child will accelerate and go beyond 'grade level' at any age, completing tasks easier and faster than you could even imagine.

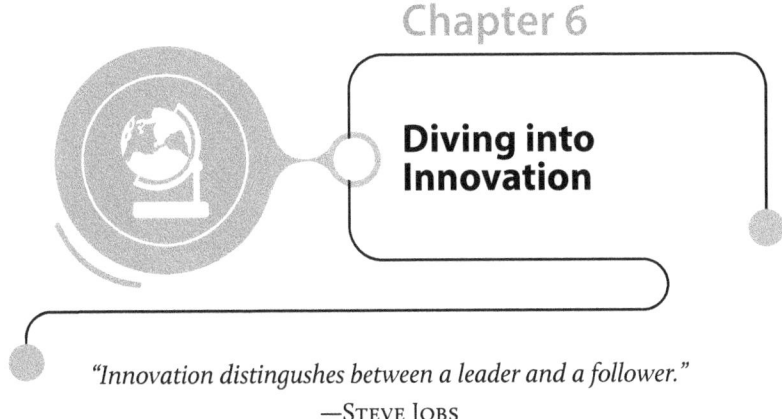

Chapter 6

Diving into Innovation

"Innovation distingushes between a leader and a follower."
—Steve Jobs

As you identify the learning style of your children, you will soon see a dramatic change in their interest and excitement. We will use that information as we move forward throughout the book, and you can refer to it often to form your *teaching* style. Keep a record of what you learned in the notes section at the end of the chapter, and become curious about all the ways you can structure learning in these new ways.

Let's do the assessment:

Instructions: Read each statement in the graph on the next page. Ask yourself how much you agree with each statement.
- If you totally agree with the statement all the time, score it with the number 5.
- If you agree with it most of the time, score it a 4.
- If you sometimes agree with it, score it with the number 3.
- If you do not agree with the statement most of the time, give it a score of 2.
- If you never agree with the statement, score it with the number 1.

After scoring each statement, refer to the next page. Add the numbered statements assigned to each type of leather and record the sum on the corresponding line.

INNOVATIVE INTELLIGENCES LEARNING INVENTORY

1. I am concerned about pollution.	
2. I like puzzles such as Rubric Cubes.	
3. I can remember information easily.	
4. I like to sing.	
5. I like to learn with graphs and pictures.	
6. I like to play sports.	
7. I like to learn by myself.	
8. I like to learn in groups.	
9. I like to learn about plants and animals.	
10. I like to play strategy games like checkers and chess.	
11. I like to write stories.	
12. I like to dance.	
13. I like to write things in the air with my finger.	
14. I like to play outside games like tag.	
15. I make new friends easily.	
16. I do not like to work in a group.	
17. I like camping, hiking, and rock climbing.	
18. I like to put jigsaw puzzles together.	
19. I like to pretend I am an actor.	
20. I think it would be fun to play a musical instrument.	
21. I learn easily and quickly.	
22. I like to swim.	
23. Noise bothers me when I am working on a project.	
24. I love to go places with other people.	

Read the statements on the adjacent clipboard, and take your time to answer.

Use the following scale to indicate how much you agree with the statement.

1= I seldom agree   4= I agree a lot
2= I agree a little bit   5= I agree all the time
3= I half agree

After you have completed how you feel about the statements, add up the score for each of the questions that correspond with each learning style.

CONSCIOUS CREATIVE
Add up your response to questions 4, 12, and 20 = _____

VIVACIOUS VERBALIST
Add up your response to questions 3, 11 and 19 = _____

EXCEPTONAL ECOLOGIST
Add up your response to questions 1, 9 and 17 = _____

MAGICAL MATHEMATICIAN
Add up your response to questions 2, 10 and 18 = _____

SUPER SPATIALIST
Add up your response to questions 5, 13, and 21 = _____

IMPRESSIVE INDEPENDENT
Add up your response to questions 7, 16 and 23 = _____

PHENOMINAL PHYSICALIST
Add up your response to questions 6, 14 and 22 = _____

AMAZING ADAPTIST
Add up your response to questions 8,15, and 24 = _____

Finally, rank the answers from greatest number to least number. The greatest number tells you the type of learner you most resemble. If there are close answers—such as the highest number being thirteen, but one or more have answers of twelve—you are mainly the highest number but have secondary interests and learning styles. Keep in mind that the highest number may also be tied with one or more of the multiple intelligences. Because a person learns on more than one level of learning simultaneously, they process information lightning-fast!

The lowest scores tell you what least interests you. You may want to strengthen those lower values, especially with new information. Keep in mind, both Gardner and I did not believe that people are stuck with one intelligence throughout their life but rather gain in intelligence as they progress through life.

Once you have taken the test to see your learning style, repeat the process with all your children and discover their various learning preferences. I encourage you to enroll your spouse or partner in the process and can even go so far as to include anyone teaching your child; caregivers, coaches, and even grandparents. How people learn is often how they teach, and this will help support your child's overall learning experience.

We are all part of this vast planet called Earth. Your child will eventually encounter people in every area of this evaluation. Improving their understanding of these types of people strengthens their abilities to understand and communicate effectively in the future with whomever they meet along life's journey. However, always focus on the top way or ways they learn best so they quickly retain that information in their long-term memory.

Below is the *Innovative Intelligences Learning Inventory questionnaire*. Score each statement using the above criteria, and get ready to find out how your child learns best. This information is going to be a game-changer!

My Family's Learning Styles

If everyone in the family has taken the Innovative Learning Inventory, it will be fun to record the various learning styles of the entire family. Compare them to give deeper meaning into how each person learns best.

Mine: _____

My Partner's/Spouse's: _____

My Oldest Child's: _____

My Middle Child's: _____

My Next Child's: _____

My Youngest Child's: _____

Additional: _____

Additional: _____

Additional: _____

Congratulations on gathering this information and taking the steps toward becoming your child's super teacher, and supporting your child in becoming a superlearner! You now have the superpowers to design the lessons that will motivate your child to love learning! Imagine your child going from bored and disinterested to excited and curious about everything you teach. See them getting up ready to embrace the day and *wanting* to do more than you had planned for the day! I guarantee what you have just discovered will help your child love learning and make teaching them so much more desirable.

How You Learn is How You Teach

Now that you know the unique ways your child processes learning you might be wondering, *"How do I teach my child using this information?"* I promise I'm going to delve further into each intelligence and give you activities that you can use and apply to your lesson plans based on age-appropriate themes. Once you get used to thinking about how you can teach in this way, it will begin to become a habit of how you design your teaching strategies for each subject and child. Instead of counting sheep to go to sleep at night, you'll be keeping yourself up by designing new ways to teach your child more effectively.

Innovative intelligence and *Learning Outside the Line* have just as much to do with the parents' style as the child's. Since you are the one teaching your child, how you teach and your learning style will play a huge factor in the overall success of your homeschooling endeavor. I am sure you can remember a favorite teacher you learned from and how they taught that spoke to your innate way of learning. You want to be the *same* kind of teacher for your child. You want to teach how they learn and teach how you learn. Utilizing both these factors will make homeschooling both fun and rewarding.

To help you understand how the different intelligences influence teaching practices, I have included a few examples of how to best utilize your strengths when teaching your child. How *you* learn is how you will teach and using your strengths will give you winning results with your kids. Think of teaching as *fusion cuisine* where two different cultures come together to form a new and yummy dish. You must use ingredients common to both cuisines and blend those flavors together into a stand-out new recipe. As a bonus, knowing your learning style and the many other styles within the Innovative Intelligences will help you add to your repertoire of teaching skills—adding more 'spices'—and improve in the areas where you are less proficient. I think I just coined a new phrase—*fusion education!* Let's look at what you, as a teacher, would fuse with your child's learning styles to become your child's Michelin Star™ teacher extraordinaire!

 **The Exceptional Teacher:** The Exceptional Teacher has the same qualities as the Exceptional Ecologist student. In other words, they love nature and anything in nature and want to preserve what this world has to offer for future generations. Therefore, this teacher will need to fuse their love of nature with the dominant intelligence of their child. But remember—both you and your child will have one or more secondary intelligences, which means you will be cross-connecting in several areas at the same time! Your math problems might reflect story problems using nature. For example, making graphs of the different types of trees in the neighborhood would not only satisfy the Exceptional Ecologist child but also the Magical Mathematician, the Super Spatialist, and the Vivacious Verbilist child. All of those children love to make graphs and like to manipulate information in visual form, and generally

like equations to some degree. Weaving what you like into the strengths of what your child likes will make you both stronger in different intelligences.

 **The Magical Teacher:** The Magical Teacher will use their strengths in many ways to teach their child of different intelligence. This teacher will use the ability to reason, solve problems, use numbers, think visually in abstract ways, and analyze cause-and-effect situations to formulate lessons for any type of learner. The Vivacious Verbilist learner will love the word games, discussions, and debates this teacher devises. The Super Spatialist learner will relate to the visuals, especially charts, graphs, and maps the Magical Teacher devises. The Phenomenal Physicalist learner will connect with hands-on activities, experiments, role-playing situations, and simulations. The Conscious Creative learner can relate to songs, rhymes, any type of music, and rhythms applied to lessons. Of course, the Amazing Adaptist learner will engage with any type of cooperative work, tutoring other siblings or children in groups, or communal projects. The Impressive Individualist child will like anything as long as they can be in a quiet place with little distraction to self-reflect and navigate and process material internally. Finally, the Exceptional Ecologist child will connect with anything that relates to the outdoors or ecology. An example of how a Magical Teacher would teach a Phenomenal Physicalist child decimals is by using the song "Cupid Shuffle," aka "To the Left To the Right," sung by the artist Cupid. Moving the decimal "To the left, to the left" makes the value smaller. Moving the decimal "To the right, to the right" results in the value getting larger. This lesson would work with the CC child, also!

 **The Vivacious Teacher:** Since the Vivacious Teacher has strong communication skills, this person is organized, objective, a good listener, and a great conversationalist. The Vivacious Teacher will need to customize the lessons taught by 'fusing' the strengths of their child with the strengths of this teacher. For instance, if the teacher is teaching fractions, use visual aids for the SS learners, songs with the Conscious Creative learner, and interactive activities with the Amazing Adaptive learner. Incorporate technology to teach the Super Spatialist learner or the Vivacious Verbilist learner and incorporate fractions into a project, such as an architectural design for the Exceptional Ecologist, Super Spatialist, and Amazing Adaptist child. This

teacher will have all their materials ready and be able to pick and choose what best addresses the needs of their child. Since the above learners share attributes with the Magical Mathematician, Phenomenal Physicalist, and Impressive Independent learners, their repertoire of tools will fuse nicely with whatever type of learner style their child possesses.

 **The Creative Teacher:** The Creative Teacher is probably the most well-rounded teacher of all of these types of teachers. They are dedicated to getting whatever they are teaching across to their student. They will definitely be creative, fun, and positive. They will set the bar high for what they want their child to accomplish, but not so high that the learner gets frustrated. This type of teacher has a clear plan on how to attack anything that needs to be taught, is very organized, and will select appropriate levels of instruction for their child. Because these teachers pay attention to detail, they are able to spot errors quickly so that information can be retaught and remediated quickly. An example of this type of teacher who is teaching the Language Arts skill, point of view, might begin with an organizational chart that gives an example of first, second, and third-person points of view. This chart will include examples: First person uses "I", second person uses "you," and third person uses "he, she, it." The Creative Teacher would then read aloud passages from each point of view and have the child identify after examples are read and identified together. The Creative Teacher would then have the child role play each point of view with them, then use an interactive notebook to cut and paste a smaller version of a graphic organizer into the notebook. This type of teacher would then have the child write on the opposite page of the interactive notebook sentences that use first, second, and third person 'voice' to illustrate point of view.

 **The Super Teacher:** The Super Teacher will have a great time teaching a topic, such as the solar system, to their child, regardless of the learning style of their child. One thing this teacher can do is teach the mnemonic, "My Very Energetic Mother Just Served Us Nine (Pizzas)." This stands for the planets in order from the sun—Mercury, Venus, Earth, Mars, Jupiter, Saturn, Uranus, and the dwarf planet, Pluto. This teacher will then have their child color and cut out representations of each of these planets.

Then, they will discuss distances from the sun and place them on a string across the largest area available as a scale model, which incorporates math. They will then look up, via the worldwide web, information on each planet; then, use various household items to show how these objects in space revolve around the sun. They can use each other to demonstrate 'revolve' and 'rotate' around each other. A 'given' field trip is to a planetarium if one is close enough to visit either as a day trip or an overnight field trip. Don't forget our moon, which controls a lot of things here on Earth, such as the tides, moon visuals—new moon, quarter moon, full moon, no moon, and what waxing and waning mean. As you can see, the Super Teacher can teach any learning intelligence. It just takes one of these teachers' qualities—adaptability.

 **The Phenomenal Teacher:** When we think of the Phenomenal Teacher, we think of someone always on the go, someone you'll find at the gym more than home, or someone who is practicing for a marathon. Does this person have a lot of energy? Yes. This person will either go to the gym or have a plethora of gym equipment at home. However, this teacher will bring all of that physical stamina into their lessons! Let's say this teacher is teaching geography, in particular, continents and oceans. This is the teacher who will make homemade play-doh with their child and create a replica of the earth via different colors of play-doh and a plastic mat that has a grid, such as a baker's mat. They will identify on the mat where each continent should be located, as well as where each ocean is located. It will take a few days, but they will put each continent on this grid and each blue ocean on it. They will form archipelagos and islands, volcanoes and mountain ranges, plains, and mesas. This teacher will take their child to the playground and draw a rough map of the world on a flat surface with sidewalk chalk and then have her child jump from continent to ocean as she calls them out. This teacher will have her child cut out continents in scaled size after they colored them and place them on an 11x15 piece of blue colored paper to replicate the continents and oceans and then label them appropriately This teacher will take their child to the beach to experience the ocean and sand and animals that they find as fossils or seashells. There are several mnemonics for remembering the oceans and continents. You can either Google them or make one up on your own! The Phenomenal Teacher puts action into their lesson plans!

 **The Amazing Teacher:** The Amazing Teacher has gifts galore when it comes to understanding *any* child! This teacher understands, empathizes, and interacts with just about everyone. The Amazing Teacher has the ability to build strong relationships with many people of different diversities. They plan lessons that are engaging but still challenging. They build the following attributes into their lessons so that the full spectrum of innovative intelligences are met at once: collaboration for the Amazing Adaptist; engaging discussions for the Vivacious Verbalist; visual aids to attract the Super Spatialist; hands-on activities for the Phenomenal Physicalist; they will build in some sort of rhythm, rhyme, or music for the Conscious Creative; spend some time outdoors for the Exceptional Ecologist; see real-world examples for the Magical Mathematician; individualize for the Impressive Independent. The Amazing Teacher will plan all of that in the blink of an eye. Just think of what this teacher can do with managing only one child, but then, add in the rest of her children. She can teach each one of her children at once on several different learning levels using one lesson. That's why they are called *Amazing!*

The Independent Teacher: The Independent Teacher is able to reflect on their own strengths and weaknesses, which allows them to judge the success of the lessons they teach. Likewise, this teacher can use this ability to build self-reflection in their child, and independent learning and studying. The Independent Teacher will use the creative arts to foster ways for their child to express themselves in many ways, then encourage the child to self-assess what they are doing. The Independent Teacher will encourage their child to set goals to allow a sense of purpose and direction. They will help keep the child on track to achieve the goals they have set to keep the child motivated and engaged in learning. By allowing the child to dig deep inside themselves, it will allow the child to grow up with strong independent qualities needed in an ever-changing worldwide society of thinkers and doers.

As you can see, you, the parent, have amazing gifts within yourself that you will use to teach the children in the family. Remember, by matching your qualities to the qualities of your child, you create an educational fusion that will ignite the passion for learning within your child. Give yourself a well-deserved pat on the back for the decision to homeschool your children and give them the quality education they deserve. Knowing how your children learn, and everyone who is teaching in your household, will create a framework that will strengthen every aspect of your family's life. Knowing your and your spouse's intelligences will allow you to mix and match that educational fusion to a whole new level of high for everyone. If you are a single parent, then try using another family member for assistance. If you belong to a co-op, share the knowledge you gain in this book. It gives the African proverb, *"It takes a village to raise a child,"* a whole new meaning.

Creating Lessons Plans For Every Learner

In the next eight chapters, I share different examples of how to strategically plan lessons for your child based on their top 'intelligences.' If you think you want to strengthen different levels of intelligence that are not prominent, it's a good idea to teach them first how they learn best, but then 'mix it up' a bit by bringing in other intelligences they do not resonate with as easily. By sprinkling a bit of other intelligences into your lessons, you allow your child to develop ways to communicate with other people and expand their interests in new areas.

I offer eight different templates to use for themed-based lessons in the areas of Language Arts, Math, Sciences, and Social Studies. Once you recognize the pattern of how to structure lessons for your child, you will begin to effortlessly do it yourself. I also encourage you to take lessons from the other intelligences and reformat them to fit your child's needs. Use my four decades of knowledge to become the Exceptional, Magical, Vivacious, Creative, Super, Phenomenal, Amazing, Independent teacher you are meant to be for your child and family!

Section 2

Knowing How to Teach
My Child

A DEEP DIVE INTO
INNOVATIVE INTELLIGENCES

The next eight chapters are dedicated to each of the Innovative learning intelligences so that you can see how to appeal to your child in the way that they learn best. Since there are countless pieces of information I could supply and many levels of understanding your child will appreciate, I have only shared some of the best examples and lessons you can use in each developmental area—the elementary learner, the middle school learner, and the high school learner.

I will begin each of these chapters by reviewing how that particular learner thinks, followed by suggestions and strategies to accommodate each learning style. Then, under each developmental area, I have included a list of suggested books that have areas of interest and appeal to that learning style.

As the chapter continues, I focus on each of the four separate subject areas: *Language Arts, Math, Science*, and *Social Studies*, giving a stated *Innovative Objective* with suggestions for a few activities to meet the requirements of each objective.

When making suggestions for Language Arts, I include activities for Reading and Writing so that a combination of elements that make up Reading, Grammar, and Writing are accomplished within the plan. I use the same principles for each additional subject area. In Math, suggestions include activities that meet a combination of Math domains, which include Counting and Numbers, Algebraic Thinking, Geometry, Measurement, Ratio and Proportion, Number Theory, Functions, and Calculus. Science activities focus on the appropriate Science of Biology, Chemistry, Physical Science, and Physics, and Social Studies includes areas of History, Geology, Civics, and Economics.

You will notice that some of the chapters on the Innovative intelligences include similar activities. That is because similar intelligences often cross-share related interests. For instance, VVs share the ability to recognize patterns and structure with CCs. MMs share the ability to identify and classify patterns with EEs, especially in nature. Both the II and the AA are able to understand and manage emotions, even though the II is an introvert and the AA is an extrovert. The PP and the SS both share the ability to manipulate objects.

To add an additional layer for you to use, I have also followed *Bloom's Taxonomy*—a set of tiered models used to classify educational learning objectives into levels of complexity and specificity—more clearly said, a way to structure the activities to include ways to build *thinking* skills that develop your child's whole-brain; intellectual and reasoning abilities. All in all, I make sure that you have a plethora of tools you can use and countless resources your child will enjoy.

Using my examples will help you develop a pattern of structuring how you teach your unique child's learning style and make homeschooling effortless. Before you know it, you will become a pro as you gain competence and confidence in your homeschooling endeavors. My lesson plans and theme-based examples will give you a running start at just what will entice and inspire your child's academic escalation. As you read each section, put to memory the highlight of each intelligence. This will help you to know the characteristics of that style. Then, flip the page to find the section that addresses your child's current learning level. Begin teaching from that area and work through the entire section to create cadence and consistency for your child. If your child is struggling with those exercises, you can move to the previous section and work through those easier resources. If your child is bored or under-challenged, level-up and move to the higher section utilizing those more thought-provoking suggestions.

Remember, grades are a construct of the public school system of education. You have the ability to determine when your child has *mastered* the aspects of what you teach. You are *not* held to a structured 180-day school schedule! You have the whole 365 days a year to structure as you please, along with the twenty-four hours in a day to accommodate your family's schedule of work and pleasure. Just because a school day begins around 7:30 AM and ends around 3:00 PM doesn't mean you can't teach something new to your child at 6:00 PM and require them to do independent work during the day when you might be at work. Now think about vacations. The best time to go to the beach is April, May, and November, which makes it nearly impossible to take a family there if they are in school. Think of the plethora of material at your fingertips for learning while at the beach! Everything you do at any time of the day can and will become a moment to *Learn Outside the Line!*

Ready to get started? Let's Teach!

Chapter 7

The Magical Mathematician (MM)

"The pure mathematician, like the musician,
is a free creator of his world of ordered beauty."
—BERTRAND RUSSELL

Magical Mathematician learners like hands-on activities, so engage them in hands-on experiments and activities that involve data collection and analysis. Real-world applications of mathematical concepts can be highly motivating. By all means, encourage questions. Welcome their questions and inspire them to explore the 'why' and 'how' behind concepts and ideas. This helps satisfy their curiosity and analytical nature.

MM learners consider sequencing fun, so present them information in a logical sequence, building upon previously learned concepts. This helps Magical Mathematicians see the connections between ideas and facts. Figuring out the patterns in a sequence speaks to their love of problem-solving tasks. Assign problem-solving tasks that require them to apply mathematical concepts to real-life scenarios. Encourage them to explain their thought processes.

Magical Mathematicians love participating in group discussions, so talking or debating about what they are learning allows them to engage in logical argumentation and evaluate different perspectives. Allow them to use technology. Incorporate educational software, simulations, and online resources that align with mathematical-logical learning preferences. When testing what they have learned, opt for assessments that challenge their analytical and problem-solving abilities rather than relying solely on traditional tests. Consider open-ended questions and projects.

Highlights:
- MMs excel in logical reasoning and enjoy solving deductive and inductive problems.
- MMs have a strong affinity for numbers, patterns, and mathematical concepts.
- MMs are skilled at breaking down complex ideas into smaller, manageable components.
- MMs are excellent critical thinkers who can evaluate arguments and evidence effectively.
- MMs can grasp abstract concepts and enjoy working with abstract symbols and ideas.

Strategies:

As you read over the following strategies, imagine the items at home you already have that will 'spiffy up' your lessons and engage your child to keep them anticipating 'what's next!' Then, read over the lesson ideas and incorporate some of them into the lesson plans you create.

- **Magical Mathematicians like to use manipulatives,** such as blocks, counters, and geometric shapes, especially to help younger children visualize mathematical concepts like addition, subtraction, multiplication, and division. They also like puzzles and brain teasers, such as logic puzzles, Sudoku, and crosswords, and math games like chess, checkers, and board games that involve strategic thinking and mathematical concepts to stimulate their problem-solving abilities and logical reasoning. Use graphs, charts, and diagrams to illustrate mathematical concepts and relationships in all subject areas.

- **Show them how math is used in everyday life**, such as budgeting, cooking (measuring ingredients), and home improvement projects. Encourage participation in math competitions like the Math Olympiad, AMC—American Mathematics Competition, or local math tournaments, if available. Visit science museums, planetariums, or places with interactive math exhibits to make learning more experiential. Look for math summer camps or enrichment programs that cater to their interests.
- **Introduce math-related books and literature** to engage their mathematical curiosity. Explore the logical aspects of literature. Discuss themes, character motivations, and plot development analytically. Consider reading books that involve puzzles or mysteries. Present creative writing challenges that involve constructing logical narratives or solving problems within a story. Teach persuasive writing and debate techniques. Discuss logical fallacies and how to construct sound arguments.
- **Show how mathematical concepts are applied in scientific disciplines.** Explore topics like physics, chemistry, and biology from a mathematical perspective. Encourage them to keep math and science journals or interactive math and science notebooks where they can record their thoughts, solutions to problems, and new discoveries. Celebrate their mathematical achievements, no matter how small, to motivate and instill a love for math.
- **Incorporate educational software and online resources** that allow your children to work independently on math activities and exercises. If you have other children to teach, this can free up your time for more individualized instruction or lesson planning. Teach your children to self-assess their progress. Have them set goals and track their learning milestones. This fosters independence and responsibility.
- **Assign open-ended projects** that allow students to delve deeply into a topic of their choice that relates to other subject areas. Encourage them to explore mathematical concepts beyond the curriculum and

present their findings to you and the family. Focus on critical reading skills. Have them dissect texts, identify arguments, and evaluate the evidence presented. This can be applied to both fiction and non-fiction reading materials.

- **Foster an environment** where your mathematical-logical learner is encouraged to ask questions, analyze information critically, and apply logical thinking to solve problems. Tailor your approach to their specific interests and strengths within each subject area to keep them engaged and motivated. Integrate STEM (Science, Technology, Engineering, and Mathematics) challenges into your curriculum. These challenges often involve complex problem-solving and logical thinking.

- **Most importantly, provide structure** for your Magical Mathematician learner. Offer clear and structured lessons with step-by-step explanations. MMs often appreciate a systematic approach to learning. Make sure you provide challenges. Offer complex problems and puzzles requiring logical reasoning and mathematical thinking. Encourage them to explore different solution strategies. All MM learners like to use visual aids to illustrate things they are learning in all subject areas. They incorporate charts, graphs, and diagrams to illustrate concepts and relationships. Visual representations can help them grasp abstract ideas more easily.

Teaching mathematics to children with strong MM intelligence can be an enjoyable and rewarding experience. You will need to stay on your toes with this child because they are extremely logical and can offer a 'pro' to any 'con' and vice versa. This learner will challenge you, but just keep in mind—you have MM qualities of your own, so just like on the gameshow, Survivor™, you can outwit, outplay, and outlast your MM child!

ELEMENTARY STUDENTS

 **Books for Elementary Students**

The following is a list of books you can acquire at the library, purchase at a bookstore, or download from Amazon™ as a digital copy. The activities in the Elementary section are all activities and suggestions modeled after a theme, trees.

"The Giving Tree" by Shel Silverstein
   This classic story explores the lifelong relationship between a boy and a tree, highlighting themes of love, selflessness, and the importance of nature.

"A Tree Is Nice" by Janice May Udry
   A beautifully illustrated book that celebrates the simple joys and benefits of trees, from climbing to picnicking in their shade.

"The Great Kapok Tree: A Tale of the Amazon RainForest" by Lynne Cherry
   In the heart of the Amazon rainforest, a man falls asleep under a tree, and as he dreams, the animals living in the tree share their wisdom about the importance of preserving the rainforest.

"The Tree Lady: The True Story of How One Tree-Loving Woman Changed a City Forever" by H. Joseph Hopkins
   This biography tells the inspiring story of Kate Sessions, a woman who transformed San Diego with her passion for trees and dedication to urban forestry.

"The Tree That Time Built: A Celebration of Nature, Science, and Imagination" edited by Mary Ann Hoberman and Linda Winston
   A collection of poems and essays celebrating the wonder of trees and the natural world, accompanied by beautiful illustrations.

"Red Leaf, Yellow Leaf" by Lois Ehlert
> *Through vivid collage illustrations, this book explores the life cycle of a maple tree, from seed to mature tree, and the changing seasons.*

"The Watcher" by Jeanette Winter
> *Based on the true story of Wangari Maathai, this book follows her journey from a young girl who loved trees to becoming an environmentalist and Nobel Peace Prize laureate who planted millions of trees in Kenya.*

"Because of an Acorn" by Lola M. Schaefer and Adam Schaefer
> *This beautifully illustrated book explores the interconnectedness of the natural world, showing how a small acorn can lead to the growth of a mighty oak tree and support a diverse ecosystem.*

"The Little Tree" by Muon Thi Van
> *A tender story about a little tree that stands alone but eventually finds its place within a bustling city, emphasizing the importance of community and growth.*

"The Wild Tree House of Kangarooboo" by Julianne Black
> *A delightful tale of imagination and adventure as children build a treehouse high in the branches and discover the magic of nature.*

"The Number Devil: A Mathematical Adventure" by Hans Magnus Enzensberger
> *This book explores mathematical concepts through an engaging narrative about a young boy's adventures with a mathematical mentor.*

"Math Curse" by Jon Sciezka and Lane Smith
> *It is a humorous and creative story where a student sees math problems everywhere in her daily life, turning everything into a 'math curse.'*

"The Phantom Tollbooth" by Norton Juster
> *This Classic novel follows a young boy's journey through a fantastical world filled with wordplay, logic puzzles, and mathematical adventures.*

These books celebrate the beauty and significance of trees while conveying important lessons about nature, conservation, and the wonders of the natural world to elementary-aged children.

 ## Language Arts for Elementary Students

Logical Story Construction & Innovative Objective: Students will understand story structure by identifying and constructing logically sequenced events around the sub-theme, the rainforest.

Read "The Great Kapok Tree" by Lynne Cherry

Summary: "Under the Great Kapok Tree" by Lynne Cherry is a poignant children's story set in the Amazon rainforest. The narrative follows two woodcutters, one of whom falls asleep under a magnificent Kapok tree. Various rainforest creatures, including frogs, snakes, sloths, birds, anteaters, and monkeys, approach him during his slumber. They each speak to the sleeping man, explaining their reliance on the Kapok tree and its significance to the world. Upon waking, the woodcutter is moved by the beauty of the rainforest and the animals' words, leading him to a moral dilemma. Ultimately, he decides against cutting down the tree, leaving it standing as he departs from the rainforest, now a changed man.

Activity 1:
- After reading "The Great Kapok Tree," discuss its beginning, middle, and end. If your child has trouble identifying the story's beginning, middle, and end, begin by asking, "Where does this story take place? Who is in the story at the very beginning of the story? What is this person trying to do? Does he get the job done or something else? What is 'the something else'?" (This is the beginning of the story.)
- Next: What does the man see and hear in his dreams? (All the conversations of the various animals are in the middle.)
- Lastly, what happens after the man awakens? First he _____ . Finally, he _____ . This is the end of the story.

Activity 2:

- Give a set of events from "The Great Kapok Tree" that are out of order. Have your child logically sequence the events to create a coherent summary of the story.

Activity 3:

- Write their own short story about a tree, emphasizing a clear and logical sequence of events. Here's a rule of thumb for writing, but remember, some paragraphs only need three sentences, even at an older level of writing. Just ensure your budding author knows when to expand and when expanding may be too much. Your child mustn't get lost in the minutia. First graders should have three paragraphs with three sentences each. Second graders—three paragraphs with four sentences each. Third graders—three or four paragraphs with four and five sentences each. Fourth graders—four to five paragraphs with four to six sentences each, and fifth graders—five to six paragraphs with five or six sentences each.

Teaching Tip: Here is a great way to structure this lesson. It is how I taught beginning writing skills to elementary children. You will need three colors of printer paper cut into sections—green, yellow, and pink—representing one paragraph. Green means 'go,' yellow means 'say something about the 'go' sentence. Sometimes, you may have several yellows in a row to clarify the sentence before it. Pink means stop the thought. I can hear you asking, *"Why not red paper?"* Answer: *"It's hard to see what is written on red printer paper."*

After this activity, have your child read what they have written to others in the family.

 ## Math for Elementary Students

Pattern Recognition and Sequences & Innovative Objective: Students will identify and continue number patterns.

Activity 1:

Begin with a story about a magical forest where trees grow in special patterns:

"The Magical Forest of Numeria"

In a land not so far away, nestled between rolling hills and winding rivers, lay the magical forest of Numeria. This wasn't any ordinary forest. The trees in Numeria grew in patterns that baffled even the wisest of sages.

Ella, a young, curious explorer, was the first to notice this phenomenon on one of her adventures. **She saw trees with colored leaves that grew in a circle, but on the next branch, the leaves grew as triangles, then up one level, squares. Then that sequence began all over again the higher the tree grew—circles, triangles, then squares. As she wandered deeper into the forest, she discovered that the trees didn't grow randomly. Instead, they grew in beautiful, mysterious sequences.

In one clearing, she found trees that were curiously spaced. **The first tree was alone, but the next had a buddy right next to it. A bit further on, there were three trees clustered together. And after that, four trees formed a little gathering. Ella pondered for a moment and then exclaimed, "They're growing in groups that increase by one!"

Further into the forest, in another glade, the trees grew in a different pattern. **One tree stood tall, followed by two slightly shorter trees, then three even shorter ones, and after that, four trees that were shorter still. "It seems the number of trees is increasing," Ella mused, "but their height is decreasing!"

Ella's heart raced excitedly as she realized the forest was sharing its secrets with her. She eagerly looked around for more patterns, scribbling her observations in her trusty notebook.

As she journeyed on, she thought of sharing these findings with her friends back in the village. But first, she wanted to challenge herself and decode one more pattern. **She soon stumbled upon a grove where the trees were neither grouped by number nor by height. They had markings on their trunks: dots that seemed to increase with each tree. The first had one dot, the next had two, then four, and the next had... eight dots!

Ella sat down, her mind whirling. "What could be the pattern here?" she wondered aloud.

At this point, discuss this last pattern, but do not give the answer away. Have your child try to draw this last pattern. Then, reread that last part slowly to see if your child drew the picture correctly.

Activity 2:
- Describe the patterns and ask students to visualize and predict the next sequence. For example, one of the magical trees has a pattern of four leaves per stem: red, blue, yellow, and purple. However, the next stem's pattern is blue, yellow, purple, red; the next is yellow, purple, red, _____ ; and so, the last is purple, _____ , _____ , _____ . To save time and allow for more fun, buy stickers in the shape of leaves and use the colors given. Allow the child to make their patterns. I used a similar activity with first graders once using colored smiley faces!

Activity 3:
- Introduce sequences like 2, 4, 6, _____ , 10 and 5, 10, 15, _____ , 25. This is a popular activity and can be adjusted to age-appropriate levels of understanding. For instance, a fifth grader may see a sequence like this: 0,1,3,6,10,15, _____ .

If you have two elementary-level children, you can teach this simultaneously, varying their difficulty levels.

Challenge them to create their own patterns for someone else in the family to solve.

 **Social Studies for Elementary Students**

Regions of the World: Rain Forests & Innovative Objective: Understanding the structured layers of the rainforest and the logic behind why certain animals and plants live in each layer.

- **Introduce the four primary layers of the rainforest:** the emergent layer, canopy, understory, and forest floor.
- **Discuss the features of each layer** (light levels, humidity, etc.) and ask students to predict which animals might live there based on those features.
- **Find pictures of rainforest** animals online and have your child categorize them into the correct layers, reinforcing the logical reasons behind their habitats.
- **Discuss different adaptations,** such as the large leaves of understory plants (to capture minimal sunlight) or the bright colors of certain frogs (to warn predators of toxicity). Provide a list of adaptations and a list of reasons. Match each adaptation to its logical reason. Extend the activity by presenting a new environment and asking students to predict what kind of adaptations might be beneficial there logically.
- **Research various rainforests online:** the Amazon (South America), the Congo (Africa), and the Daintree (Australia), for example.
- **Create a table or chart.** List common features of rainforests (size, average rainfall, primary animals, etc.) and fill in the details for each forest.
- **Analyze the data** to make logical conclusions: which rainforest is the largest, which gets the most rainfall, etc.

Objective: Grasp the magnitude and rate of deforestation through mathematical visualization.

Activity:
- **Research online statistics** about the rate of rainforest deforestation. For example, "Every minute, forty football fields of rainforest are cut down."

- **Use grid paper** to represent the rainforest. Each square might represent ten acres, and students can color in the squares to represent the land lost to deforestation over time.
- **Discuss the long-term implications** using logical predictions. "If we continue at this rate, how much forest will be left in ten years?"

By weaving logical patterns, classifications, and structured comparisons into these activities, we cater to the strengths of mathematical-logical learners, making the topic of rainforests both engaging and educational for them.

 ## Science for Elementary Students

Scientific Method Investigation & Innovative Objective: To understand the logical sequence of the scientific method.

Activity:
Pose a simple question, e.g., "What conditions do plants need to grow best?" Guide your child through the scientific method:
- **Question:** What do plants need to grow?
- **Hypothesis:** Students predict (e.g., sunlight, water, soil).
- **Experiment:** Set up plant growth under different conditions.
- **Observation:** Document growth over a week. The following is a list of appropriate reading literature that your MM middle school learner might enjoy reading with a short summary following each title. These books contain qualities in the story that will appeal to your child.
- **Conclusion:** Discuss findings and validate or refute the hypothesis.

Emphasize the importance of following the steps of the scientific method to obtain accurate results.

MIDDLE SCHOOL LEARNERS

 **Books for Middle School Learners**

"Chasing Vermeer" by Blue Balliett
A mystery novel that involves two friends solving an art heist using logic and mathematical clues.

"The Miscalculations of Lightning Girl" by Stacy McAnulty
This novel tells the story of a math prodigy who needs to learn about the world beyond math and numbers.

"The Adventures of Penrose the Mathematical Cat" by Theoni Pappas
A collection of short stories that introduce mathematical concepts in a fun and accessible way through the adventures of a cat.

"The Logic Book" by Eleanor Abrams, Howard Handelman, and Allen P. Sotek
This is a more advanced option, suitable for those with a strong interest in logic and critical thinking. It covers various topics in logic and is designed for young learners interested in formal reasoning.

"Math Potatoes: Mind-stretching Brain Food" by Greg Tang
A fun and creative book that offers math riddles and puzzles to engage young readers' mathematical thinking.

"Theoni Pappas Books" (Various Titles)
Theoni Pappas has authored several books that make math concepts accessible and enjoyable for young learners. Titles like "Math Talk" and "Math for Kids and Other People Too" are worth exploring.

"Murderous Maths" series by Kjartan Poskitt
A series of books that cover various math topics in a humorous and engaging way, making math fun and accessible.

These books can foster an interest in mathematics and promote critical thinking and problem-solving skills in middle school-aged children with a mathematical-logical learning style. Be sure to check the reading level and content to ensure they are appropriate for your students' specific needs and interests.

 **Reading Unit for Middle School Learners**

Unit Title: Exploring Mathematics and Logic in "The Phantom Tollbooth"

Objective: To engage your middle school child with an MM learning style in critical thinking, problem-solving, and mathematical concepts through the reading of "The Phantom Tollbooth."

Summary: "The Phantom Tollbooth" is a whimsical and imaginative children's novel written by Norton Juster. It tells the story of a young boy named Milo who, bored with his mundane life, discovers a magical tollbooth that leads him to the fantastical Kingdom of Wisdom. Milo embarks on a journey filled with wordplay, clever puns, and allegorical adventures in this captivating land. Along the way, he meets memorable characters like Tock the Watchdog and the Humbug. He learns important lessons about the value of curiosity and learning and the importance of not taking the world for granted. The book combines elements of fantasy, wit, and wisdom to encourage readers of all ages to appreciate the wonders of the world around them and the joy of learning.

Discussion: Explore Milo's boredom and indifference as a starting point for discussing problem-solving. Introduce the concept of 'wasting time' and how it relates to mathematics.

Activity:

- Ask your child to identify situations in the story where Milo encountered problems and brainstorm possible mathematical solutions.

Reading Assignment: Chapters 4–6

Discussion: Explore the wordplay and puns in the book and discuss how they relate to mathematical concepts. Discuss "Tock" as a representation of time.

Activity:

- Have your child create wordplay or puns using mathematical terms (e.g., math jokes or math-related riddles).

Reading Assignment: Chapters 7–10

Discussion: Analyze the word-based culture of Dictionopolis and relate it to the importance of precision in mathematics. Explore the concept of spelling and accuracy.

Activity:

- Create a spelling bee competition at home with a list of challenging mathematics-related words.

Reading Assignment: Chapters 11–14

Discussion: Discuss the concept of lethargy and explore how it might relate to mathematical problem-solving. Talk about the implications of not caring about mathematics.

Activity:

- Encourage your child to create a visual representation of what a world filled with mathematical lethargy might look like.

Reading Assignment: Chapters 15–18

Discussion: Explore the Dodecahedron's role as the "Mathemagician" and discuss various mathematical ideas presented in the book.

Activity:
- Have your child solve mathematical puzzles related to geometry and shapes. You can find age-appropriate geometry puzzles online or create your own.

Reading Assignment: Chapters 19–22

Discussion: Analyze the concept of "Punishments" and discuss the use of idiomatic expressions. Explore how language and math can be intertwined.

Activity:
- Ask your child to create mathematics-related idioms and illustrate them.

Reading Assignment: Chapters 23–26

Discussion: Discuss the banquet's absurdity and its potential mathematical aspects, such as perspective and geometry.

Activity:
- Organize a "mathematically absurd" banquet at home featuring unconventional food and table settings, and discuss the mathematical elements involved.

Reading Assignment: Chapters 27–29

Discussion: Explore the Mountains of Ignorance and the demons of Ignorance and Fear. Discuss the importance of knowledge and its relationship to problem-solving.

Activity:
- Challenge your child with mathematical problems that require critical thinking and knowledge application.

Reading Assignment: Chapters 30–32

Discussion: Analyze Milo's character development and how his journey has developed his problem-solving skills and mathematical thinking.

Activity:
- Ask your child to write a letter from Milo to a friend, reflecting on his adventures and the importance of curiosity, learning, and mathematical thinking.

Chapter 10: Culminating Projects

Activity:
- Have your child create a final project related to the mathematical concepts explored in the book. Options include creating a mathematical board game, designing a geometric art project, constructing a dodecahedron, making each side a picture of something that happened in the book, or writing a mathematical analysis of a specific scene or concept from the book. *Model dodecahedrons can be found on the internet.
- Throughout the unit, emphasize mathematical thinking, problem-solving, and logical reasoning while reading "The Phantom Tollbooth." This tailored approach will help engage your mathematical-logical learner and deepen their understanding of mathematical concepts in a fun and creative way.

 ## Language Arts for Middle School Learners

Objective: The child will structure and present a logical argument on a given topic.

Activity:
- Introduce the structure of an argument: claim, evidence, and reasoning.
- Provide a statement, such as "solar energy is good to place on houses," and ask them to logically argue for or against it using the given structure.

To debate this claim, your child must research many aspects of solar energy on houses, such as, *"How are solar cells produced? How do solar cells work? Can solar cells work in northern areas of the world? What happens to solar cells that break?"* and other significant questions.

- Encourage your child to research both sides of this statement, pros and cons, focusing on the arguments' logical sequence and validity.

Middle school children typically have more developed cognitive skills and a greater capacity for abstract thinking than elementary students. Here are lessons designed for middle school students emphasizing the Magical Mathematician intelligence:

 ## Math for Middle School Learners: Algebraic Expressions and Equations

Objective: The child will understand and apply the concept of variables and solve simple algebraic equations.

Activity:
- Reinforce what the equal sign means in an equation, i.e., $3 + 2 = 1 + 4$. Both sides balance out to five. Reinforce that in any equation, you must do the same thing to both sides of the equal sign. Introduce the concept of a variable with a mystery box analogy: "Imagine a box that contains a certain number of candies. We don't know how many there are, so we call it 'x' candies."

Write down algebraic expressions, e.g., $x + 5 = 27$, and ask students to solve for x.

$$x + 5 = 27$$
$$x + (5 - 5) = 27 - 5$$
$$x + 0 = 22$$
$$x = 22$$

Ask your child to explain what has happened in the equation. Let your child create equations for you and others to solve, emphasizing logical construction.

 ## Social Studies for Middle School Learners

Objective: Your child will understand and evaluate the logical progression of events leading to major historical outcomes.

Activity:
- Before beginning this activity, your child must research the fall of the Roman Empire.
- List potential causes (economic decline, invasions, etc.) and discuss the logical sequence of events.
- Discuss significant historical events that led to the fall of the Roman Empire.
- Ask your child to choose another historical event and analyze it for causes and effects, presenting their findings in a flowchart or presentation.

 ## Science for Middle School Learners

Objective: Design a simple experiment, conduct it, and interpret the results logically.

Need to know: Observations, variables, controls, data, scientific method.

Activity:
- Introduce the scientific question, "Does the type of soil affect plant growth rate?"
- After discussing the possible variables and controls in this experiment, guide your child to design an experiment and select variables and controls.
- Allow your child to conduct the experiment over a set period, recording observations and results.
- Discuss the importance of logical interpretation of data.
- Have them present their findings and draw logical conclusions from their data.

For middle school students, these lessons provide a deeper exploration into the MM realm, promoting critical thinking, problem-solving, and a structured approach to various academic topics.

HIGH SCHOOL STUDENTS

 **Books for High School Students**

The following is a list of novels that include books your Magical Mathematician learner might enjoy reading, which contain many areas of interest for this type of learner that will appeal to their unique learning style.

"Contact" by Carl Sagan
> *Dr. Ellie Arroway, a brilliant scientist, receives a message from extraterrestrial beings containing mathematical and scientific information. She embarks on a journey to decipher the message and make contact with the aliens.*

"The Curious Incident of the Dog in the Night-Time" by Mark Haddon
> *The novel is narrated by Christopher, a fifteen-year-old boy with a high-functioning form of autism. Christopher's logical and mathematical mind leads him to investigate the murder of a neighbor's dog, uncovering family secrets in the process.*

"The Housekeeper and the Professor" by Yoko Ogawa
> *A brilliant mathematician, known simply as "The Professor," forms a unique bond with his housekeeper and her young son. Despite his short-term memory loss, he shares his passion for mathematics and introduces them to the beauty of numbers.*

"Foucault's Pendulum" by Umberto Eco
> *Three editors at a publishing house become obsessed with conspiracy theories and hidden codes. They create a fictional conspiracy, only to find themselves drawn into a world of secret societies and cryptic symbols.*

"The Solitude of Prime Numbers" by Paolo Giordano

This novel follows the lives of two individuals, Alice and Mattia, who share a unique connection with prime numbers. They both struggle with personal traumas and find solace in their mathematical affinity.

"The Number Devil: A Mathematical Adventure" by Hans Magnus Enzensberger

A young boy named Robert encounters a mathematical mentor, the Number Devil, who takes him on a series of dreamlike adventures to explore mathematical concepts, making math fun and accessible.

"Uncle Petros and Goldbach's Conjecture" by Apostolos Doxiadis

This novel tells the story of Uncle Petros, a brilliant mathematician who becomes obsessed with proving Goldbach's Conjecture, a famous unsolved problem in number theory. It explores the sacrifices one might make in pursuit of mathematical knowledge.

"Anathem" by Neal Stephenson

In a parallel universe, a group of scholars known as "avout" live in seclusion, studying mathematics and philosophy. When the world faces an existential threat, these scholars must use their knowledge to save their civilization.

"The Oxford Murders" by Guillermo Martínez

A mathematician and a student become entangled in a series of murders that are seemingly connected by mathematical patterns and symbols. They must use their logical thinking to decipher the clues and solve the crimes.

"The Tenth Circle" by Jodi Picoult

This novel weaves together themes of family, relationships, and mathematics. The story follows a comic book artist and his daughter, who becomes embroiled in a high school scandal involving a complex mathematical formula.

"1984" by George Orwell

A dystopian novel set in a totalitarian society where the government controls every aspect of citizens' lives. The story follows Winston Smith as he rebels against the oppressive regime and seeks truth and freedom in a world marked by surveillance and thought control.

These fiction books incorporate mathematical and logical elements into their narratives, making them engaging choices for high school students with an MM learning style. They explore mathematical concepts, problem-solving, and how mathematics can intersect with everyday life and human relationships.

 **Language Arts for High School Learners:**

Critical Analysis of Literature

Objective 1: Your child will dissect a piece of literature, identifying themes, character motivations, plot development, and presenting a logical analysis.

Objective 2: To critically analyze the novel "1984," by George Orwell from a mathematical and logical perspective, exploring themes, characters, and the dystopian society depicted in the book.

This literature unit should engage your high school student's logical and mathematical skills while delving into the thought-provoking themes of "1984." Feel free to adapt the unit to your student's specific needs and pace of learning.

Summary: In the dystopian world of "1984," the totalitarian regime of the Party, led by Big Brother, tightly controls every aspect of citizens' lives. Winston Smith, a disillusioned Party member, dares to question the regime's version of reality. As he explores forbidden ideas and falls in love with Julia, he becomes a symbol of resistance against the relentless surveillance and manipulation. "1984" is a chilling exploration of totalitarianism's consequences and the human spirit's enduring power to seek truth and freedom.

Activity: Reading Assignment: Read Part 1 of "1984."

Discussion Topics:
- **Introduce George Orwell** and the historical context of the novel. Define the concept of a dystopian society. Discuss the setting, characters, and initial themes in the story.

- **Logical Analysis:** Analyze the logical inconsistencies and contradictions in the Party's ideology.

Themes and Symbols:
- **Reading Assignment:** Continue reading Parts 2 and 3 of "1984."
- **Discussion Topics:** Explore themes of surveillance, manipulation, and the suppression of truth. Identify and discuss important symbols in the novel (e.g., Big Brother, the Thought Police, Newspeak).
- **Analysis:** Analyze the use of statistics and numbers in the Party's propaganda.

Character Development:
- **Reading Assignment:** Finish reading "1984."
- **Discussion Topics:** Examine what motivates the actions of characters in a story; identify doublethink.
- **Analysis:** Analyze the development of Winston Smith as the protagonist. Examine the motivations and actions of other key characters (e.g., Julia, O'Brien). Logical Analysis: Explore the concept of doublethink and its impact on characters.

Government and Control:
- **Study** the Party's control mechanisms, including Newspeak and the Memory Hole. Explore the concept of totalitarianism and its logical consequences.
- **Analysis:** Create graphs and charts to illustrate the Party's manipulation of information and history.

Final Reflection and Project:
- **Discuss** the implications of the novel's ending. Reflect on the relevance of "1984" in contemporary society. Project: Have the student choose a specific aspect of the novel to explore in-depth, such as the linguistic manipulation of Newspeak, and present their findings logically with charts and diagrams.
- **Additional Resources:** Supplement the literature unit with related articles, essays, and documentaries on topics like surveillance, totalitarianism, and linguistic manipulation to provide a broader context for discussion.

Math: Calculus—Introduction to Derivatives

Objective: The student will grasp the instantaneous rate of change concept and calculate simple derivatives.

- **Activity:** Start with a real-life scenario: "Imagine you're driving a car, and the speedometer is constantly changing. How do you determine your speed at an exact moment?" Introduce the concept of a derivative as an instantaneous rate of change. Give examples. Work through basic differentiation rules using polynomial functions. Assign problems for your child to solve, progressively increasing in difficulty, and then discuss solutions, emphasizing the logic behind each step.

Social Studies for High School Students: Comparative Political Systems

Objective: The student will analyze and compare different political systems, evaluating strengths, weaknesses, and logical foundations.

- **Need to know:** What is each world political system, such as democracy, republic, monarchy, communism, etc.?
- **Activity:** Introduce different political systems (democracy, monarchy, communism, etc.) Ask your child to pick two political systems, one being their country's political system. Your child must present the logic behind their country's system, its foundational principles, how it operates in practice, strengths, and weaknesses, as well as that of the second system chosen. Construct a Venn Diagram showing where the political systems have the same values. Write an essay that compares and contrasts each political system.

Science for High School Students: Genetics—Punnett Squares and Probability

Objective 1: Students will understand the principles of genetic inheritance and predict probabilities of certain traits.

Objective 2: Create Punnett squares to make predictions based on genetic scenarios for various results on heredity.

Prior Knowledge:
- **Research information:** "Who was Mendel, and what significant contribution to science did he make?"
- **Explanation of 'Punnett squares'**—monohybrid cross and dihybrid cross.
- **Genetic scenarios** with determined dominant and recessive traits.
- **Premade Punnett squares** or paper and pencils to construct Punnett squares.

Activity: Punnett squares:
- Introduce Mendel's experiments and the basics of genetic inheritance. Teach students how to set up and interpret Punnett squares.
- Pose hypothetical genetic scenarios (e.g., crossing two heterozygous tall pea plants) and guide students in predicting offspring probabilities using Punnett squares.
- Expand to more complex genetic scenarios involving multiple genes or incomplete dominance, challenging students' logical reasoning skills.

For high school students, these lessons delve deeper into the subject matter, emphasizing the understanding of content and the ability to think critically, analyze, and present logical arguments or solutions.

Conclusion

Remember that individuals may possess a combination of multiple intelligences, so it's essential to provide a variety of teaching methods and resources to accommodate different learning styles within your classroom. Tailoring your lessons to cater to MM learners can help them thrive academically and stay engaged in the learning process.

Each lesson emphasizes logical reasoning and mathematical concepts in different subjects, catering to students with strong logical-mathematical intelligence.

Here are a few websites that I recommend for all learners, but particularly the Magical Mathematician learner. For elementary and middle school students, I recommend the website www.BrainPOP.com. This site is user-friendly and geared to those age groups—one is specifically designed for elementary ages and one for middle school students. It has lessons no longer than five minutes, reviews of information for each lesson, extra activities, and interactive quizzes that can be done directly on the computer. I have included this site at the end of the book in the chapter dedicated to various websites.

Another website I strongly recommend is www.IXL.com. It has interactive practice and instructions for the parent to guide lessons for all learners pre-K through twelfth grade and can be taken from one place to another easily for those who may need to travel around and be mobile. It, too, has been added to my vetted lists of websites. There is also a Spanish version of this site, and it can be used in many different countries as long as the student understands Spanish or English.

Other websites excellent for practice in all subjects are www.curiositystream.com, www.pbslearningmedia.org, www.EdHelper.com, www.education.com, www.ABCTeach.com, and www.Superteachers.com. I offer all the above paid websites, and many others, at no cost to parents I consult with. CuriosityStream™ and PBS Learning Media™ have tons of videos for interactive learning.

The above lessons are designed to allow your creative juices to begin to flow. As you can see, elementary children love to learn with themes—it keeps them on task and allows them to bring them together with all the various disciplines of education. As children master skills, they can then relate what they've learned to higher-level thinking strategies. By allowing your MM learner the freedom to learn in a way that suits their thinking, they can achieve much more in a shorter period of time, thus advancing to higher thinking strategies.

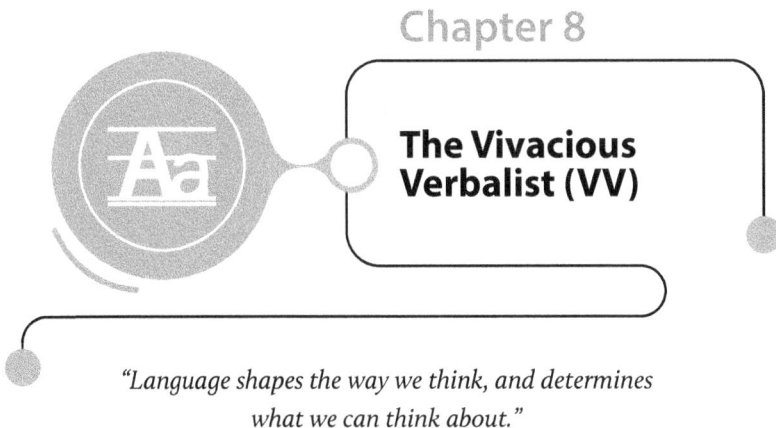

Chapter 8

The Vivacious Verbalist (VV)

"Language shapes the way we think, and determines
what we can think about."
–Benjamin Lee Whorf

*D*o you have a child who likes to challenge you with an argument periodically? *Have you noticed that the older this child gets, the more effort is put into arguing about anything and everything?* This child is the one who keeps you on your toes! The trick to teaching Vivacious Verbalist learners is to cultivate their 'arguing attitude' into better focus. Give them something to argue about! Change the verb from 'argue' to 'debate.' Ask your child things like, "*What do you think about...?*" Listen closely to their answer and immediately take the opposite viewpoint, but this time, assign that topic to research and require them to 'put their money where their mouth is' by backing up their opinion with facts. You're welcome!

People with high VV intelligence may also have strengths in other areas, and their overall cognitive profile can vary widely from individual to individual. Additionally, individuals can develop and enhance their intelligence through learning and practice, regardless of their innate tendencies.

In this chapter, we are deep-diving into the world of VV intelligence. It is associated with written and spoken language proficiency. People with strong VV intelligence tend to think and learn in the following ways:

Highlights:

- Vivacious Verbalist learners are adept at using words to express themselves. They have a rich vocabulary, a good understanding of grammar and syntax, and can easily articulate their thoughts and ideas.
- They excel in reading comprehension and written communication. They enjoy reading books, newspapers, and other written materials and often express themselves best through writing.
- VV learners are skilled at conveying information, persuading others, and debating issues. They are often effective public speakers and debaters.
- Storytelling: They have a natural talent for storytelling and can captivate an audience with their narratives. They often remember and can retell stories in great detail.
- They may use language and verbal reasoning to solve complex problems. They are often good at reasoning through arguments and finding logical solutions to issues.
- VV learners have a strong memory for words and phrases. They may be able to recall quotes, passages from books, or conversations with precision.
- They typically enjoy activities such as reading, writing, crossword puzzles, word games, and engaging in debates or discussions.
- Vivacious Learners can use words, and language to understand and convey the emotions and perspectives of others, making them effective at empathetic communication.
- They tend to learn and develop their vocabulary easily, often picking up new words and their meanings quickly.
- VV learners often use language to analyze and critically evaluate information, making them adept at tasks that require logical reasoning and the assessment of arguments.

Strategies:

Teaching VV learners effectively involves utilizing strategies that tap into their strengths in language and communication. Here are some specific strategies to consider:

- **Provide a variety of reading materials**, including books, articles, and literature, that align with the learner's interests and reading level to expand vocabulary and comprehension skills. Assign writing tasks such as essays, journals, creative writing, and research papers. Encourage them to express their thoughts and ideas in writing and provide constructive feedback to help improve their writing skills. Encourage discussions, debates, and family activities that involve verbal expression. Allow them to share their opinions, defend their arguments, and engage in meaningful dialogues.

- **Incorporate storytelling into lessons**. Share anecdotes, narratives, or real-life examples to illustrate concepts. Encourage your child to create and share their own stories related to the subject matter. Integrate word games, crossword puzzles, anagrams, and vocabulary-building activities into the curriculum. These activities can be both fun and educational. These activities can be both fun and educational.

- **Provide opportunities to give presentations**. This allows them to practice public speaking, organization of ideas, and effective communication. Highlight key vocabulary words related to the subject matter and encourage using these words in discussions, presentations, and written assignments. Provide context for new vocabulary words. Encourage critical thinking and analysis by presenting complex texts or issues to dissect and discuss. Ask open-ended questions that require them to analyze, evaluate, and form arguments.

- **Incorporate digital tools and resources**, such as educational websites, blogs, and online forums, to engage in language-related activities and research. Provide constructive feedback on written assignments and presentations, emphasizing both content and language use. Allow time to revise their work to improve their communication skills.

- **Allow your child to read passages aloud** to improve pronunciation, fluency, and comprehension. This can also help identify areas where they may need assistance. Help connect language and other subjects by showing how language skills can be applied in various contexts, such as science, history, or mathematics. Recognize that VV learners may have different interests and learning preferences. Allow for some flexibility in assignments to accommodate individual strengths and passions.

- **Encourage the use of storytelling techniques and mnemonic devices—** memory aids or techniques that help individuals remember information more effectively, such as acronyms—to help students remember important information or concepts. See examples of acronyms below.

- **Assign writing tasks** that serve different purposes, such as persuasive essays, informative reports, narrative writing, and creative writing. This variety can keep learners engaged.

Remember that not all VV learners are the same, so it's important to be flexible and adapt your teaching strategies to meet your child's specific needs and interests. Tailoring instruction to individual learning styles and providing a supportive and language-rich environment can help verbal-linguistic learners thrive academically.

 ## Mnemonic Devices

Mnemonic devices are memory aids or techniques that help individuals remember information more effectively. These devices work by organizing or encoding information to make it easier to recall. Mnemonics can be particularly useful for remembering lists, sequences, facts, or complex information. There are several types of mnemonic devices, including:

- **Acronyms:** Acronyms are words or phrases formed by taking the initial letters of a list of items and creating a new word or phrase. For example, HOMES stands for the five great lakes in North America: H=Huron, O=Ontario, M=Michigan, E=Erie, and S=Superior.

- **Acrostics:** Acrostics are sentences or phrases where the first letter of each word represents something to be remembered. For instance, "Please Excuse My Dear Aunt Sally" is an acrostic used in mathematics to remember the order of operations (Parentheses, Exponents, Multiplication and Division, Addition and Subtraction).

- **Rhymes and Songs:** Rhyming phrases or songs can be memorable ways to remember information. For example, "i before e, except after c" is a rhyme used to help with English spelling.
- **Chunking:** Chunking involves breaking down a long list of items or numbers into smaller, more manageable groups or chunks. This makes it easier to remember the information. For instance, remembering a phone number as three chunks (e.g., 555-123-4567) is easier than remembering it as a single string of digits.
- **Method of Loci:** This technique involves associating items on a list with specific locations or places you are familiar with. When you need to recall the items, you mentally walk through these locations, retrieving the associated information. It's beneficial for remembering a sequence of items or facts by linking them to physical or mental locations in a familiar environment.
- **Visual Imagery:** Visual imagery mnemonics involve creating mental images or scenes that help you remember information. You can imagine vivid and memorable pictures related to the content you want to remember. For example, if you need to remember a shopping list, you can visualize each item as a vivid image in a specific location in your mind.

ELEMENTARY STUDENTS

 **Books for Elementary Students**

I have chosen the theme 'apples' for the elementary section of this chapter. Every theme-based teaching unit should have a list of books readily available to be read and enjoyed. Each book can give insight into the theme, as well as insight into characters in the stories, facts about the theme, and all of the story elements that you might be teaching your child, such as sequence, cause, and effect, comparison and contrast, etc. When I taught elementary children, I found that using a theme kept the focus of everything I taught: math, language arts, science, social studies, and even health. I have taught every theme-based group of activities in this book, and I know the tips and tricks work. *Enjoy!*

"The Apple Pie Tree" by Zoe Hall
>*Follow a young brother and sister as they witness the changing seasons of an apple tree, from blossoms to picking apples and baking a delicious apple pie.*

"Apple Farmer Annie" by Monica Wellington
>*Join Annie, an apple farmer, as she tends to her orchard and prepares for the farmers' market, showcasing the variety of apple products she creates.*

"Apple Picking Day!" by Candice Ransom
>*A family goes apple picking, providing an engaging look at the process of harvesting apples and the joy of spending time together.*

"Ten Apples Up On Top!" by Dr. Seuss
>*This playful rhyming book features animal characters balancing apples on their heads, counting from one to ten in an entertaining way.*

"Apples, Apples, Apples" by Nancy Elizabeth Wallace
>*Join the Wallace family on a trip to the apple orchard and learn about different apple varieties, from picking to making applesauce.*

"Applesauce Season" by Eden Ross Lipson
>*Experience the joys of making applesauce from scratch with family and friends during the autumn season.*

"Apple Trouble!" by Ragnhild Scamell
>*Hedgehog's quest to carry an apple to his nest without it sticking to his spines leads to humorous and unexpected encounters with other animals.*

"Apple Cake" by Dawn Casey
>*Follow a little girl as she goes on a journey to make a special apple cake using apples from her tree, highlighting the anticipation of baking.*

"The Apple Orchard Riddle" by Margaret McNamara
> *Join the students of Miss Tippi's class on a field trip to an apple orchard, where they solve a riddle and learn about apple varieties.*

"The Biggest Apple Ever" by Steven Kroll
> *Two mice, Clayton and Desmond, both find the same giant apple, leading to a collaborative adventure of sharing and teamwork.*

These short stories centered around apples are perfect for young children, celebrating the harvest season, teaching about apples, and promoting themes of sharing, teamwork, and family activities.

 ## Language Arts for Elementary Students: "Apple Storytelling"

Objective: The child will practice developing the skills of 'sequencing' and 'summarizing.'

Activity 1:
- Read the book "Johnny Appleseed" by Stephen Kellogg aloud and have your child follow along.
- Ask questions as you read. Allow your child to ask questions as you read, such as, *What does that word mean? Why did Johnny Appleseed walk around planting apple trees?* Make a list of 'need to know' words.
- Refer to the websites at the end of this book for free materials to use with this book.

Activity 2:
- Depending on your child's level of understanding, make a worksheet of important one-sentence things that happened in the story. (Printing them on cardstock makes an activity you can save for another child.)
- Cut out the sentences as strips.
- Mix them up and ask your child to put them in order.

Activity 3:
- Have the child practice reading the story out loud to you.
- Test your child by writing a summary of the story.

Follow-up activity: Needed—starter cards (e.g., "Once upon a time, there was a magical apple...").
- Provide your child with blank paper and pencils.
- Introduce story starter cards with apple-themed prompts. Your child should choose a card and use it as a starting point to write a creative story about apples.
- Encourage them to include descriptive language and imagery to make their story engaging.
- After writing, they can illustrate their story with markers and share it with you. Hang it on the brag board.

 ## Math for Elementary Students

Apple Math Puzzles

Objective 1: The child will design and solve story problems and equations.

Activity 1:
- Give your child apple-shaped cutouts and markers.
- Ask them to create math puzzles on each apple. For example, they can write addition or subtraction problems on one side and the answers on the other.
- Challenge your child to solve the puzzles they've created, or you can solve the puzzles they make for you.
- Extend the activity by introducing multiplication or division puzzles for more advanced learners.

Objective 2: Using various kinds of apples, the child will find the circumference of the apples and the weight of the apples, find the average weight of various kinds of apples, such as all of the Gala apples and all of the Red Delicious apples, and make various charts and graphs of the collected data.

Activity 1:
- Use several apples of each kind—for instance, five Granny Smith apples, five Gala apples, five Red Delicious apples, etc.
- Use the measuring tape to find each apple's circumference in inches and centimeters.
- Then, weigh each apple on a kitchen scale to find their weight in ounces and grams.

Activity 2:
- Average each kind of apple for circumference and weight.
- Make graphs of each data group—one for average circumference in inches, one for average circumference in centimeters, one for average weight in ounces, and one for average weight in grams.

Activity 3:
- Using graph paper, make line and bar graphs to represent and compare your findings from activities 1 and 2.

 **Science for Elementary Students**

Objective: The child will use the scientific method to investigate apples.

Activity 1:
- Start by discussing different types of apples with your child, such as Granny Smith, Red Delicious, and Gala.
- Provide a variety of apples for them to observe.
- Encourage your child to use a magnifying glass to examine the apples closely. Have them describe the apple's color, texture, and any unique features in their interactive science notebook.

Activity 2:
- Discuss with them how apples grow, their life cycle, and the parts of an apple (skin, flesh, seeds).

*Optional: Conduct an experiment to see how different apple types taste and compare their flavors.

 ## Social Studies for Elementary Students

Objective: The child will investigate the cultivation of apples around the world.

Activity 1:
- Provide your child with a world map.
- Explore the origins of various apple varieties worldwide, such as Fuji apples from Japan, Granny Smith apples from Australia, or Braeburn apples from New Zealand.
- Provide images of apples from different countries and ask your child to match each image with the corresponding location on the map.

Activity 2:
- Ask your child to locate these countries on the map and mark them.
- Create index cards with interesting facts about apple orchards in different countries.
- Have your child read the facts aloud and place each card on the map where it belongs.

Activity 3:
- Discuss the cultural significance of apples in different regions and how they are used in various cuisines.

These activities are designed to engage elementary VV learners while incorporating the theme of APPLES into different subject areas. Feel free to adapt and modify them based on your child's age and interests.

MIDDLE SCHOOL STUDENTS

Middle school students are the 'tweeners' of the family. They want to appear to be 'all grown up,' but at the same time, they struggle with still wanting to do things associated with their younger selves. It's very important for you to bring in elements to their education that will appeal to their 'inner little child' by offering some more playful ideas as you teach them higher learning content.

 **Books for Middle School Students**

The following is a list of books your middle school VV learner might enjoy. Many have been made into movies. I always loved having my students read a book and then watch the movie. I would have them compare and contrast the book to the movie, making note of sequences that may have been left out, actions that may be out of order from the book, or enhanced in ways that were not in the book.

"Harry Potter" series by J.K. Rowling
> *Follow the adventures of a young wizard, Harry Potter, as he battles dark forces and unravels mysteries at Hogwarts School of Witchcraft and Wizardry.*

"Percy Jackson and the Olympians" series by Rick Riordan
> *Join Percy Jackson, a demigod and the son of Poseidon, on thrilling quests to prevent calamities in both the mortal and mythological worlds.*

"The Giver" by Lois Lowry
> *In a seemingly perfect but controlled society, a boy named Jonas discovers the true meaning of freedom and individuality.*

"Wonder" by R.J. Palacio
> *Witness the remarkable journey of August Pullman, a boy with a facial deformity, as he navigates his first year in a mainstream school.*

"A Wrinkle in Time" by Madeleine L'Engle
> *Travel through space and time with Meg Murry and her companions to rescue her missing father from a dark force.*

"The Lightning Thief" by Rick Riordan
> *Follow Percy Jackson's quest to prevent a catastrophic war among the gods while uncovering his true identity.*

"The Diary of a Young Girl" by Anne Frank
> *Experience the poignant and powerful diary of Anne Frank, a Jewish girl hiding from the Nazis during World War II.*

"The Hunger Games" by Suzanne Collins
> *Enter the dystopian world of Panem, where Katniss Everdeen becomes a symbol of resistance against a brutal regime.*

"The Hobbit" by J.R.R. Tolkien
> *Join Bilbo Baggins, a reluctant hero, on a grand adventure to help a group of dwarves reclaim their homeland from a fearsome dragon.*

"The Secret Garden" by Frances Hodgson Burnett
> *Follow the transformation of Mary Lennox and her discovery of a neglected garden that holds the key to healing.*

"Matilda" by Roald Dahl
> *Cheer for Matilda Wormwood, a brilliant girl with telekinetic powers, as she stands up to her neglectful family and tyrannical headmistress.*

"Bridge to Terabithia" by Katherine Paterson
> *Explore the imaginative world created by two friends, Jess and Leslie, as they face the challenges of childhood and loss.*

"The Tale of Despereaux" by Kate DiCamillo
> *Join Despereaux Tilling, a mouse with an oversized heart, on a quest to rescue a princess and restore honor to his kind.*

"Holes" by Louis Sachar
> *Follow Stanley Yelnats as he unravels the mysteries of Camp Green Lake, a juvenile detention center with a strange history.*

"The Westing Game" by Ellen Raskin
> *Engage in a thrilling mystery where a diverse group of heirs must solve puzzles to inherit a deceased millionaire's fortune.*

"Ender's Game" by Orson Scott Card
> *Witness the training of Ender Wiggin, a young military genius, as he prepares to defend Earth from an alien invasion.*

"Charlotte's Web" by E.B. White
> *Celebrate the heartwarming friendship between Wilbur, a pig, and Charlotte, a clever spider who spins messages in her web.*

"The Outsiders" by S.E. Hinton
> *Explore the lives of Ponyboy and his friends, members of a tight-knit gang, as they navigate the challenges of teenage life and societal divisions.*

 ## Language Arts for Middle School Students

Objective: The child will analyze characters from a short story to determine personality, motivations, reactions to situations, and a change of personality.

Summary: In "The Gift of the Magi," a young couple, Della and Jim, deeply love each other but face financial hardship. In a touching display of selflessness, Della sells her long, beautiful hair to buy Jim a gift, while Jim sells his prized pocket watch to buy Della a gift. On Christmas Day, they exchange their gifts, only to discover the sacrifices they've made for each other. This heartwarming story illustrates the true spirit of love and giving, where the greatest gift is the love they share.

Activity:

- Read the short story, "The Gift of the Magi."
- Ask your child to choose a character from the story and create a character analysis.
- Have them describe the character's personality, motivations, and how they change throughout the story.
- Encourage textual evidence and quotes to support their analysis.
- Discuss how understanding characters enhances the reading experience.

Creative Writing: "The Enchanted Orchard"

Objective: The child will create a story adventure using all the elements needed to create it using the given prompt.

Activity:

- Give your child a creative writing prompt: "Imagine you discover an enchanted orchard filled with magical apple trees."
- "Write a story about your adventure." Encourage them to develop a narrative with engaging characters, a plot, and vivid descriptions of the orchard's magical elements.
- After writing, have your child illustrate key scenes from their story.
- Share the stories with family members and discuss the use of descriptive language and storytelling techniques.

*This activity can be modified to fit a genre study, i.e., if studying science fiction, the story prompt would be to create a science fiction story.

Literary Debate: "The Great Coffee Debate"

Objective: The child will begin to learn the skills needed to debate issues with clear two-sided (or more) viewpoints.

- *You will need the internet and/or public library for this activity. Allow several days to work on this project.

Activity:
- Select an article about coffee to read with your child.
- After reading, organize a friendly debate where your child defends their viewpoint on topics related to the theme of the debate (e.g., coffee has nutritional value).
- Encourage them to use evidence from the text to support their arguments.
- Engage in a discussion exploring different perspectives, fostering critical thinking and communication skills.

 ## Math for Middle School Learners:

Several years ago, I taught middle school math and science in an inclusion setting—i.e., many of the students were on an Individual Education Plan (IEP). They always loved it when I set up a lesson with a make-believe story and appeared to be talking to 'someone' they couldn't see. Imagine the following story where I converse with the main character, Lina, as I introduce and teach this difficult geometry theorem, the Pythagorean Theorem.

Objective: The child will solve various problems using the Pythagorean Theorem.

Activity 1:
- Introduce "The Quest for the Missing Formula," a math-themed adventure story where your child becomes a detective searching for a missing formula.
- Give your child a worksheet with a picture of a woodland area with a brook in the center.
- Draw several right triangles along a path that ends at a waterfall.
- Your child must solve for x to advance in the story and uncover clues as they progress.
- Finally, discuss the story and review the math concepts they encountered. *This story can be adjusted for various math formulas.*

"The Quest for the Missing Formula: Pythagoras' Discovery"

In the ancient city of Geometria, nestled amidst rolling hills and lush valleys, there lived a curious young mathematician named Lina. Lina had always been captivated by the mysteries of geometry and arithmetic. She spent her days poring over scrolls and manuscripts in the city's grand library, searching for hidden mathematical gems.

One sunny afternoon, as Lina was engrossed in her studies, a peculiar old man with a long, white beard approached her. He introduced himself as Pythagoras, the renowned mathematician of antiquity who was said to have unlocked the secrets of triangles and right angles.

Pythagoras handed Lina a delicate parchment, its edges tattered with age. "I need your help, young mathematician," he said, his eyes gleaming with urgency. "I have lost a precious formula, the cornerstone of my discoveries."

Intrigued, Lina unfurled the parchment to reveal a half-finished proof that bore a striking resemblance to the Pythagorean Theorem:

$a^2 + b^2 = ?$ (Refer to the worksheet with right triangles from above).

With each discovery, she carefully measured the lengths of the triangle's legs and sought to unveil the secret that Pythagoras had lost.

One day, while wandering through a tranquil forest, Lina stumbled upon a magnificent waterfall. To her amazement, the flowing water formed a perfect right triangle, with the waterfall's base as one of the legs. The other leg extended across a serene pond.

Lina measured the lengths of the waterfall's base and the extending leg, and a sudden realization struck her. She rushed back to her quarters in Geometria and fervently began her calculations.

(On the back of this paper, draw the picture Lina saw at the waterfall).

After days and nights of meticulous work, Lina finally completed the missing formula:

$c^2 = a^2 + b^2$

With triumphant excitement, Lina returned to Pythagoras, who was overjoyed at the recovery of his lost formula. He explained that this theorem was not just a mathematical curiosity but had profound applications in fields ranging from architecture to navigation.

As a token of gratitude, Pythagoras shared his extensive knowledge with Lina, revealing the intricate connections between geometry, mathematics, and the natural world. Lina's quest had not only restored a valuable formula but had deepened her understanding of the timeless beauty of mathematics.

The story of Lina's quest for the missing formula became a cherished legend in Geometria, a testament to the enduring power of mathematical exploration. It served as a reminder that within the world of numbers and shapes, endless adventures awaited those with inquisitive minds and the courage to seek answers to the most intriguing mysteries.

Objective: The child will relate definitions of various terms to their definitions.

Activity 2:
- Provide your child with a list of math vocabulary words and their definitions.
- Have your child choose a word from the list and draw a visual representation on the whiteboard.
- Other family members or friends can try to guess the math term based on the drawing.
- After the game, discuss the meanings of the terms and their relevance to math concepts.

Objective 3: Determine all fractions are ratios. By increasing the terms of the ratio, one can double the amount of a product.

*Need to know—All fractions can be represented as a ratio. A ratio is a mathematical expression that represents the relationship between two quantities or values. It is typically expressed as a fraction or with a colon (":") between two numbers. Ratios are used to compare the sizes or quantities of two different things relatively or proportionally. The two numbers in a ratio are often referred to as the "terms" of the ratio—e.g., ½ or 1:2 and verbalized as "one to two".

Activity 3:
- Select a recipe from a cookbook or a cooking website that involves various measurements, such as cups, tablespoons, and teaspoons.
- Ask your child to calculate the ratios of ingredients needed to double or halve the recipe.
- Have them write down the measurements and explain their reasoning.
- Using the modified measurements, prepare the recipe together to see if the calculations were correct.
- Discuss the importance of math in real-life scenarios like cooking.

 ## Science for Middle School Students

Objective 1: The child will observe change over time using the scientific method.

Activity 1:
- Encourage your child to keep a scientific journal dedicated to observing changes in nature.
- Regularly visit an outdoor area (e.g., a park, garden, or backyard) and document seasonal changes, weather patterns, or plant growth observations.
- Have your child write detailed descriptions of their observations, including any patterns or trends they notice.
- Discuss the importance of keen observation in the scientific process.

Objective 2: The child will create a closed terrarium.

A terrarium is an enclosed indoor garden, usually small and made in a glass container so you can see inside and observe every day. When completed, it becomes a small ecosystem that self-sustains itself with evaporated water that collects on the top. When the water gets too heavy, it will 'rain' on the plants and soil below, thus creating a water cycle so that the plants live and grow.

Materials Needed:
- A sealed glass or plastic container (e.g., a clear 2-liter water or soda bottle)
- Soil
- Small plants
- Rocks
- Water
- Plastic animals (e.g., insects)

Activity 2:
- Create a mini ecosystem in a clear plastic container, starting with a layer of soil.
- Plant small vegetation, add rocks, and simulate a water source within the container, such as a pond.
- Introduce plastic animals to represent different parts of the ecosystem (predators, prey, scavengers).
- Your child should observe and document how the ecosystem changes over time, noting interactions among the components.
- Discuss the concept of ecosystems, food chains, and the balance of nature.

 **Social Studies for Middle School Students**

Objective: The child will research Johnny Appleseed to discover this historical figure's significance. *This activity can be done with any historical person of interest, such as Jane Goodall.*

Activity:
- Introduce your child to the historical figure Johnny Appleseed and his role in American history.
- Ask your child to research and write a report on the life and contributions of Johnny Appleseed.
- Encourage them to explore his impact on westward expansion and the cultivation of apple orchards in early America.
- Discuss the significance of individuals in shaping history.

HIGH SCHOOL STUDENTS

High school students have reached a definite point where they are taking on a role of more independence. As a result, they take on more family responsibilities, such as chauffeuring for younger children and caretaking younger children when you, the parents, need to be away from home for a short while. You give them more freedom of choice, more freedom when they use the internet, and more freedom to go with their friends on outings outside of the family unit. Because of their gradual transition to making adult choices, their assignments should reflect more social, political, and worldwide topics of interest. The following ideas are ways to direct your VV Learner to become a more informed adult as they begin exploring outside the home.

 **Books for High School Students**

The following is a list of literature your high school student might enjoy. Some of these selections have more mature themes, so it is advisable for you, the parent, to decide if you would want your child to read some of the selections. For example, "The Handmaid's Tale" by Margaret Attwood has a more mature theme that some high school students might not be ready to read. These books encompass a range of genres, themes, and writing styles, making them suitable for a high school verbal-linguistic learner with diverse reading interests.

"To Kill a Mockingbird" by Harper Lee
> *Set in the American South during the 1930s, this classic novel explores themes of racism and justice through the eyes of young Scout Finch.*

"1984" by George Orwell
> *A dystopian masterpiece that examines the dangers of totalitarianism and the loss of individual freedoms in a surveillance society.*

"The Great Gatsby" by F. Scott Fitzgerald
> *A portrayal of the American Dream and its disillusionment during the Roaring Twenties, told through the enigmatic Jay Gatsby.*

"Brave New World" by Aldous Huxley
> *In a highly controlled future society, this novel delves into the consequences of a world obsessed with pleasure and conformity.*

"The Catcher in the Rye" by J.D. Salinger
> *Follow the journey of Holden Caulfield as he grapples with alienation, identity, and teenage angst in New York City.*

"The Lord of the Flies" by William Golding
> *Stranded on a deserted island, a group of boys descends into chaos and brutality, highlighting the dark side of human nature.*

"Frankenstein" by Mary Shelley
> *Explore themes of scientific ethics and the consequences of playing god in this classic novel about the creation of a monster.*

"The Scarlet Letter" by Nathaniel Hawthorne
> *Set in 17th-century Puritan Massachusetts, this novel examines the consequences of sin and societal judgment through the character of Hester Prynne.*

"Jane Eyre" by Charlotte Brontë
> *Follow the life of the orphaned Jane Eyre as she faces adversity, love, and societal expectations in 19th-century England.*

"Pride and Prejudice" by Jane Austen
> *A timeless tale of romance, class, and societal expectations as Elizabeth Bennet navigates the world of eligible bachelors.*

"The Odyssey" by Homer
> *An epic poem that chronicles Odysseus' adventures and trials on his journey home after the Trojan War.*

"The Picture of Dorian Gray" by Oscar Wilde
> *A Gothic novel that explores the moral decay of Dorian Gray, whose portrait ages while he remains youthful.*

"Fahrenheit 451" by Ray Bradbury
> *In a future where books are banned, follow the journey of Guy Montag, a fireman tasked with burning them, as he questions the status quo.*

"The Road" by Cormac McCarthy
> *A post-apocalyptic story of a father and son's harrowing journey through a desolate landscape in search of safety.*

"The Iliad" by Homer
> *Another epic poem by Homer, this one tells the story of the Trojan War and the hero Achilles.*

"The Handmaid's Tale" by Margaret Atwood
> *In a theocratic dystopia, follow the story of Offred, a handmaid who seeks to reclaim her identity and freedom.*

"The Hobbit" by J.R.R. Tolkien
> *Join Bilbo Baggins on an adventure with dwarves and a wizard as they seek to reclaim their homeland from a dragon.*

"The Road Less Traveled" by M. Scott Peck
> *A self-help classic that explores personal growth, spiritual development, and the path to a fulfilling life.*

 **Language Arts for High School Students**

Objective 1: The child will compare and contrast two Dystopian novels.

Definition of a Dystopian Novel: *A dystopian novel is a genre of speculative fiction that presents an imagined society or world in which conditions are nightmarishly oppressive, grim, and often characterized by authoritarian or totalitarian control. Dystopian novels typically depict a future or alternate reality far from ideal, often highlighting the darker aspects of human nature, government, technology, or social systems.*

Prominent examples of dystopian novels include George Orwell's "1984," Aldous Huxley's "Brave New World," Margaret Atwood's "The Handmaid's Tale," and Ray Bradbury's "Fahrenheit 451." These works, along with others in the genre, have become important vehicles for exploring societal issues, warning against the dangers of totalitarianism, and reflecting on the consequences of unchecked power and societal conformity.

Activity 1:
- Assign your child two or more dystopian novels to read.
- Ask them to conduct a comparative analysis of the novels, focusing on themes, character development, and societal critiques.
- Have them write a literary essay that explores similarities and differences between the novels.
- Encourage in-depth analysis and textual evidence to support their arguments.

Objective 2: The child will write a Shakespearean sonnet using its structure and theme development.

Activity 2:
- Introduce your child to Shakespearean sonnets and discuss their structure and themes.

- Challenge your child to write their own Shakespearean sonnet on a contemporary topic or issue.
- Emphasize the iambic pentameter and rhyme scheme (ABAB CDCD EFEF GG) typical of sonnets.
- Encourage creativity in expressing modern ideas within a traditional form.

What are Shakespearean Sonnets?

A Shakespearean sonnet, also known as the 'English sonnet' or the 'Shakespearean sonnet form,' is a poetic structure popularized by William Shakespeare and has since become one of the most recognized and frequently used sonnet forms in English literature. It comprises fourteen lines written in iambic pentameter and follows a specific rhyme scheme.

The rhyme scheme of a Shakespearean sonnet is typically as follows: ABAB CDCD EFEF GG. In this rhyme scheme, the sonnet is divided into three quatrains (four-line sections) followed by a final rhymed couplet (a two-line section). Each quatrain follows the ABAB rhyme pattern, meaning that the first and third lines rhyme with each other, and the second and fourth lines rhyme with each other. The final rhymed couplet usually has a distinct rhyme (GG) and often contains a twist, change in tone, or resolution of the themes explored in the quatrains.

The Shakespearean sonnet form allows for flexibility in the expression of ideas and themes. It is known for its versatility and has been used by many poets, but William Shakespeare is perhaps the most famous practitioner of this form. He wrote a collection of one hundred and fifty-four sonnets, many of which adhere to the Shakespearean sonnet structure.

Shakespearean sonnets often explore themes of love, beauty, time, mortality, and the complexities of human emotion. They are celebrated for their lyrical qualities, wordplay, and ability to convey profound thoughts and feelings within a concise and structured framework.

<u>Sonnet 18 Written by William Shakespeare</u>

Shall I compare thee to a summer's day?
Thou art more lovely and more temperate:
Rough winds do shake the darling buds of May,
And summer's lease hath all too short a date:

Sometime too hot the eye of heaven shines,
And often is his gold complexion dimmed;
And every fair from fair sometime declines,
By chance or nature's changing course untrimmed;

But thy eternal summer shall not fade
Nor lose possession of that fair thou owest;
Nor shall Death brag thou wanderest in his shade,
When in eternal lines to time thou growest:

So long as men can breathe or eyes can see,
So long lives this, and this gives life to thee.

 ## Math for High School Students

Objective: The child will collect statistics on the given topic and create appropriate graphs. Then, the child will logically form a stance to discuss or debate the data presented.

*The following activity requires someone else to take an opposing viewpoint.

Activity:
- Provide your child with articles related to data privacy and the ethical considerations of data collection and analysis.
- Organize a debate in which your child takes a position on whether certain data collection practices are ethical or not.
- Encourage them to research and prepare arguments to support their stance.

- Engage in a structured debate where they present their arguments and counterarguments.
- Discuss the broader implications of data privacy and ethics in the digital age.

Objective 2: The child will create an artistic project using math patterns and geometry principles.

Activity 2:
- Introduce your child to the concept of mathematical patterns in art and design.
- Provide art supplies and ask them to create an original artwork incorporating geometric shapes, symmetry, or fractal patterns.
- Have them explain the mathematical principles behind their artwork in a written or oral presentation.
- Explore famous works of art that use mathematical concepts and discuss their significance.

Objective 3: The child will explore cryptography and design their own secret code. *Cryptographic codes or puzzles involve using cryptography, the science of securing communication and information by transforming it into a secret code. Cryptographic codes and puzzles are designed to be challenging to decipher without the proper key or knowledge, making them a popular area of interest in computer science, mathematics, and puzzle-solving.*

Activity 3:
- Find some cryptographic puzzles or codes on the internet and give them to your child to solve.
- Encourage them to research different encryption methods and decipher the codes.
- Provide step-by-step guidance on how to decode one of the puzzles.
- Have your child create their own coded message and challenge a family member or friend to decode it.
- Discuss the applications of cryptography in mathematics and computer science.

 **Types of Cryptography**

- **Ciphers:** Ciphers are algorithms that encode or encrypt messages. The recipient can decode or decrypt the message if they possess the correct key or algorithm. Classic examples include the Caesar cipher, Vigenère cipher, and substitution ciphers.
- **Cryptograms:** Cryptograms are puzzles in which letters in a message are replaced with other letters or symbols based on a specific cipher. Solvers must figure out the original message by deciphering the code.
- **Transposition Ciphers:** Transposition ciphers involve rearranging the order of letters in a message according to a specific rule. The message's content remains the same, but the arrangement is altered.
- **One-Time Pads:** One-time pads use a random key of the same length as the message to encrypt it. They are theoretically unbreakable if used correctly and only once, as long as the key remains secret.
- **Hash Functions:** Hash functions are one-way functions that take an input (message) and produce a fixed-size output (hash). They are used for data integrity and password hashing. Cryptographic hash functions should be difficult to reverse engineer.
- **Public Key Encryption:** Public key encryption, such as RSA, relies on a pair of keys: a public key for encryption and a private key for decryption. Messages encrypted with the public key can only be decrypted with the corresponding private key.
- **Block Ciphers:** Block ciphers encrypt data in fixed-size blocks, typically sixty-four or one hundred and twenty-eight bits at a time. Examples include the Data Encryption Standard (DES) and the Advanced Encryption Standard (AES).
- **Mystery Codes:** Mystery codes are puzzles that involve decoding messages using clues or patterns provided in the puzzle. They may include a mix of different cryptographic techniques.
- **Escape Room Puzzles:** Many escape rooms incorporate cryptographic puzzles as part of the challenge. These puzzles often require teamwork and problem-solving to decipher codes and unlock clues to progress in the game.

Cryptographic codes and puzzles serve various purposes, from securing sensitive information to providing entertainment and mental stimulation. They require logical thinking, pattern recognition, and a good understanding of cryptographic principles to solve. Cryptography is also fundamental in computer security, data protection, and information technology. Various websites and platforms host cryptographic challenges and competitions where participants solve puzzles and crack codes to test their skills.

 ## Science for High School Students

Objective: The child will use technology to produce a finished video.

*You will need to install a recording app on your phone or computer for this project. There are several free or inexpensive ones available on the worldwide web.

Activity:

- Introduce your child to the world of science journalism and podcasting.
- Ask them to select a science topic or discovery they find fascinating.
- Have them create a script for a podcast episode, including an introduction, a discussion of the topic, and a conclusion.
- Record and edit the podcast, adding music or sound effects if desired.
- Share the podcast with friends and family, promoting science communication skills.

 ## Social Studies for High School Students

Objective: The child will explore and identify various forms of propaganda while researching how propaganda influences society's views around the world.

Activity:

- Explore WWII propaganda posters and videos and discuss their historical context and purpose.
- Ask your child to research the role of propaganda in shaping public opinion during the war.

- Have them analyze specific posters and their messaging, such as "Uncle Sam."
- Encourage the creation of a presentation or essay on the impact of propaganda on society during WWII.

Conclusion

As you can see, learning does not have to be a constant worksheet-after-worksheet learning situation. Although worksheets have their place in any 'school,' they do not always engage the upper learning areas that need to be developed. Typically, the best lessons include explanations with examples of what you are teaching to acquire knowledge, time for exploring and identifying what you are teaching, time to experience what you have taught, and time to reflect and analyze what you have taught. Incorporating these attributes in your homeschooling efforts assures your child's intellectual intelligence is developed and used, even when your child isn't engaged in your 'lesson plans,' but in independent activities and discussions with friends and family!

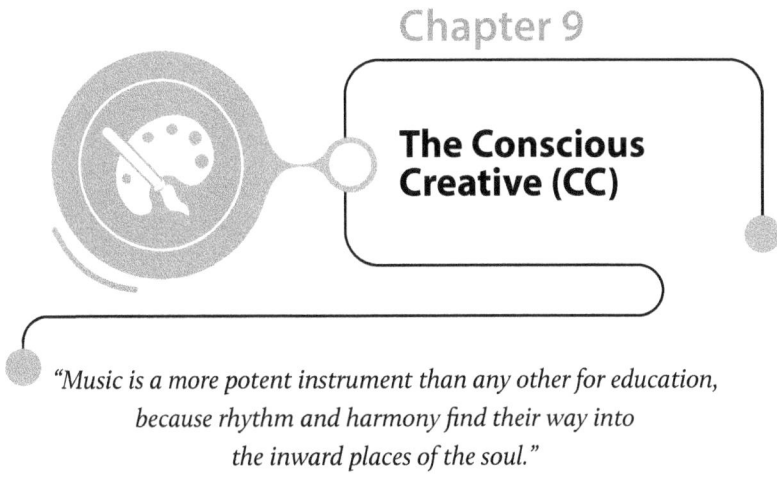

Chapter 9

The Conscious Creative (CC)

*"Music is a more potent instrument than any other for education,
because rhythm and harmony find their way into
the inward places of the soul."*
—Plato

It was always interesting to have the CC learner in the class. Having several at the same time made for a really fun adventure! Even the children with little characteristics of a CC learner became engaged in the topics at hand because these children are hard to resist. However, a word of caution: If you teach more than one child in your home, and someone is *not* a CC learner, make sure your CC learner is elsewhere. Other intelligences cannot think critically around the one who likes to listen to music or is drumming out a rhythm with their pencil to an unheard song in their head.

According to CC intelligence, these children have high musical and rhythmic abilities. They are extremely creative and learn just about anything if they can think of the information in some sort of rhythm, poem, acrostic, song lyrics, or melody. Here is a detailed list of characteristics of a CC learner. They are very easy to identify because they are the children who sing songs out of the blue, dance to about any music, make up rhymes, and pound out drum rhythms on your pots and pans.

Highlights:

- CCs have a heightened sensitivity to various sounds, tones, and rhythms.
- They may have natural musical talents, such as singing, playing instruments, or composing music.
- They can easily detect and follow rhythms in music and everyday sounds.
- The Conscious Creative has a strong ability to remember melodies and tunes.
- They often have a strong emotional connection to music and can use it to express themselves.
- CCs may use music and rhythm as a means of creative expression.
- They can distinguish between subtle differences in pitch, tone, and rhythm.
- They can use music as a mnemonic device to aid memory and learning.
- The Creative Conscious learner derives great enjoyment from listening to, creating, or performing music.
- They may naturally tap their fingers or feet or move to the rhythm of music without conscious effort.
- CCs may pay attention to the nuances of musical compositions, including lyrics, instrumentation, and arrangement.

It stands to reason that the best way to teach your CC learner is to include music and rhythm in all of your lessons, including allowing them to listen to music as they work on their assignments. If you have other children in the house, especially if they are not CC learners, headphones connected to their favorite playlist works quite well. The following list of strategies are tried and true ways for the child of music to learn effectively. They help engage and support the learning of CC learners in various educational settings in your home.

Strategies:
- **Use music and rhythm** to teach various subjects, such as using songs to remember facts or creating musical mnemonics. Provide opportunities for your child to learn to play musical instruments or experiment with rhythm-making tools. To engage these learners, teach concepts using rhythmic patterns, clapping, or body percussion.
- **Assign projects that involve creating music** or exploring musical themes related to the subject matter. Use visual aids with musical elements, such as diagrams with musical notes or rhythmic patterns.
- **Use music to tell stories or narratives**, and encourage students to create their own musical stories. Create rhythmic mnemonics and chants to help students remember key information. Organize field trips to musical performances, museums, or exhibits related to music and rhythm.
- **Allow students to move or tap along with the rhythm** during lessons to help them focus. Provide opportunities for students to express themselves through music and rhythmic compositions. Encourage group activities like group singing, composing songs, or collaborative musical performances. Some families even have a 'performance night.'

In the next section, I demonstrate all the major subjects for elementary children surrounding a central theme: *The African savannah.* I think it would be fun if you had some ongoing projects and activities that would support this theme and add interest and excitement to your day. Even older children can get involved because, let's face it, most people do enjoy music and performances! I'll add some thoughts on other activities at the end of this section before moving on to middle school students.

ELEMENTARY STUDENTS

 **Books for Elementary Students**

The following lessons are designed around a central theme: The African savannah. Many of the activities are centered around the book, "Bringing the Rain to Kapiti Plain." The following books should be either purchased for your child's home library or acquired at their local library. If you have an Amazon Prime account, these books can be acquired there.

"Bringing the Rain to Kapiti Plain" by Verna Aardema
> Origin: Based on a Kenyan folk poem
> *Association with the African savannah: This story is set on the African savannah and tells the tale of a boy's quest to bring rain to the dry Kapiti Plain.*

"The Leopard's Drum" by Jessica Souhami
> Origin: Nigerian folktale
> *Association with the African savannah: While the story doesn't explicitly mention the savannah, it is a West African folktale and likely takes place in a natural African setting, which could include the savannah.*

"Why Mosquitoes Buzz in People's Ears" by Verna Aardema
> Origin: Based on a West African folktale
> *Association with the African savannah: This story is set in the African wilderness and features animals commonly found in savannah environments, making it suitable for association with the savannah.*

"The Girl Who Married a Lion" by Alexander McCall Smith
> Origin: Botswana folktale
> *Association with the African savannah: While the story doesn't explicitly mention the savannah, Botswana is known for its diverse landscapes, including savannah regions.*

"The Hunterman and the Crocodile" by Baba Wagué Diakité
  Origin: Malian folktale
  Association with the African savannah: Mali includes both savannah and other landscapes, and this story might be set in or near savannah areas.

These stories are either explicitly set in African savannah settings or are from regions with savannah landscapes, making them suitable for association with the African savannah theme.

For the following activities, it is advantageous for you to acquire a recording device, such as on your phone or a computer app. Also, these websites—www.curiositystream.com or www.PBSlearningmedia.org—have some nice documentaries and other videos that pair well with this unit.

 ## Language Arts for Elementary School Students

Objective: To improve comprehension and engage with the story.

Summary: In "Bringing the Rain to Kapiti Plain," we follow the journey of Ki-pat, a determined herdsman, as he faces a severe drought on Kapiti Plain. With rhythmic, cumulative storytelling, Ki-pat devises an ingenious plan involving a thunderous sound to summon the much-needed rain. This beautifully illustrated tale celebrates resourcefulness and the power of an individual's determination to bring about positive change, even in the face of adversity, making it a timeless and inspiring story for young readers.

Activity:
- Read "Bringing the Rain to Kapiti Plain" aloud to your child, emphasizing the rhythmic language.
- Have your child read the story and try to mimic the rhythmic nuances of the story.
- Record it when your child agrees that they have mastered the story's rhythm. Afterward, facilitate a discussion about the story's plot, characters, and the rhythmic elements of the text.

Objective: To explore character development and expression.

Activity:
- Have your child create rhythmic chants or songs that represent the character's emotions, actions, or traits in the book.
- Use percussion instruments, such as a homemade drum, to emphasize the cadence of their creations.
- Use a recording device so your child can hear their performance as they perform these chants to the family.

Objective: To improve sequencing and comprehension skills.

Activity:
- Provide pictures representing key events from the story.
- Have your child arrange the pictures in the correct order while creating a rhythmic chant or song that summarizes each event.
- Share the chants/songs with the family, or record your child with their chants and songs.

Objective: To explore poetry and creative writing.

Activity:
- Introduce various African Savannah animals and their characteristics.
- Have your child write short poems or rhymes about these animals, focusing on rhythm and sound.
- Encourage them to perform their poems with rhythmic elements like clapping or snapping.

Objective: To enhance storytelling skills.

Activity:
- Have your child create their own short stories set in the African Savannah.
- They should incorporate facts about the environment and wildlife.
- Have your child perform their story with rhythmic narration, using musical instruments or body percussion to emphasize key moments.

Objective: To develop listening skills and vocabulary.

Activity:
- Play audio recordings of African savannah sounds, including animal calls, winds, and rain. Have students listen and write descriptive words or sentences to capture the sounds.
- Encourage them to create a rhythmic sound collage using their descriptions.
  This can also double as a science lesson on how sound reaches the ear, the parts of the ear, the inner ear, and how the sound is interpreted by the brain.

 **Math for Elementary School Students**

Objective 1: To reinforce counting skills while learning about African savannah animals.

Activity 1:
- Provide pictures of different animals found on the African savannah.
- Have students count the number of each animal they see and create a rhythmic chant, song, or clapping pattern based on the count. For example, " zebras, two lions, three giraffes."
- Ask your child to use stickers to illustrate their pattern or draw and color circles that represent these animals. If you are studying geometry, use various geometric shapes to illustrate each animal species. You can also use this to create patterns or equations. For instance, five zebras - three giraffes = two lions or a pattern such as this: ___, five, three, two. What is the first term in this pattern?

Objective 2: To introduce and reinforce the concept of patterns.

Activity 2:
- Using pictures of animals, plants, and other elements of the African savannah, create pattern cards (e.g., zebra, lion, lion, zebra, lion...).
- Have students replicate the patterns through body movements, rhythmic clapping, or using objects like beads.

- If you can find stickers of the African savannah, it's fun to create the pattern with the stickers but it must be replicated by the above suggestions.

Objective 3: To incorporate storytelling and math concepts.

Activity 3:
- Read "Bringing the Rain to Kapiti Plain" and have your child identify and count the animals and objects mentioned in the story.
- Encourage them to create their own math stories or word problems based on the characters and events in the book. *This story has a specific rhythm and it's fun to read in cadence.*
- Find worksheets that have word problems on a concept you are teaching your child, and change the objects in the problems to fit the Savannah without changing the problem's parameters. Example: Instead of "Mary had three apples," change it to read "Mary saw three zebras."

 ## Science for Elementary School Students

Objective: To understand animal adaptations in the savannah ecosystem.

Activity:
- Explore the unique adaptations of animals that inhabit the African savannah.
- Allow your child to choose an animal to research and create a rhythmic presentation that showcases the animal's adaptations and behavior.

 ## Social Studies for Elementary School Students

Objective 1: To introduce geography and map skills.

Activity 1:
- Explore maps of Africa and identify the regions where African savannahs are located.

- Research and discuss the importance of the savannah ecosystem.
- Have your child create their own rhythmic chants or songs that highlight the key geographic features of the savannah.

Objective 2: To learn about the cultures of people living near the African savannah.

Activity 2:
- Introduce students to the cultures of African tribes or communities that inhabit savannah regions.
- Provide rhythmic music or dance examples from these cultures and encourage students to create their own rhythmic interpretations.

Other ideas to do for this themed unit:
- Make a drum from an oatmeal container.
- Use paper towel cardboard centers for 'sticks' to use as rhythm makers.
- Use dried gourds to make rhythmic shakers.
- Use art supplies to make and decorate their bedroom or learning space with African savannah plants and animals.
- Art project: Make tribal masks out of paper mache.

MIDDLE SCHOOL CHILDREN

Most of the Language Arts lessons below are based on various lessons I have taught to public school children over my forty-two-year career as an educator. While each of the selections I have chosen involves music and rhythm, the ideas you choose to bring out in the reading selection are up to you, the parent. For example, poetry tends to use abstract imagery and word choice to illustrate how the author was feeling and seeing when the poem was written. It is up to you to be able to ask questions to uncover these emotions of the author as you discuss poetry with your child, as well as what feelings the poem evokes in your child.

 **Books for Middle School Learners**

These poems and books study nature poems and their rhythmic qualities. Encourage students to write their own nature poems, focusing on rhythm, rhyme, and vivid descriptions of the natural world. Here are a few nature-themed poems that speak to the musical-rhythmic learner:

Theme: Poetry and Nature

Objective: To write nature-themed poems with rhythmic elements.

"The Eagle" by Alfred Lord Tennyson
> *This poem describes the majestic flight of an eagle and its interaction with nature, featuring strong imagery and rhythmic language.*

"A Dream Within A Dream" by Edgar Allan Poe
> *This poem explores the fleeting nature of time and life, and its rhythmic repetition adds to its musical quality.*

"The Lake Isle of Innisfree" by W.B. Yeats
> *Yeats' poem reflects on the tranquility of nature and the desire for a peaceful retreat, with a soothing rhythm that mirrors the calm of nature.*

"The Tyger" by William Blake
> *This poem contemplates the fierce and beautiful aspects of nature, with a rhythmic and repetitive structure that emphasizes the power of the tiger.*

"Daffodils" by William Wordsworth
> *Wordsworth's poem celebrates the beauty of a field of daffodils and evokes a sense of wonder through its rhythmic descriptions.*

"The Road Not Taken" by Robert Frost
> *Frost's famous poem reflects on choices in life and the paths we take, with a contemplative rhythm that adds depth to its meaning.*

"Jabberwocky" by Lewis Carroll

Carroll's whimsical poem features playful and nonsensical words that create a unique rhythmic experience, making it enjoyable for musical-rhythmic learners.

"Sea Fever" by John Masefield

This poem captures the allure of the sea and the call of adventure, with a rhythmic and repetitive refrain that mirrors the ocean's waves.

"The Wind" by Robert Louis Stevenson

Stevenson's poem personifies the wind and its playful nature, with rhythmic verses that evoke the sensation of the wind's movement.

"The Tree" by Ezra Pound

Pound's poem explores the life cycle of a tree and its connection to the seasons, with a rhythmic structure that mirrors the tree's growth.

 ## Language Arts for Middle School Students

Objective 1: To analyze African folktales and their rhythmic qualities.

Activity 1:
- Read African folktales and identify rhythmic elements in the storytelling.
- Have students choose a folktale and adapt it into a rhythmic performance using spoken word, percussion, or music.

In the following list of African folktales, rhythm is the central element that brings the stories to life:

"The Magic Drum" by Idries Shah

This West African folk tale tells the story of a magic drum that can change the seasons, and it incorporates rhythm and music as integral elements of the narrative.

"Why the Sky Is Far Away: A Nigerian Folktale" by Mary-Joan Gerson
This Nigerian folktale explores themes of nature and balance and features rhythmic language and storytelling.

"The Hunterman and the Crocodile: A West African Folktale" by Baba Wagué Diakité
Set in Mali, this beautifully illustrated book features a rhythmic narrative as a clever hunter outwits a crocodile in a rhythmic storytelling style.

"The Talking Eggs" by Robert D. San Souci
This Southern folktale blends rhythm and magical elements as a young girl meets a mysterious old woman and her talking eggs, leading to a rhythmic and musical adventure.

"The Palm of My Heart: Poetry by African American Children" edited by Davida Adedjouma and R. Gregory Christie
While not traditional stories, this collection of poems showcases the creativity of African American children, often featuring rhythmic and musical language.

"Song of the Water Boatman and Other Pond Poems" by Joyce Sidman
This collection of poems explores the rhythms of nature, including pond life, and can resonate with musical-rhythmic learners.

"Bintou's Braids" by Sylviane Diouf
While not a traditional story, this picture book features rhythmic text and explores the cultural significance of braiding in West African communities.

"The Barefoot Book of Earth Tales" by Dawn Casey and Anne Wilson
This collection includes various folk tales from different cultures, some of which are from African regions, and features storytelling with rhythmic elements. These African stories and tales incorporate rhythmic and musical elements into their narratives, making them suitable for middle school musical-rhythmic learners while offering insights into African cultures and traditions.

One excellent book to create a CC unit for homeschooled middle school children is "The Crossover" by Kwame Alexander. This novel-in-verse combines basketball, family, and the lyrical art of hip-hop poetry. Here's how you can structure a unit around this book:

Unit Title: "Verse, Hoops, and Family Ties: Exploring 'The Crossover' Through Music and Poetry"

Summary: In "The Crossover," we meet Josh Bell, a talented young basketball player with a deep passion for the game. Written in verse, the story explores Josh's life on and off the court as he navigates the challenges of adolescence, sibling rivalry, and his changing relationship with his twin brother, Jordan. Through the lens of basketball, the novel delves into themes of family, friendship, and identity themes. With a distinctive poetic style, "The Crossover" captures the rhythm and emotions of the sport while providing a heartfelt and relatable glimpse into the struggles and triumphs of growing up.

Objective 2: Students will explore the themes, characters, and poetic elements in "The Crossover" by Kwame Alexander and create their own original poetry and musical compositions inspired by the book.

Activity 2: Introduction to the book, "The Crossover," by Kwame Alexander
- **Introduce the book and author:** Discuss the themes of family, friendship, and basketball. Read the first few chapters together or individually.
- **Hip-Hop and Poetry:** Introduce the elements of hip-hop and poetry, including rhythm, rhyme, and wordplay. Analyze hip-hop lyrics and discuss how they convey emotion and tell stories. Explore various forms of poetry and their musicality.
- **Character Analysis and Themes:** Analyze the main characters in "The Crossover" (Josh and Jordan). Discuss the themes of sibling rivalry, teamwork, and loss. Write short character-based poems inspired by the characters' perspectives.
- **Basketball and Rhythm:** Explore the role of basketball in the book and how it's tied to rhythm and movement. Discuss the concept of rhythm in poetry and music. Create basketball-themed rhythm patterns and chants.

- **Music and Sound:** Introduce the concept of sound in poetry and music. Experiment with creating soundscapes and musical elements to accompany poems. Analyze how Kwame Alexander incorporates musicality into his writing.
- **Creative Projects:** Choose a scene or character from the book as inspiration. Create original poems or lyrics with musical accompaniment. Perform and share their creations with you and the family.
- **Reflection and Discussion:** Reflect on the unit and how music and poetry enhance storytelling. Discuss the impact of "The Crossover" and its themes on your child.

 ## Math for Middle School Students

Objective 1: To explore fractions through musical rhythms.

Activity 1:
- Introduce musical notes and rhythms.
- Teach students how to represent fractions using musical notation (e.g., eighth, quarter, half, and whole notes).
- Have them compose short rhythmic patterns using fractions and perform them with percussion instruments or hum or sing the rhythm with a melody. (See the above suggestions under "Elementary Students" for making quick percussion instruments.)

Objective 2: To reinforce geometry concepts through dance.

Activity 2:
- Teach geometric shapes and angles.
- Have students choreograph a dance routine incorporating different geometric shapes (e.g., squares, triangles, circles) and angles.
- Each shape and angle corresponds to a specific dance move. Some specific dances use geometric shapes, such as the Waltz, and this could be a fun-filled activity that incorporates movement and exercise.

Objective 3: To practice multiplication tables through drumming.

Activity 3:
- Provide students with African drums or drumming apps.
- Assign each drum a different number.
- Create multiplication equations, and students will drum the answer by striking the corresponding drums in a rhythmic pattern (e.g., 4 x 3 = 12). You can also use children's toys that have tonal qualities, such as the colored-coded xylophone I bought for my children when they were toddlers.

I have also personally developed a way to memorize multiplication tables using fingers, similar to learning to play a piano. Using the 'twos' multiplication table, I will demonstrate:

- Lay hands flat in front of you with thumbs facing each other.
- Starting with the *left-hand pinky*—press it to the table and say 'two.'
- Then the ring finger—press it to the table and say 'four.'
- Then the middle finger—press and say 'six.'
- Then the pointer finger—press and say 'eight.'
- Finally, the left-hand thumb—press and say 'ten.'
- Now rotate to the right hand and repeat the same order, beginning with the right-hand pinky, and say 'twelve.'
- Right-hand ring finger = 'fourteen,' right-hand middle finger = 'sixteen,' right-hand pointer finger = 'eighteen,' and finally the right-hand thumb = 'twenty.'
- Repeat this process over and over again.

You can use this same process with every multiplication table! Notice that every thumb is a multiple of either five or ten. Add musical scales to the process so you now incorporate sound and tonal properties to the finger pressing process. It works like a charm for any child's CC intelligence!

 ## Science for Middle School Students

Objective 1: To learn about volcanic activity and plate tectonics.

Activity 1:
- Study the science of volcanoes and plate tectonics.
- Create a rhythmic 'volcanic eruption' simulation where your child uses rhythmic patterns to represent the stages of a volcanic eruption.
- Discuss the geological processes.

Objective 2: To explore the solar system and planetary characteristics.

Activity 2:
- Study the planets in our solar system.
- Assign a planet and have them create a rhythmic presentation that includes facts about their assigned planet.
- Perform the rhythmic planetary presentations.

Objective 3: To study rainforest ecosystems and biodiversity.

Activity 3:
- Explore the rainforest ecosystem and its rich biodiversity.
- Create a rhythmic rainforest soundscape using percussion instruments to mimic the diverse rainforest sounds.
- Discuss the importance of preserving rainforests.

These lessons are designed to engage middle-school-aged CC learners across various subjects while incorporating different thematic elements to make learning more enjoyable and meaningful.

 **Social Studies for Middle School Students**

Objective 1: To learn about cultural traditions and celebrations.

Activity 1:
- Explore various cultural celebrations from around the world.
- Assign a different celebration and culture every other day.
- Have them research and create a rhythmic presentation with traditional music and dance.

Objective 2: To study world geography and continental features.

Activity 2:
- Focus on one continent each week.
- Research and create a rhythmic presentation about the continent's geography, landmarks, and cultures. Incorporate rhythmic elements to highlight key aspects.

*Antarctica has different animals with various patterns of life, not necessarily 'cultural,' but many specific to individual species who come to Antarctica for various rhythms of their lives.

Objective 3: To explore the civil rights movement through rhythm.

Activity 3:
- Study key figures and events from the civil rights movement.
- Assign different historical figures to research.
- Have them create rhythmic presentations that tell the stories of these figures, their contributions, and the movement's impact.

HIGH SCHOOL STUDENTS

 **Books for High School Students**

Here's a list of books from various genres suitable for high school students who are Conscious Creative learners. These books encompass a range of genres and themes, making them suitable for high school students who are CC learners. They incorporate music, rhythm, and emotional depth, offering a unique reading experience for those who appreciate the lyrical aspects of storytelling.

"If I Stay" by Gayle Forman
> *After a car accident, Mia, a talented cellist, has an out-of-body experience and must decide whether to fight for her life or let go. This emotional and musical journey explores themes of love, loss, and the power of music.*

"Out of the Easy" by Ruta Sepetys
> *Set in 1950s New Orleans, this novel follows Josie, the daughter of a brothel prostitute, as she dreams of a better life and navigates a world filled with secrets and jazz music.*

"Ender's Game" by Orson Scott Card
> *In a futuristic world, Ender Wiggin is a gifted strategist trained to defend Earth against alien invaders. The book's strategic challenges and Ender's journey make it appealing to analytical minds with a musical twist.*

"The Name of the Wind" by Patrick Rothfuss
> *This epic fantasy follows Kvothe, a talented musician and magician, as he recounts his life's adventures and quest for knowledge at the University. The novel is enriched with lyrical prose and music-related elements.*

"Thirteen Reasons Why" by Jay Asher
> *Clay Jensen receives a set of cassette tapes recorded by his classmate, Hannah Baker, who tragically took her own life. As he listens to her recordings, he unravels a web of secrets and mysteries. The book's suspenseful narrative is reminiscent of a compelling song.*

"Eleanor & Park" by Rainbow Rowell
> *Two misfit teenagers, Eleanor and Park, bond over their shared love of music and comics on a school bus. Their heartwarming and lyrical journey explores themes of first love and belonging.*

"The Sound of a Wild Snail Eating" by Elisabeth Tova Bailey
> *A memoir that chronicles the author's experience of being bedridden due to illness and her unlikely companionship with a wild snail. It beautifully explores the quiet, musical rhythms of nature.*

"Miles: The Autobiography" by Miles Davis
> *This autobiography of jazz legend Miles Davis offers insights into his musical journey, creative process, and the evolution of jazz.*

"Ariel" by Sylvia Plath

Sylvia Plath's collection of confessional poetry delves into the depths of emotion, mental health, and personal struggles, making it a powerful exploration of the lyrical and emotional aspects of life.

"Blankets" by Craig Thompson

A coming-of-age graphic novel that weaves a heartfelt story of family, first love, and spirituality, with intricate artwork that adds a musical quality to the narrative.

 ## Language Arts for High School Students

These lessons are designed to engage high-school-aged CC learners in various subjects, incorporating rhythm, music, and creative expression into their learning experiences.

Objective 1: To analyze the story's elements and themes through rhythm.

Summary: In "All Summer in a Day" by Ray Bradbury, the story unfolds on the planet Venus, where the sun only shines for two hours every seven years. The narrative revolves around a group of schoolchildren eagerly awaiting this rare event. The story primarily focuses on Margot, a girl who vividly remembers the sun from her earlier years on Earth. However, the other children, jealous of her memories, cruelly lock her in a closet during the precious two hours of sunshine. Bradbury's poignant tale explores themes of jealousy, the fleeting nature of happiness, and the consequences of cruelty, leaving readers with a haunting reflection on the impact of human actions.

Activity 1:
- Read "All in a Summer's Day" and discuss its themes and characters.
- Have students identify key moments in the story and create rhythmic soundscapes or percussion arrangements that reflect the mood and emotions of these moments.

Objective 2: To explore character development and expression.

Activity 2:
- Assign your child a character from the story, or let them pick one.
- Have them create rhythmic monologues or spoken-word performances reflecting their characters' thoughts and feelings.
- Encourage them to use rhythm to convey the character's unique perspective.
  Your child may want to do more than one character, using their voice to indicate male or female tones.

Objective 3: To analyze the story's literary elements through poetry.

Activity 3:
- Study the story's themes, symbolism, and imagery.
- Ask students to write poems inspired by "All in a Summer's Day," incorporating rhythmic elements such as rhyme and meter.
- Perform and discuss their poems in class.

Optional activity: Watch the short thirty-minute video, "All in a Summer's Day," on YouTube™ and compare and contrast it to the story they read.

 **Math for High School Students**

Objective 1: To understand algebraic equations through music composition.

Activity 1:
- Teach algebraic equations and variables.
- Create their own musical compositions where they assign musical notes to variables (e.g., $x = C$, $y = E$, $z = G$). They must compose melodies and rhythms based on algebraic equations.
- Perform and share compositions in 'class.'

Objective 2: To explore algebraic patterns through rhythm.

Activity 2:
- Introduce algebraic sequences and patterns.
- Provide rhythmic patterns with missing elements (e.g., 1, _, 4, _, 7).
- Solve for the missing values and create rhythmic representations of the sequences.
- Perform and analyze the rhythmic patterns.

Objective 3: To connect algebraic expressions with storytelling.

Activity 3:
- Assign word problems involving algebraic equations.
- Create rhythmic narrations or spoken-word performances that tell the story of solving these problems.
- Encourage them to use rhythm and tone to convey the problem-solving process.

 **Science for High School Students**

Objective 1: To understand biological systems through rhythmic modeling.

Activity 1:
- Teach biological systems (e.g., circulatory, respiratory).
- Create rhythmic models that represent the functions and interactions within these systems.
- Perform and explain their rhythmic models.

Objective 2: To explore evolution and adaptation through rhythm.

Activity 2:
- Discuss the concept of evolution and adaptation.
- Assign specific animal species and have them create rhythmic adaptations that represent how these species have evolved over time.
- Share and discuss adaptations.

Objective 3: To study cellular processes through rhythm.

Activity 3:
- Explore cellular processes (e.g., mitosis, cellular respiration).
- Create rhythmic performances that illustrate these processes using body percussion or music.
- Explain and perform the processes to you.

 # Social Studies for High School Students

Objective 1: To explore historical events through music and rhythm.

Activity 1:
- Select key historical events from different time periods and regions.
- Research and create musical compositions that represent these events using rhythm, melody, and instruments. (e.g., Ellie Mannette invented the steel drum.)
- Perform and discuss the compositions.

Objective 2: To learn about world cultures through rhythm.

Activity 2:
- Choose various world cultures and traditions.
- Assign a culture to research.
- Have them create rhythmic presentations that showcase the culture's music, dance, and rhythmic traditions.
- Perform and share these presentations.

Objective 3: To create a rhythmic timeline of significant historical events.

Activity 3:
- Provide a world history timeline with major events and eras.
- Assign a period or event.
- Have them compose rhythmic pieces that represent their assigned period/event. Assemble the pieces into a rhythmic timeline performance.

Conclusion

Dear Conscious Creative Learner,

As we journeyed through the world of homeschooling together, I hope you found the words on the pages dancing to the beat of your heart and the rhythm of your soul. Music and words are kindred spirits, each with its unique melody, and you've tapped into their harmonious connection.

Remember, stories are not just meant to be read; they're meant to be sung, danced, and lived. Whether you're strumming your own story on a guitar or penning lyrics to the soundtrack of your life, know that the magic of words and music will always be there to guide your creative journey.

I hope you 'heard' the patterns and rhythms of the universe speaking and singing to your musical heart through math, science, history, and social studies.

Keep singing, dancing, and writing your unique melody in this grand symphony of life. The world is your stage, and your song is worth sharing with the world.

With lyrical wishes and a musical embrace,
—Melanie Summers

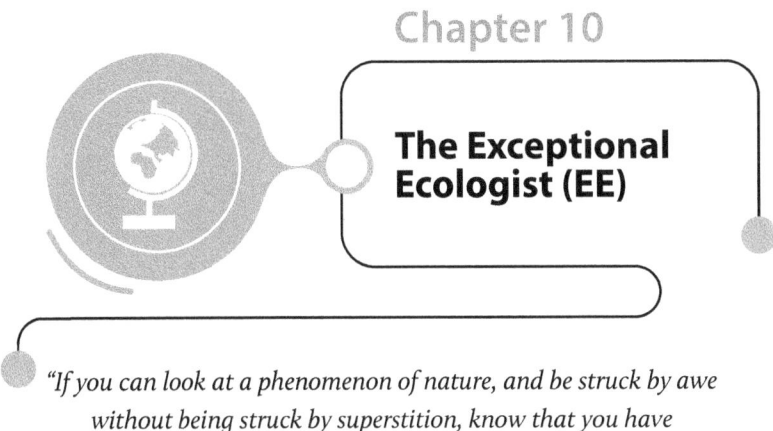

Chapter 10

The Exceptional Ecologist (EE)

"If you can look at a phenomenon of nature, and be struck by awe without being struck by superstition, know that you have finally grown up."
—ABHIJIT NASKAR

I was a lucky child in many ways. I grew up on a farm in rural West Virginia, unlike small-town West Virginia. I helped plant our vegetable garden in the spring, and in late spring, I found wild blackberries or raspberries to pick. In the summertime, I went swimming or rode horses, but on lazy afternoons, I loved lying under the big maple tree in our backyard as I peeked through the leaves to watch the clouds as they morphed into different shapes. Sometimes, I read a book under it stretched out on a quilt Grandma had made, while Polly, my Appaloosa, nibbled on the rich green grass of the backyard. In late summer, I helped Mom preserve the garden veggies for wintertime use. In the fall, I wandered the woods looking for West Virginia black walnuts and hickory nuts for holiday goodies. Although winter wasn't my favorite season, I did enjoy sled riding. While traveling to my Uncle Clair's dairy farm, I sat in Daddy's farm sled pulled by a team of horses. We always made ice cream while sitting around their pot-bellied stove while Daddy and Uncle Clare told stories about their childhood. I guess you could say I was a bit of an Exceptional Ecologist learner.

Howard Gardner proposes that EE learners have a particular way of thinking and learning centered around their sensitivity and ability to understand the natural world. Here are some key ways in which EE learners think. They possess unique thinking skills and a deep affinity for the natural world. They excel in observing, categorizing, and understanding the complexities of nature, and they often use their knowledge to advocate for environmental conservation and sustainability.

Highlights:

- EE learners excel in observing and recognizing patterns and details in the natural environment. They are keen observers of plants, animals, weather, geological formations, and other elements of the natural world.
- They are skilled at categorizing and classifying objects and phenomena in nature. They can often identify and differentiate between different species of plants and animals and recognize ecological relationships.
- EE learners are strongly aware of environmental issues and the interconnectedness of ecosystems. They are concerned about conservation and sustainability and may deeply appreciate the beauty and complexity of the natural world.
- They thrive when they have the opportunity to engage in hands-on experiences in natural settings. Activities such as hiking, gardening, birdwatching, or exploring natural habitats are particularly effective for their learning style.
- Exceptional Ecologist learners tend to have a good memory for specific details of the natural world. They can easily recall specific plant species, animal behaviors, and ecological facts.
- They often feel strongly connected to nature and may find solace, inspiration, and motivation in natural environments. Being in nature can be a source of comfort and energy for them.
- EE learners may excel in solving problems related to the natural world. They can analyze environmental issues, propose solutions, and understand the consequences of human actions on the environment.
- They often effectively convey their knowledge and insights about the natural world to others through storytelling, writing, or teaching. They can engage others in discussions about nature and ecology.
- EE learners may integrate their knowledge of the natural world into other areas of study, such as biology, ecology, geology, or environmental science. They see connections between different fields of knowledge.
- They have a deep appreciation for the beauty and aesthetics of the natural world, which may manifest in artistic expressions, such as painting, photography, or nature-inspired crafts.

Strategies

Since EE learners love anything that has something to do with planet Earth, there are some specific strategies that homeschooling parents can use to effectively teach Exceptional Ecologist learners. Capitalizing on your specific region of the world is a prime place to start. If you live near woods, use the deciduous forests. If you live near the ocean, use the ocean and surrounding beaches, dunes, cliffs, estuaries, and wetlands. If you live near the Southwest, use the deserts, sand dunes, and volcanic mountains. The Northwest has redwood forests and coastal tropical rainforests. No matter where you live in the world, nature has bountiful choices for your EE learner to dive into and learn from.

The following are a few strategies for homeschooling parents to use when teaching an Exceptional Ecologist learner:

- **Take regular nature walks** in local parks, forests, or natural areas to observe and explore the environment. Plan field trips to natural history museums, botanical gardens, wildlife sanctuaries, and other places that offer hands-on learning experiences. Provide opportunities for hands-on exploration, such as gardening, birdwatching, or collecting specimens like leaves, rocks, or insects. Set up a backyard or balcony garden where they can observe and care for plants and animals.
- **Encourage them to keep a nature journal** where they can record their observations, sketches, and notes about what they discover during their outdoor adventures. Use the journal as a tool for reflection and documentation of their naturalist experiences. Build a library of nature-related books, field guides, and reference materials for them to explore. Utilize online resources, documentaries, and educational websites focused on nature and environmental topics.
- **Assign projects that involve creating nature-inspired art**, dioramas, or exhibits showcasing their understanding of ecosystems, wildlife, or plant life. Challenge them to design and implement small-scale conservation projects in your community or backyard. Engage in citizen science projects together, where you contribute valuable data to scientific research while learning about nature. Participate in bird counts, insect surveys, or environmental monitoring programs. Incorporate nature-themed games and activities like scavenger hunts, nature bingo, or outdoor

puzzles to make learning fun. Create nature-themed board games or card games to reinforce concepts.

- **Encourage them to write stories, poems, or essays** inspired by their experiences in nature. Explore nature-themed literature and discuss books with ecological themes. Watch nature documentaries and films that showcase the beauty and wonders of the natural world. Discuss the content and encourage them to ask questions and make connections.
- **Provide art supplies for nature-inspired art projects**, including painting, drawing, and sculpture. Foster their creativity by encouraging them to create their own field guides or illustrated nature catalogs. Teach them about environmental ethics, conservation, and the importance of preserving nature. Discuss real-world environmental issues and involve them in age-appropriate discussions and actions to address them.
- **Plan camping trips or outdoor adventures** that teach essential survival and outdoor skills. Learn about foraging, fire-making, wilderness safety, and navigation in a natural setting.

Remember that the key to teaching EE learners is to foster their curiosity, hands-on exploration, and deep connection to the natural world. Tailor your homeschooling approach to their interests and provide ample opportunities for them to observe, explore, and learn from nature.

THE ELEMENTARY STUDENT

The following lessons are designed around a central theme, owls, and many of the activities are centered around the book, "Owl Moon," by Jane Yoland. I am drawing from my memory from several years ago when I taught this same unit in my classroom. It took about a week to complete the activities. The lessons offer a holistic approach to teaching math, science, social studies, and language arts while focusing on the engaging theme of owls and the book "Owl Moon." They combine hands-on activities, critical thinking, and creativity to make learning both enjoyable and educational.

 **Books for Elementary Students**

As I planned this unit, I checked out the following books from the school library and the community library, and purchased a few that I couldn't find elsewhere. These books are not only informative but also engaging for naturalist learners, fostering their love for the natural world and the creatures that inhabit it. "Owl Moon" happened to be one of the stories in their reading book.

"The Watcher" by Jeanette Winter
> *This beautifully illustrated book tells the true story of Jane Goodall and her lifelong fascination with and study of chimpanzees in the African wilderness.*

"The Tree Lady: The True Story of How One Tree-Loving Woman Changed a City Forever" by H. Joseph Hopkins
> *The book chronicles the life of Kate Sessions, a pioneering botanist who transformed San Diego's arid landscape by introducing diverse plant species, leaving a lasting legacy.*

"The Camping Trip that Changed America: Theodore Roosevelt, John Muir, and Our National Parks" by Barb Rosenstock
> *Join President Theodore Roosevelt and naturalist John Muir on a historic camping trip that led to the creation of America's national parks.*

"Over and Under the Pond" by Kate Messner
> *Dive into the underwater world beneath a peaceful pond and explore the interconnected ecosystems in this beautifully illustrated book.*

"The Boy Who Drew Birds: A Story of John James Audubon" by Jacqueline Davies
> *Follow the life of John James Audubon, a young boy who grew up to become one of the world's most renowned bird artists and naturalists.*

"The Wild Robot" by Peter Brown
> *In this imaginative novel, a robot named Roz becomes stranded on an uninhabited island, where she learns about the natural world and forms connections with its animal inhabitants.*

"The Salamander Room" by Anne Mazer

A young boy dreams of turning his bedroom into the perfect habitat for a salamander in this delightful story about the love of nature.

"Beaks!" by Sneed B. Collard III

Explore the fascinating world of bird beaks and how they are adapted for different diets and environments in this engaging nonfiction book.

"The Leaf Man" by Lois Ehlert

Follow the journey of a leaf man who is blown by the wind and transformed into various natural objects, showcasing the diversity of the natural world.

"Owl Moon" by Jane Yolen

Join a young girl and her father on a moonlit owl-watching adventure, celebrating the beauty and mystery of the nighttime forest.

 ## Language Arts for Elementary Students

This five-day reading unit for "Owl Moon" incorporates reading comprehension, vocabulary exploration, creative writing, and artistic expression, allowing your child to fully engage with the book and its themes.

Summary: In "Owl Moon," a young girl and her father venture into the winter woods on a quiet, moonlit night in search of owls. The story beautifully captures the anticipation and connection between the two as they embark on their nighttime adventure. Through the girl's perspective, readers experience the magical hush of the snowy forest and the thrill of finally spotting an owl. "Owl Moon" is a tender and atmospheric exploration of the bond between a parent and child and the wonder of nature's mysteries, making it a timeless bedtime favorite for families.

Objective 1: The child will practice developing their skills in predictions and story elements: plot, characterization, and setting.

Activity 1:
- Begin by discussing the cover and title of the book. Ask your child what they think the story might be about based on the cover illustration.
- Read the first few pages of the book together, stopping to discuss any unfamiliar words or phrases.
- Have your child make predictions about the story's plot and characters.
- Ask them to share their thoughts on the book's setting (winter night, woods).
- Discuss the concept of owl watching and how it connects to the title.

Objective 2: Develop reading comprehension skills.

Activity 2:
- Read the first half of the book with your child. Pause at key points in the story to ask comprehension questions. For example, *"Why do you think the characters are going owling at night?"* or *"How does the author describe the winter night?"*
- Encourage your child to make connections with their own experiences, such as nighttime adventures or family traditions.
- Discuss the emotions of the characters in the story and how they change throughout the adventure.

Objective 3: Expand vocabulary and understanding of descriptive language.

Activity 3:
- Select a few descriptive words or phrases from the book (e.g., "silvery," "pale moths," "moon-blanched"). Have your child look up the meanings of these words in a dictionary or online.
- Discuss how these words contribute to the imagery and mood of the story.
- Encourage your child to create drawings or illustrations inspired by these descriptive words.

Objective 4: Foster creative expression through writing.

Activity 4:
- Ask your child to imagine that they are the main character in "Owl Moon" or a new character joining the owling adventure.
- Have them write a journal entry or a short story from the perspective of this character, describing their thoughts and feelings during the owling experience.
- Encourage them to use descriptive language and sensory details to bring their writing to life. Share and discuss their creative writing.

Objective 5: Reflect on the book and create an artistic representation.

Activity 5:
- Re-read the final part of "Owl Moon."
- Discuss the book's resolution and how the characters' feelings have changed.
- Encourage your child to create an art project inspired by the book. They can draw a scene from the story, paint a snowy night, or even make a diorama of an owl in its habitat.
- Have them share their artwork and explain why they chose that particular scene or image.

Objective 6: The child will create an owl-themed story incorporating descriptive adjectives and adverbs.

Activity 6:
- Have your children write their own owl-themed stories, drawing inspiration from "Owl Moon" or other owl-related books.
- Encourage them to use descriptive language to capture the atmosphere of a moonlit owl-watching adventure.

Objective 7: The child will create a journal entry describing a moonlit nature walk accompanied by an adult.

Activity 7:
- After reading "Owl Moon," take your children on a moonlit nature walk or owl-watching adventure.
- Have them keep a nature journal describing their observations, feelings, and sensory experiences of the nighttime forest.

 ## Math for Elementary School Students

The following are sample examples of how to teach your curious EE learner math:

Objective 1: Read "Owl Moon" together and discuss the size and features of the owls mentioned in the book.

Activity 1:
- Have your children measure and create drawings or cutouts of owls to scale using rulers and measuring tapes.
- Compare the sizes of different owl species mentioned in the story.

Objective 2: Research different owl species and their characteristics, including size, habitat, and diet.

Activity 2:
- Create a bar graph or a pictograph to represent the data, allowing your children to practice graphing and interpreting information about owls.

Objective 2: Craft word problems related to owls and "Owl Moon." For example, *"If Jane saw three owls in the story and two more joined later, how many owls did she see in total?"*

Activity 3:
- Encourage your children to write their own owl-themed word problems and solve them.

 ## Science for Elementary School Students

Objective 1: Study the anatomy of owls, focusing on their unique features like silent flight, keen eyesight, and adaptations for hunting at night.

Activity 1:
- Create owl anatomy diagrams or models using clay, craft materials, or drawings.

Objective 2: Explore the concept of nocturnal animals, including owls, and their adaptations for nighttime living.

Activity 2:
- Create a poster or a diorama showcasing various nocturnal animals and their habitats.

Objective 3: The child will dissect owl pellets as a hands-on activity. (Order owl pellets [sterilized regurgitated food remains] online).

Activity 3:
- Identify and classify the bones and other objects found in the pellets, learning about owl diet and digestion.

 ## Social Studies for Elementary School Students

Objective 1: Investigate how owls are viewed in different cultures and traditions around the world, from symbols of wisdom to superstitions.

Activity 1:
- Create a cultural collage or presentation showcasing owls' significance in various societies.

Objective 2: Explore other books and stories that feature owls, such as "Winnie-the-Pooh" or "Guardians of Ga'Hoole," and discuss the roles of owls in these narratives.

Activity 2:
- Encourage your children to write their own short stories or poems involving owls.

Objective 3: Research the natural habitats of owls, including the types of forests and regions where they are found.

Activity 3:
- Create a world map and mark the locations of different owl species, discussing the geographical distribution of owls.

MIDDLE SCHOOL CHILDREN

 **Books for Middle School Learners**

The following list of books are ones that your EE learner will enjoy. They are not only educational but also engaging for middle school Exceptional Ecologist learners, encouraging them to explore and appreciate the wonders of the natural world and the work of scientists and naturalists who have contributed to our understanding of it.

"Hoot" by Carl Hiaasen
> *This novel follows the adventures of a young boy who discovers a population of burrowing owls and becomes an environmental advocate in his Florida community.*

"The Tarantula Scientist" by Sy Montgomery
> *Join a real-life tarantula scientist in the rainforests of French Guiana as she conducts field research and uncovers the fascinating world of these arachnids.*

"The Hidden Life of Trees: What They Feel, How They Communicate—Discoveries from a Secret World" by Peter Wohlleben

> *Dive into the intriguing world of trees and forests, exploring their complex social networks, communication systems, and the ways in which they support each other.*

"The Boy Who Drew Birds: A Story of John James Audubon" by Jacqueline Davies

> *Follow the life of John James Audubon, a young boy who grew up to become one of the world's most renowned bird artists and naturalists.*

"The Call of Distant Mammoths: Why the Ice Age Mammals Disappeared" by Peter D. Ward

> *Investigate the mystery of the extinction of Ice Age mammals and the scientific methods used to uncover their history, with a focus on paleontology and environmental science.*

"Owls" by Gail Gibbons

> *This nonfiction book provides comprehensive information about various owl species, their habitats, behavior, and adaptations, making it an excellent resource for young naturalists.*

"Wildlife of the Galápagos" by Julian Fitter, Daniel Fitter, and David Hosking

> *Explore the unique wildlife of the Galápagos Islands through stunning photographs and informative descriptions, learning about the animals that inspired Charles Darwin's theory of evolution.*

"The Burgess Bird Book for Children" by Thornton W. Burgess

> *Join Peter Rabbit and his animal friends as they learn about different bird species through stories and adventures in the Green Forest, making it an engaging introduction to ornithology.*

"The Big Book of Bugs" by Yuval Zommer

> *Dive into the world of insects and arachnids with colorful illustrations and fascinating facts about these tiny creatures, encouraging young naturalists to appreciate the diversity of the insect world.*

"Life in the Ocean: The Story of Oceanographer Sylvia Earle" by Claire A. Nivola
Discover the life and work of renowned oceanographer Sylvia Earle, who dedicated her life to exploring the oceans and advocating for their conservation.

 ## Literature Unit for Middle School Students

These activities cater to middle school naturalist learners, fostering their curiosity and love for the natural world while integrating math, science, language arts, and social studies.

The following unit of study centers around the book, "The Call of the Wild," a unit I taught many years ago with sixth grade students. This literature unit provides an in-depth exploration of "The Call of the Wild," allowing middle school naturalist learners to delve into the novel's themes, characters, and historical context while fostering critical thinking and creative expression.

In this unit, students will explore the themes of nature, survival, and adaptation in Jack London's "The Call of the Wild." The novel follows the journey of Buck, a domesticated dog who is thrust into the wilds of the Yukon during the Klondike Gold Rush. Through Buck's experiences, students will examine the relationship between humans and nature, the primal instincts of animals, and the challenges of survival in a harsh environment.

Summary: In "The Call of the Wild," readers are transported to the rugged terrain of the Yukon during the Klondike Gold Rush. The story revolves around Buck, a domesticated dog who is stolen from his home in California and thrust into the harsh wilderness of the North. As Buck adapts to the brutal life of a sled dog, he undergoes a transformation, tapping into his primal instincts and inner strength. The novel vividly portrays the struggle for survival, the wild beauty of nature, and the timeless clash between civilization and the untamed. "The Call of the Wild" is an epic tale of resilience, adventure, and the indomitable spirit of a creature rediscovering its primal roots.

Unit Overview:
- **Analyze** the characters, plot, and themes of "The Call of the Wild."
- **Explore** the historical and geographical context of the novel.
- **Engage** in critical thinking and discussions related to nature, survival, and adaptation.
- **Develop** writing skills through creative and analytical writing assignments.

Objective 1: Introduce students to the author, Jack London, and the novel's setting.

Activity 1:
- Research background information about Jack London's life and experiences in the Klondike.
- Discuss the significance of the Klondike Gold Rush in the late 19th century.
- Show images and maps of the Yukon region to help students visualize the setting.

Objective 2: Analyze the protagonist, Buck, and his transformation throughout the story.

Activity 2:
- Read and discuss book passages describing Buck's life as a domesticated dog.
- Create a character profile for Buck, including his physical traits, personality, and the evolution of his instincts in the wild.

Objective 3: Explore nature, survival, and adaptation themes.

Activity 3:
- Engage in a discussion about how the novel portrays the relationship between humans and nature.
- Identify key scenes that illustrate Buck's survival instincts and adaptation to the wild.

Objective 4: Analyze literary devices used in the novel and explore symbolic elements.

Activity 4:
- Identify literary devices such as foreshadowing, personification, and symbolism.
- Discuss the significance of the "call" of the wild as a recurring motif in the story.

Objective 5: Write from the perspective of an animal character in the novel.

Activity 5:
- Choose an animal character from the book (e.g., Buck, Spitz, or other dogs).
- Write a diary entry or a short story from the chosen character's point of view.

Objective 6: Explore the historical context of the Klondike Gold Rush.

Activity 6:
- Research and present information about the Gold Rush, including its impact on people and animals.
- Discuss the challenges and hardships faced by prospectors during this period.

Objective 7: Create and present projects related to the novel.

Activity 7:
- Choose from various project options: character interviews, a visual timeline, a dramatic reenactment, or a multimedia presentation.
- Conduct presentations to showcase the project and share insights about the book.

Additional Resources:

Maps, photographs, and documentaries related to the Klondike Gold Rush. Excerpts from Jack London's non-fiction writings about his experiences in the Yukon.

 **Math for Middle School Students**

The website www.BrainPop.com has a great video on the Fibonacci sequence that I have used many times.

Objective 1: Explore the Fibonacci sequence in nature. The sequence is seen in the arrangement of leaves, pinecones, and sunflower seeds.

Activity 1:
- Go on a nature walk and collect samples of plants displaying Fibonacci patterns.
- Count the spirals or the number of petals, leaves, or seeds in each sample.
- Discuss how the Fibonacci sequence appears in these natural patterns.

Objective 2: Study the population growth of a local bird species over several years.

Activity 2:
- Research the population data of a specific bird species in your area over the last decade.
- Create a line graph to visualize the population changes.
- Analyze the data to make predictions about future population trends.

Objective 3: Investigate the geometric shapes used in bird nests.

Activity 3:
- Collect images or diagrams of various bird nests.
- Identify and measure the angles and shapes present in the nests.
- Discuss how different birds use geometry to construct their nests for specific purposes.

 # Science for Middle School Students

Objective 1: Dissect owl pellets to learn about the diet and food chains of owls.

Activity 1:
- Obtain owl pellets (available online or from science supply stores).
- Dissect the pellets, carefully identifying and classifying the bones and other remains found.
- Create a food web to illustrate the owl's role in the ecosystem.

Objective 2: Investigate microhabitats in your local area.

Activity 2:
- Select different microhabitats like a pond, a rotting log, or a tree canopy.
- Observe the plants, animals, and conditions unique to each microhabitat.
- Discuss how biodiversity varies in different microenvironments.

 # Social Studies for Middle School Students

Objective 1: Have your child research an environmental issue related to wildlife or natural habitats.

Activity 1:
- Identify an environmental concern, such as habitat destruction or pollution.
- Create a presentation or persuasive essay advocating for a solution to the issue.
- Explore ways to get involved in local conservation efforts.

Objective 2: Investigate how different cultures perceive and interact with nature.

Activity 2:

- Research how indigenous cultures in your region or around the world view the natural world.
- Create a presentation or report that highlights cultural connections to nature and how they differ from mainstream perspectives.

HIGH SCHOOL STUDENTS

 **Books for High School Students**

These non-fiction and fiction books offer diverse perspectives on the natural world, making them suitable choices for a high school Exceptional Ecologist learner interested in exploring nature through literature and storytelling. They are recommended reading for your EE learner. I've categorized them by fiction and non-fiction:

Non-Fiction:

"Pilgrim at Tinker Creek" by Annie Dillard
> *A poetic exploration of the natural world around Tinker Creek, Virginia, where Annie Dillard observes and reflects upon the beauty and mysteries of nature.*

"Last Child in the Woods: Saving Our Children from Nature-Deficit Disorder" by Richard Louv
> *Richard Louv discusses the importance of reconnecting with nature and outdoor experiences in a world dominated by technology, emphasizing the benefits for children's well-being.*

"The Hidden Life of Trees: What They Feel, How They Communicate—Discoveries from a Secret World" by Peter Wohlleben
> *Peter Wohlleben reveals the fascinating world of trees, describing their communication, social behaviors, and interconnectedness in forests.*

"The Forest Unseen: A Year's Watch in Nature" by David George Haskell
David Haskell takes readers on a year-long journey through a Tennessee forest, exploring the intricacies of nature and the interconnectedness of all living things.

"Braiding Sweetgrass: Indigenous Wisdom, Scientific Knowledge and the Teachings of Plants" by Robin Wall Kimmerer
Robin Wall Kimmerer combines indigenous wisdom, scientific knowledge, and personal stories to celebrate the relationship between humans and the natural world.

Fiction:

"The Overstory" by Richard Powers
A novel that weaves together the lives of nine individuals and their profound connections to trees and forests, highlighting the importance of environmental activism.

"The Secret Garden" by Frances Hodgson Burnett
A classic children's novel that tells the story of a young girl who discovers a neglected garden and the transformative power of nature.

"The Call of the Wild" by Jack London
A gripping adventure novel that follows the journey of a domesticated dog, Buck, as he adapts to the challenges of the wild, offering insights into primal instincts and survival in nature.

"Prodigal Summer" by Barbara Kingsolver
A novel that weaves together three intertwined stories of individuals living in the Appalachian Mountains, celebrating the beauty and complexity of the natural world.

These activities cater to the interests of an EE learner while incorporating math, science, and social studies concepts. They encourage hands-on exploration, critical thinking, and a deeper understanding of the natural world and its historical context. Invoking thinking and a deeper understanding of the natural world and its historical context.

 **Language Arts for High School Students**

The following is a Language Arts unit centered on the book "The Diversity of Life." This will provide a well-rounded experience for your high school homeschooling student. This enhanced Language Arts unit focuses on reading and comprehension and incorporates writing, research, essays, and a creative culminating project to provide a well-rounded educational experience for your high school homeschooling student. Feel free to adapt and modify the unit based on your child's interests and learning style.

Unit Title: Exploring Biodiversity: A Language Arts Unit

Book: "The Diversity of Life" by Edward O. Wilson

In "The Diversity of Life" E.O. Wilson takes readers on a captivating journey into the rich tapestry of Earth's biodiversity. Drawing on his vast knowledge as a biologist and naturalist, Wilson explores the intricate web of life on our planet, from the smallest microbes to the grandest ecosystems. He underscores the urgent need to protect and conserve this diversity as species continue to disappear at an alarming rate due to human activities. Through eloquent prose, Wilson's book serves as a passionate call to action, emphasizing the importance of understanding, appreciating, and preserving the remarkable array of life forms that share our world. "The Diversity of Life" is a compelling exploration of the interconnectedness of all living things and a plea for the stewardship of our planet's biological heritage.

Unit Objectives:
- To deepen understanding of biodiversity, ecology, and conservation.
- To enhance reading comprehension, critical thinking, writing skills, and research abilities.
- To encourage thoughtful reflection on humanity's role in preserving biodiversity.

Objective 1: Introduce the concept of biodiversity.

Activity 1:
- Read the book's introduction and discuss the meaning and importance of biodiversity.
- Have your child create a mind map or concept web illustrating the interconnectedness of species in an ecosystem.

Objective 2: Develop reading comprehension skills.

Activity 2:
- Read and discuss the book's first part (chapters one-four).
- Have your child summarize key points, identify the author's main arguments, and highlight unfamiliar vocabulary words.
- Assign comprehension questions or prompts related to the material.

Objective 3: Explore ecological concepts.

Activity 3:
- Study the chapters related to ecosystems and food webs (chapters five-eight).
- Create a food web diagram based on the ecosystems discussed in the book.
- Discuss how disturbances can affect ecological balance.

Objective 4: Understand the impact of human activities on biodiversity.

Activity 4:
- Read chapters on conservation and human impact (chapters nine-twelve).
- Research and discuss real-world examples of species conservation efforts.
- Encourage your child to reflect on their own environmental footprint.

Objective 5: Continue developing reading comprehension skills.

Activity 5:
- Read and discuss the book's remaining chapters (chapters thirteen-seventeen).

- Engage in discussions about the author's vision for biodiversity conservation.
- Analyze key quotes and passages from the book.

Objective 6: Encourage critical thinking and reflection.

Activity 6:
- Have your child write a reflective essay on the book's themes and their personal thoughts on biodiversity and conservation.
- Emphasize the importance of citing evidence from the book to support their arguments.

Objective 7: Enhance research skills and in-depth understanding.

Activity 7:
- Assign a research project on a specific conservation topic or an endangered species.
- Provide resources for research, including books, articles, and reputable websites.
- Instruct your child to write a well-researched report, including citations and a bibliography.

Objective 8: Improve presentation skills.

Activity 8:
- Have your child prepare a multimedia presentation based on their research project.
- Encourage the use of visuals, graphics, and data to make the presentation engaging.
- Deliver the presentation to you or a small audience.

Objective 9: Encourage creative writing and empathy for other species.

Activity 9:

- Ask your child to choose an animal or plant species mentioned in the book.
- Write a short story or poem from the perspective of that species, exploring their experiences and challenges.

Objective 10: Apply knowledge to a practical project.

Activity 10:

- Challenge your child to design an eco-friendly habitat for a specific animal species.
- Provide materials for creating a model or digital design.
- Ask your child to present their habitat design, explaining how it meets the species' needs while conserving biodiversity.

 ## Math for High School Students

Objective: Explore geometry concepts through gardening.

Activity:

- Plan a small vegetable or flower garden together.
- Provide a list of plants available, their cost, and a budget for your child. Your child must plan the garden based on what plants they can purchase according to what plants grow well together and the budget.
- Discuss geometric shapes that can be incorporated, such as rectangular beds, circular plots, or triangular trellises.
- Calculate the area and perimeter of the garden beds using appropriate formulas.
- Consider arranging plants in patterns, such as rows or concentric circles, and calculate planting distances.
- Include a drawing on graph paper of the garden's appearance when completed.
- Document the garden's growth and measure plant heights over time, graphing the data to analyze growth rates.

 ## Science for High School Students

Objective: Develop observation and recording skills in the natural environment.

Activity:
- Choose a nearby natural area (e.g., a park, forest, or wetland) to visit regularly.
- Provide your child with a field journal, binoculars, and a camera.
- Encourage them to observe and document local flora and fauna.
- Record details such as species names, behaviors, weather conditions, and seasonal changes. Include drawings.
- Discuss their observations, research species they encounter, and explore the ecological interactions they witness.

 ## Social Studies for High School Students

Objective: Investigate your local environment's historical and cultural aspects.

Activity:
- Research the history of your region's natural landscape, including changes due to human activities.
- Explore how indigenous cultures interacted with and valued the local environment.
- Visit local museums, historical sites, or nature preserves to learn more about the area's environmental history.
- Conduct interviews with local experts or elders who can provide insights into past environmental practices.
- Create a multimedia presentation or write a research paper about your region's evolving relationship between humans and nature.

Conclusion

In contemplating the array of exercises and educational experiences shared throughout this exploration of the Exceptional Ecologist learner, it becomes apparent that the connection between one's personal background and one's preferred learning style can profoundly shape one's educational journey. Much like my own childhood experiences on a rural West Virginia farm, these exercises emphasize the significance of fostering an innate curiosity and appreciation for the natural world. Encouraging your child to engage with the environment through observation, exploration, and hands-on activities can nurture their innate naturalist tendencies.

Furthermore, incorporating literature, such as "The Call of the Wild" by Jack London and "The Diversity of Life" by Edward O. Wilson, provides an enriching platform for naturalist learners to connect with the written word on a deeper level. These books resonate with my upbringing and offer a gateway to explore the complexities of biodiversity, ecology, and conservation. Ultimately, by tailoring educational approaches to the naturalist learner's affinity for nature and experiential learning, we can empower them to develop a lifelong bond with the environment and become dedicated stewards of the natural world.

Chapter 11

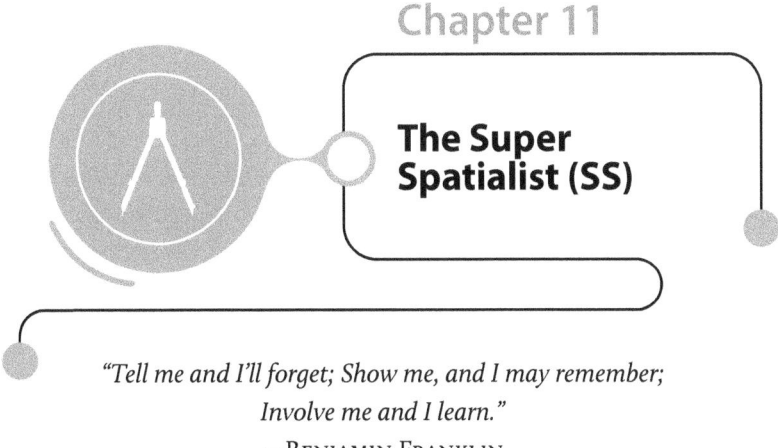

The Super Spatialist (SS)

"Tell me and I'll forget; Show me, and I may remember;
Involve me and I learn."
—Benjamin Franklin

Many years ago, my former husband and I bought a house. At the time, our children were two and four years old. It wasn't a huge house, but it had a large kitchen and dining combo room, a nice-sized living room, three bedrooms, one bathroom, and a full-sized basement where the laundry room was located. The two smaller bedrooms were tiny, one so small it barely fit a twin-size bed. We had to put our youngest son's chest of drawers outside his bedroom door. His bedroom was directly across the hallway to the one bathroom, so we had to turn sideways to get to the toilet!

As the children grew a bit older and larger, it became a better arrangement to put the boys in bunk beds in the larger two 'small' bedrooms, with both their chest drawers in that tiny room that was originally the younger child's bedroom. But then, the boys outgrew even that arrangement. We loved our property, but we had outgrown the small house.

After much discussion, we decided it would be more economical if we kept the property and added on to the original house, adding a second story as a master suite, adding a formal dining room, and converting the three bedrooms into two with walk-in closets and one huge bathroom complete with a linen closet, and a shower. We expanded the basement with the house, making a convenient second kitchen for summertime cookouts, food preparation, a second shower for boys getting home from sports practice, and a super cool place where our kids could hang out with their friends. This was easy to talk about but not so easy to design. *So, what do you think we did?* We called an architect.

I didn't really think about it at the time, but Ron had to have been a Super Spatialist learner. As we sat around our kitchen table, we described what we wanted to do, and he began to sketch. As we talked, he added details here and there and made a few suggestions, and within the hour, he had put into drawing what we had described. Gone was the teeny-tiny house we had bought, and before our eyes was a home where our kids could have their own rooms with plenty of space for double beds, a study desk, a chest of drawers, and huge closets for all their other clothes and shoes. *(Don't ever say that boys don't like shoes!)* A few days later, Ron showed up with the blueprints for our expansion, and a week later, a backhoe was digging the basement expansion. That's what SS people can do—they visualize in their heads with 3D effects, even rotating that thought in the air like in a science-fiction movie. So, let's take a more detailed look at the attributes of the Super Spatialist learner.

SS learners excel in thinking and problem-solving tasks that involve visualizing objects, shapes, and spaces. They have a strong ability to perceive and understand the visual world. Here are some key ways SS learners think:

Highlights:

- Super Spatialist learners are skilled at mentally manipulating and representing objects and spatial information. They can easily visualize objects from different angles, understand how objects fit together in space, and navigate through complex environments.
- They have vivid and accurate mental imagery that allows them to create mental pictures of objects, scenes, and concepts. This ability to visualize information helps them remember and understand complex information.
- SS learners are adept at recognizing patterns and relationships among visual elements. They can quickly identify similarities and differences between objects, images, or designs.
- They tend to notice small details that others may overlook. This attention to detail can be advantageous in tasks that require precision or an eye for aesthetics, such as art, design, or architecture.
- SS learners often exhibit creative thinking and problem-solving skills. They can devise innovative solutions to problems by visually manipulating ideas and concepts in their minds.
- They have a strong sense of direction and spatial awareness, which can be helpful in activities like map reading, navigation, and understanding spatial relationships in various contexts.
- Many Super Spatialist learners naturally gravitate toward artistic and design-related pursuits. They can express themselves through visual mediums like drawing, painting, sculpture, or graphic design.
- SS learners may find sequential and linear tasks (requiring step-by-step procedures) challenging because their thinking style is more holistic and non-linear. They prefer to see the big picture first.
- These learners often prefer visual aids, diagrams, maps, and other visual representations when learning new information. They may benefit from visual learning strategies and tools.

Strategies:

Notice that the SS learners share many commonalities with other types of learners. Teaching Super Spatialist learners effectively involves tailoring your instructional methods to accommodate their strengths and preferences for visual and spatial thinking. The following are some specific strategies to use when teaching SS learners:

- **Incorporate visual aids** such as diagrams, charts, maps, and illustrations in your lessons. Visual-spatial learners benefit greatly from seeing information presented visually.
- **Encourage the use of mind maps** or concept maps as tools for organizing information. These visual diagrams can help visual-spatial learners connect concepts and see relationships more clearly.
- **Motivate students to create visual stories** or narratives to explain complex ideas or processes. This can help them make connections between different pieces of information. Use visual analogies and metaphors to explain abstract concepts. Relating new information to familiar visual images can enhance understanding.
- **Incorporate hands-on activities** and manipulatives that allow visual-spatial learners to physically interact with the subject matter. Building models, puzzles, or using tangible objects can be very effective. If available, consider using VR or AR applications that provide immersive visual experiences to enhance learning. Utilize multimedia resources, such as educational videos, interactive simulations, and online visual resources, to supplement your teaching materials. Introduce software tools for creating digital concept maps or mind maps. These tools often offer the flexibility to create dynamic visual representations of ideas.

Virtual Reality (VR) is a technology that creates a completely immersive, computer-generated environment that users can interact with and become a part of, typically through a VR headset or goggles. VR aims to transport users to a simulated reality where they can experience and interact with a digital environment as if it were real. Augmented Reality (AR) is a technology that overlays digital information, such as images, videos, or 3D models, onto the real-world environment, enhancing the user's perception of reality. AR typically relies on devices like smartphones, tablets, or AR glasses to seamlessly blend the physical and digital worlds.

- **Encourage artistic expression** through drawing, painting, or other creative activities. SS learners often excel in artistic endeavors and can use these to understand and express ideas. Use color coding to emphasize important information or categorize concepts. Visual-spatial learners may benefit from color-coded notes and materials. Prompt students to visualize concepts and scenarios in their minds. Ask open-ended questions that require them to manipulate visual images related to the topic mentally.
- **Incorporate collaborative group activities** involving brainstorming, problem-solving, and visualizing solutions. This encourages peer-to-peer learning and engagement. Provide flexibility in assignments and assessments to allow SS learners to showcase their understanding through visual projects, presentations, or creative work.
- **Provide constructive feedback** on Super Spatialist learners' work, emphasizing the strengths of their visual thinking and suggesting improvements where needed. Whenever possible, take students on field trips or provide real-world experiences that allow them to see and explore concepts in their natural context.
- **Remember that not all SS learners are the same**, so observing your students' preferences and adjusting your teaching methods is essential. Additionally, offering a variety of teaching strategies and materials can benefit all students, regardless of their predominant learning style, as it promotes a more inclusive and engaging learning environment.

So, now you are probably asking, *What are ways to incorporate all this information into lessons in which my visual-spatial learner can excel?* The following are lesson suggestions. Feel free to use these models in designing lessons for your child.

ELEMENTARY CHILDREN

 **Books for Elementary Students**

These books offer a wide range of genres and themes to captivate the imaginations of elementary-aged children, making them perfect choices for reading at home or in a homeschooling setting. They are a list of suggested reading for your elementary child who is a visual-spatial learner:

"Charlotte's Web" by E.B. White
> *A heartwarming tale of friendship between a pig named Wilbur and a spider named Charlotte, who work together to save Wilbur's life.*

"Matilda" by Roald Dahl
> *Follow the adventures of Matilda, a brilliant and book-loving girl with telekinetic powers, as she outsmarts her neglectful parents and tyrannical headmistress.*

"The Magic Tree House" series by Mary Pope Osborne
> *Join siblings Jack and Annie on their time-traveling adventures through history and mythology using a mysterious tree house filled with books.*

"The Tale of Peter Rabbit" by Beatrix Potter
> *A classic story about Peter Rabbit's misadventures in Mr. McGregor's garden as he disobeys his mother's warnings.*

"Diary of a Wimpy Kid" series by Jeff Kinney
> *Dive into the humorous and relatable diary entries of Greg Heffley, a middle school student navigating the challenges of growing up.*

"Harry Potter and the Sorcerer's Stone" by J.K. Rowling
The beginning of the beloved series follows Harry Potter as he discovers he's a wizard and embarks on his magical journey at Hogwarts School of Witchcraft and Wizardry. (Or any Harry Potter book)

"The Very Hungry Caterpillar" by Eric Carle
Follow the journey of a hungry caterpillar as it transforms into a beautiful butterfly through colorful illustrations and die-cut pages.

"Where the Wild Things Are" by Maurice Sendak
Max sails to the land of the Wild Things, where he becomes their king, but ultimately realizes the importance of home and family.

"Charlie and the Chocolate Factory" by Roald Dahl
Join Charlie Bucket on a tour of Willy Wonka's magical chocolate factory, filled with whimsical characters and mouthwatering surprises.

"The Cat in the Hat" by Dr. Seuss (Theodore Geisel)
The mischievous Cat in the Hat brings chaos and fun to the home of two bored children on a rainy day.

"Wonder" by R.J. Palacio
A touching story about August Pullman, a boy with a facial difference, as he faces the challenges of starting fifth grade in a mainstream school.

"Pippi Longstocking" by Astrid Lindgren
Meet Pippi Longstocking, the strongest, quirkiest, and most adventurous girl in the world, as she embarks on wild escapades.

"The BFG" by Roald Dahl
Follow the friendship between Sophie, an orphan, and the Big Friendly Giant as they set out to stop the other giants from eating children.

"The Little Engine That Could" by Watty Piper
The classic tale of a determined little blue engine that overcomes obstacles with the mantra, "I think I can, I think I can."

"Stuart Little" by E.B. White
Join Stuart Little, a small mouse with a big heart, on his adventurous journey to find his missing friend in the big world of humans.

 ## Language Arts and Reading for Elementary School Students

The following is a sample Language Arts and Reading unit centered around the book "Tooter Pepperday" by Jerry Spinelli. The theme is 'Adjusting To a New Home.'

Summary: In "Tooter Pepperday," we meet a spunky and adventurous young girl named Tooter, known for her distinctive name and even more distinctive personality. Tooter is determined to prove herself to her family, school, and community. As she navigates the challenges of growing up, she finds herself on a journey of self-discovery, discovering the power of friendship, family, and embracing her unique identity. Jerry Spinelli's heartwarming story portrays Tooter's spirited and relatable character, making it a delightful and memorable read for young readers who are celebrating the joys and trials of childhood.

Objective 1: Introduce the theme of 'Adjusting to a New Home' and engage students in discussing what it means to move to a new place.

Activity 1:
- Read the first few chapters of "Tooter Pepperday" by Jerry Spinelli aloud with your child.
- After the reading, facilitate a discussion about Tooter's feelings about leaving her old home, the experiences in the new neighborhood, and how she is adjusting to her new home.
- Ask your child to share any personal experiences or feelings related to moving to a new place.

- Ask them to write a short paragraph (three–five sentences) about a time when they or someone they know had to adjust to a new home.

Objective 2: Analyze the main character, Tooter Pepperday, and how she deals with her new home.

Activity 2:
- Continue reading "Tooter Pepperday" (chapters three–six) and discuss Tooter's character traits, feelings, and actions.
- Have your child create a character web or poster about Tooter, including visual representations of her personality traits.
- Ask your child to choose a character from the story and write a paragraph describing their chosen character's personality traits.

Objective 3: Explore how the setting influences the story's plot and how Tooter's new home affects the story's events.

Activity 3:
- Read a few more chapters of the book (chapters seven–ten) and discuss how the setting impacts Tooter's experiences and decisions.
- Create a visual map or drawing of the neighborhood in the story, highlighting key locations.
- Ask your child to write a paragraph about how the setting in "Tooter Pepperday" affects the story's events.

Objective 4: Discuss the story's theme and identify symbols or metaphors related to adjusting to a new home.

Activity 4:
- Read the remaining chapters of the book (chapters eleven–fifteen) and analyze how the theme of adjusting to a new home is portrayed.
- Encourage your child to find symbols or metaphors in the story that represent Tooter's journey.
- Have your child write a short essay (one–two pages) discussing the theme and symbols in "Tooter Pepperday."

Objective 5: Summarize the book, reflect on the theme, and share personal connections.

Activity 5:
- Have your child create a visual collage or presentation that summarizes the story, highlights the theme, and includes personal reflections.
- Allow your child to present their project to you and the family and share their thoughts on adjusting to a new home.
- Answer this question: *What did Tooter discover about the flower, 'Queen Anne's Lace'? What lesson in life did she learn when she really observed that flower?*

Summarize: Conclude the unit by discussing the importance of understanding and empathizing with others adjusting to new homes or environments.

 **Math for Elementary School Students**

Objective: Visualize and design a neighborhood map.

Activity:
- Begin by discussing the concept of a neighborhood and its various components (houses, streets, parks, etc.) with the students.
- Provide a blank sheet of paper and art supplies (colored pencils, markers, rulers, etc.).
- Instruct your child to create a visual representation of their ideal neighborhood. They should include houses, streets, parks, and other important features.
- Encourage them to use geometric shapes to represent the houses and other elements. For example, rectangles for houses, circles for trees, and lines for streets.
- After completing their neighborhood maps, your child can explain their designs to you, emphasizing the visual-spatial aspects of their creations.

 ## Science for Elementary School Students

Objective: Explore the concept of ecosystems through visual representation.

Activity:
- Introduce the concept of ecosystems and discuss the different components that make up an ecosystem (plants, animals, soil, etc.).
- Provide a large sheet of paper and art supplies.
- Instruct your child to choose a specific ecosystem (e.g., a forest, pond, desert) and create a visual representation of that ecosystem. They should include drawings or representations of the key elements in the chosen ecosystem, paying attention to spatial relationships and interactions.
- Label and explain their ecosystem diagrams, highlighting the interdependence of different elements.
- Present their ecosystem diagrams and explain how the visual representation helps understand the ecosystem.

 ## Social Studies for Elementary School Students

Objective: Create a visual timeline of historical events.

Activity:
- Select a historical period or topic relevant to your curriculum (e.g., American Revolution, Ancient Egypt, Civil Rights Movement, The Roman Empire).
- Give your child a long strip of paper and art supplies.
- Instruct them to create a visual timeline of the chosen historical events using drawings, symbols, and labels.
- Emphasize the chronological order of events and the spatial arrangement of the timeline. Include key dates, important figures, and significant events in their timelines.
- Explain their historical timeline, explaining the significance of each event and its placement on the timeline.

These lessons are designed to engage visual-spatial learners by incorporating visual representations and spatial thinking into Reading and Language Arts, Math, Science, and Social Studies activities. Adapt the lessons as needed to suit your elementary child's specific needs and grade level.

MIDDLE SCHOOL CHILDREN

 **Books for Middle School Learners**

Here's a list of books appropriate for middle school-aged children that may appeal to visual-spatial learners, along with short summaries and the authors of each book. These books offer a mix of adventure, fantasy, mystery, and science fiction themes that may engage and captivate visual-spatial learners in middle school.

"The Maze Runner" by James Dashner
> *In a mysterious and deadly maze, a group of young boys must work together to escape and uncover the secrets of their confinement.*

"Percy Jackson & the Olympians" series by Rick Riordan
> *Follow Percy Jackson, a demigod and the son of Poseidon, as he embarks on adventures to prevent catastrophic events involving Greek gods and monsters.*

"Ender's Game" by Orson Scott Card
> *Join Ender Wiggin as he undergoes rigorous training to prepare for a future alien invasion, all within a virtual battle simulation.*

"Artemis Fowl" by Eoin Colfer
> *Enter the world of Artemis Fowl, a teenage genius and criminal mastermind, as he seeks to steal fairy gold and unlock hidden secrets.*

"The Giver" by Lois Lowry

> *In a seemingly perfect society with no emotions or pain, Jonas is chosen to be the Receiver of Memories, bearing the burden of knowledge.*

"Hatchet" by Gary Paulsen

> *After a plane crash, Brian must survive alone in the wilderness with only a hatchet, relying on his resourcefulness and determination.*

"The City of Ember" by Jeanne DuPrau

> *Lina and Doon discover a hidden message that leads them on a quest to save their underground city, which is running out of resources.*

"The Lightning Thief" by Rick Riordan

> *Follow the adventures of Percy Jackson as he embarks on a quest to prevent a war among the gods by recovering Zeus's stolen lightning bolt.*

"The Westing Game" by Ellen Raskin

> *A group of seemingly unrelated people is brought together to solve the mystery of a wealthy man's death and a potential inheritance.*

"The 39 Clues" series by various authors, including Rick Riordan, Jude Watson, and more.

> *Siblings Amy and Dan Cahill embark on a worldwide adventure to discover the truth about their family's powerful and mysterious legacy.*

"The Mysterious Benedict Society" by Trenton Lee Stewart

> *Four gifted children with unique talents are recruited to stop an evil mastermind's plan to control minds.*

"The Secret Keepers" by Trenton Lee Stewart

> *Follow the adventures of Reuben as he discovers an ancient watch with incredible powers and becomes entangled in a dangerous conspiracy.*

"The Apothecary" by Maile Meloy
Janie, Benjamin, and Pip uncover a world of espionage, magic, and alchemy in 1950s London when they befriend a mysterious apothecary.

"The Chronicles of Narnia" series by C.S. Lewis
Enter the magical land of Narnia, where children discover a world of talking animals, mythical creatures, and epic adventures.

"The School for Good and Evil" by Soman Chainani
Follow Sophie and Agatha as they are unexpectedly enrolled in a school that trains children to become fairy-tale heroes or villains.

 **Language Arts and Reading for Middle School Students**

When I was developing this section for middle school students, I asked my son (who is now an adult with sons who are members of Boy Scouts of America), *"What is the one book you would recommend for a book unit that middle school children would want to read that would be appropriate for Super Spatialist learners?"* His response was immediate: *"'Hatchet' by Gary Paulsen."* I remember reading this book aloud to my sixth graders one year, and I agreed that this book would be a perfect recommendation for parents with an SS learner who were homeschooling. I also included it in the above-recommended reading list.

By incorporating visual elements and hands-on activities throughout the unit, you can engage visual-spatial learners while enhancing their comprehension and appreciation of "Hatchet" by Gary Paulsen. This comprehensive approach allows students to connect with the story on multiple levels and develop a deeper understanding of the themes and characters.

If you want a good source for implementing parts of this unit, I would consult with the Boy Scouts of America™ or The World Organization of Scout Movement™. Feel free to adjust this in any way you want! The following lessons are designed to engage your visual-spatial learner in math, social studies, and science while incorporating hands-on and visual elements to enhance their understanding and retention of the concepts. I really believe these lessons could be shared if you have more than one child in the family. Even if they are different intelligences, there are aspects to every project in which just about everyone can participate in. Feel free to adapt the lessons to suit your child's specific interests and learning style. Heck! I think it would be fun to join in their fun!

Summary: In "Hatchet," we follow the harrowing adventure of Brian Robeson, a thirteen-year-old boy who survives a plane crash in the wilderness of the Canadian woods. Alone and with only a hatchet as his tool, Brian must rely on his wits, determination, and resourcefulness to survive in the unforgiving environment. As he faces challenges like finding food, building shelter, and combating his own despair, Brian undergoes a profound transformation, tapping into his inner strength and primal instincts. Gary Paulsen's gripping tale is a testament to the resilience of the human spirit and the power of survival, offering readers a riveting journey into the heart of the wilderness and the depths of self-discovery.

Objective 1: Introduce students to the book "Hatchet" and its author, Gary Paulsen.

Activities 1:
- Show the book cover and read the blurb to pique interest.
- Discuss the concept of survival and its importance.
- Show images of the Canadian wilderness, where the story is set, and discuss its characteristics.
- Create a visual timeline to highlight important events in Brian's life before the airplane crashes.
- Introduce key vocabulary words from the book.
- Create a visual word wall to place images and definitions for each word.
- Provide a graphic organizer with details about Brian's personality, thoughts, and actions as you read the book.
- Research and present visuals or diagrams of essential survival skills, such as building a shelter, making a fire, and finding food and water.

Objective 2: Build comprehension skills through visualization and the creation of survival skills.

Activity 2:

Chapters 1–5
Read the first five chapters of "Hatchet," emphasizing visualization and comprehension. Continue to create a timeline to track significant events.

Chapters 6–10
Read chapters 6–10. Discussing the obstacles Brian faces. Draw or create visuals representing key moments from these chapters.

Chapters 11–15
Read chapters 11-15. Focus on Brian's growing abilities. Create a survival guide with visual instructions for the skills Brian learns.

Chapters 16–20
Read chapters 16–20. Discuss Brian's evolving mental state and physical condition. Create visual representations of Brian's thoughts and emotions during these chapters.

Chapters 21–25
Read chapters 21–25 aloud. Examine Brian's accomplishments and setbacks, listing Brian's progress and challenges. Discuss how Brian's survival skills have developed visually.

Additional Activities:
- Choose a scene or event from "Hatchet" and create a visual representation of it (e.g., drawings, dioramas, or a storyboard).
- Create a visual survival guide that includes key skills and information learned from the book.
- Reflect on how Brian's character and experiences relate to the theme of survival. Then, write an essay on how this book relates to survival.
- Watch "Hatchet," the movie, and note the similarities and differences with the book, focusing on visual aspects.
- Plan a camping trip with the family as an overnight adventure.

In the following subjects, I have given ideas that can also be applied to the reading and language arts unit above.

 **Math for Middle School Students**

Objective 1: Recognize and analyze geometric shapes and patterns.

Activity 1:
- Start by discussing the basics of geometric shapes (e.g., polygons, circles, angles) and their properties. Ask your child to draw different geometric shapes, such as triangles, quadrilaterals, and hexagons. Have them measure and label angles and sides using a ruler, compass, protractor, and colored pencils.
- Introduce the concept of geometric patterns and tessellations. Provide examples and encourage your child to create their own tessellating patterns using various shapes and colors, such as pattern blocks and pentominoes.
- Extend the lesson by exploring symmetry in geometric shapes. Have your child draw symmetrical figures and discuss lines of symmetry. Challenge your child to find examples of geometric shapes and patterns in their environment, such as in architecture or art.

Objective 2: Understand units of measurement and practice converting between them.

Activity 2:
- Start with a discussion about different units of measurement, such as inches, feet, centimeters, meters, pounds, and kilograms.
- Use objects around the house to practice measuring length and weight. Have your child measure the length of furniture, the height of family members, or the weight of items in the kitchen, etc.
- Introduce measurement word problems and challenges related to everyday scenarios, such as cooking or DIY projects.
- Have your child create a visual reference chart or poster with unit conversions for future use.

Objective 3: Collect and represent data using bar graphs.

Activity 3:
- Choose a data collection topic that interests your child, such as favorite colors, hobbies, or sports.
- Collect data by surveying family members, neighbors, or friends.
- Record the data in a table.
- Explain how to create a bar graph using the collected data.
- Help your child label the axes (x-axis and y-axis) and choose appropriate scales.
- Guide your child in drawing and coloring bars to represent the data. Encourage them to use different colors for each category.
- Discuss the bar graph interpretation, including the most and least popular categories, trends, and comparisons.
- Challenge your child to come up with questions based on the graph and answer them using the data.

 ## Science for Middle School Students

Objective 1: Explore the concept of simple machines through hands-on construction. Introduce the concept of simple machines (e.g., levers, pulleys, inclined planes) and their functions.

Activity 1:
- Explain the idea of a Rube Goldberg machine—a complex device that accomplishes a simple task through a series of chain reactions.
- Provide a variety of household objects and materials and challenge your child to design and build a Rube Goldberg machine that performs a simple task (e.g., turning off a light switch or ringing a bell).
- Encourage your child to sketch a blueprint or plan for their machine, incorporating multiple simple machines into the design.
- Guide your child in constructing and testing the machine to ensure it accomplishes the task.

- Discuss the role of each simple machine within the Rube Goldberg machine and how they work together.
- Have your child present their Rube Goldberg machine to the family, explaining the visual elements and how each part functions, or plan a time to demonstrate your Rube Goldberg machine on video.
- Post on social media.

Objective 2: Explore Earth's layers and create a 3D model of the Earth's interior.

Activity 2:
- Discuss the composition of Earth's layers, including the crust, mantle, outer core, and inner core.
- Provide reference materials and visuals that explain the characteristics and temperatures of each layer.
- Encourage your child to create a 3D model of the Earth's interior using craft materials.
- They can use different colors and textures to represent each layer. Guide your child in labeling and describing the properties of each layer on their model.
- Discuss how scientists have learned about Earth's layers and their importance in understanding our planet.
- Present and display their 3D model to the family, explaining the visual representations and key facts about Earth's layers.

 **Social Studies for Middle School Students**

Objective 1: Analyze historical maps to learn about ancient civilizations.

Activity 1:
- You will need historical maps of ancient civilizations (print or online resources), markers, and colored pencils.
- Choose a specific ancient civilization (Ancient Egypt, Mesopotamia, Greece, etc.) to study.

- Provide your child with historical maps or atlases that depict the region where the chosen civilization existed.
- Guide your child in examining the maps and identifying key geographical features, such as rivers, cities, and landmarks.
- Encourage your child to use markers and colored pencils to highlight and label important locations on the maps.
- Discuss how geography influenced the development of the civilization, including factors like agriculture, trade, and defense.
- Ask your child to create a visual presentation or a report that includes their findings and annotated maps.

Objective 2: Create a visual timeline of important historical events.

Activity 2:
- You will need a blank timeline template or poster board, markers, and historical events information.
- Choose a specific historical period or topic to explore, preferably the same civilization from above.
- Provide your child with information about key events from the chosen period and their dates.
- Discuss the concept of a timeline and its importance in understanding history. Help your child create a visual timeline, drawing and labeling events chronologically.
- Encourage your child to use markers and illustrations to represent each event visually.
- Discuss the cause-and-effect relationships between events and their impact on history.
- Display the completed timeline in a prominent place for reference.

HIGH SCHOOL STUDENTS

 **Books for High School Students**

It's common for Super Spatialist learners to share characteristics of intelligence with a Magical Mathematician learner. The following list of books is suitable for high school-aged students who display both categories of intelligence, along with short summaries and the authors of each book:

"The Da Vinci Code" by Dan Brown
> *A thrilling mystery that follows Harvard symbologist, Robert Langdon, as he unravels a series of clues left by a murdered curator, leading to a conspiracy that could change history.*

"The Night Circus" by Erin Morgenstern
> *A mesmerizing tale of a magical competition between two young illusionists, set in a fantastical, black-and-white circus that appears only at night.*

"The Secret History" by Donna Tartt
> *A dark and psychological novel that explores the lives of a group of classics students at an elite college and the consequences of their actions.*

"The Name of the Wind" by Patrick Rothfuss
> *Follow the extraordinary life of Kvothe, a gifted musician and magician, as he recounts his journey from a young boy to a legendary figure.*

"The Book Thief" by Markus Zusak
> *Narrated by Death, this novel tells the story of Liesel Meminger, a young girl in Nazi Germany who finds solace in stealing books and sharing them with others.*

"The Goldfinch" by Donna Tartt
> *A gripping coming-of-age story that follows Theo Decker, who survives a tragic event and becomes entangled with a priceless painting, "The Goldfinch."*

"The Nightingale" by Kristin Hannah
> *Set in Nazi-occupied France, this novel explores the bravery and sacrifices of two sisters as they resist the German occupation during World War II.*

"The Shadow of the Wind" by Carlos Ruiz Zafón
> *A mystery set in post-war Barcelona that follows a young boy who discovers a forgotten book by a little-known author, leading him into a world of secrets and danger.*

"All the Light We Cannot See" by Anthony Doerr
> *A beautifully written story that weaves together the lives of a blind French girl and a German boy during World War II, demonstrating the power of human connection.*

"The Alchemist" by Paulo Coelho
> *A philosophical novel that follows Santiago, a shepherd who embarks on a journey to discover his personal legend and fulfill his dreams.*

"The Girl with All the Gifts" by M.R. Carey
> *In a dystopian world overrun by a fungal infection, a gifted young girl named Melanie may hold the key to humanity's survival.*

"The Martian" by Andy Weir
> *When astronaut Mark Watney is stranded on Mars, he must use his resourcefulness and ingenuity to survive while awaiting rescue.*

"The 7 1/2 Deaths of Evelyn Hardcastle" by Stuart Turton
> *A mind-bending murder mystery where the protagonist wakes up in a different host's body each day, tasked with solving a murder to escape a time loop.*

"The Ocean at the End of the Lane" by Neil Gaiman
> *A magical and nostalgic story of a man who returns to his childhood home and recalls a series of extraordinary events involving a mysterious girl and her family.*

"The Martian" by Andy Weir
> *When astronaut Mark Watney is stranded on Mars after a mission and must learn to survive long enough to be rescued.*

 ## Language Arts and Reading for High School Students

This literature unit will delve into the novel "The Book Thief," exploring its themes, characters, and historical context. Additionally, it will introduce important college-preparatory skills such as critical thinking, research, writing, and presentation.

This literature unit not only delves into the content and themes of "The Book Thief" but also equips your high school visual-spatial learner with crucial college-preparatory skills such as research, critical thinking, writing, and presentation. It fosters a deep understanding of the novel while honing valuable skills for future academic endeavors.

Summary: "The Book Thief" is a profoundly moving and uniquely narrated novel set in Nazi Germany. Through the eyes of Death as the narrator, readers are drawn into the life of Liesel Meminger, a young girl with a love for words who steals books during a time of war and oppression. The story beautifully explores the power of words, love, and humanity's resilience amid the darkest of circumstances. It's a tale of hope and connection that lingers in the heart long after turning the last page.

Objective 1: Introduce the book, its author, and the historical context of Nazi Germany.

Activity 1:
- Read the book's blurb and discuss the title's significance. Provide an overview of Nazi Germany and World War II.

Objective 2: Analyze key characters in the novel.

Activity 2:
- Discuss and create character profiles for Liesel Meminger, Hans Hubermann, Rosa Hubermann, and other significant characters.
- Encourage visual-spatial learners to sketch or create character collages to represent the characters' traits.

Objective 3: Develop research and presentation skills.

Activity 3:
- Assign a specific aspect of Nazi Germany or World War II to research (e.g., Hitler Youth, Lebensborn program).
- Create visual presentations (e.g., slideshows, infographics) to share their findings with you and the family.

Objective 4: Identify and discuss major themes in the novel.

Activity 4:
- Discuss themes such as the power of words, human resilience, and the impact of war.
- Create visual representations (e.g., concept maps or drawings) of the themes.

Objective 5: Explore literary devices used in the novel.

Activity 5:
- Identify and discuss literary devices like symbolism, foreshadowing, and metaphors in "The Book Thief."
- Find examples of these devices in the text and create visual representations to illustrate their understanding.

Objective 6: Develop critical thinking and writing skills.

Activity 6:
- Assign essay topics related to the novel's themes or characters.
- Give guidance to outline their essays, including visual diagrams or concept maps to organize their ideas.

Objective 7: Conduct in-depth research on a historical aspect related to the novel.

Activity 7:
- Select a specific historical topic (e.g., the Holocaust, book burning) for research.
- Teach how to access and evaluate primary and secondary sources.

Objective 8: Synthesize research findings into a cohesive presentation.

Activity 8:
- Create visual presentations (e.g., posters or digital slides) summarizing their research.
- Emphasize effective visual communication through layouts, images, and graphics.

Objective 9: Develop strong presentation skills.

Activity 9:
- Conduct a mock presentation, providing constructive feedback on delivery, content, and visual aids.
- Discuss strategies for engaging the audience and addressing questions.

Objective 10: Foster critical thinking and discussion skills.

Activity 10:
- Discuss the novel's impact and relevance today.
- Reflect on what they've learned and how it applies to their lives.

Objective 11: Apply creative and visual skills to express understanding.

Activity 11:
- Choose from various creative projects, such as creating a book cover, designing a board game based on the novel, or producing an art piece inspired by the story.
- Share with family members.

 **Math for High School Students**

Here are math lessons covering various math courses tailored for your SS homeschooled child. These math lessons aim to engage your SS homeschooled child in different math courses while incorporating visual and hands-on activities to enhance their understanding and retention of mathematical concepts. Feel free to adapt these lessons to suit your child's specific interests and learning style.

Objective 1: Understand and solve equations using visual representations.

Activity 1:
- Introduction to Equations.
- Discuss the concept of algebraic equations and their importance in problem-solving.
- Provide examples of simple equations (e.g., $2x + 3 = 7$) and their solutions.

Objective 2: Introduce the idea of representing equations graphically on graph paper.

Activity 2:
- Show how to plot points and create visual representations of equations.
- Provide algebraic equations for your child to graph, using different colors for each equation.
- Discuss how the intersection points on the graph represent solutions.

Objective 3: Explain systems of equations and how they involve multiple equations with common solutions.

Activity 3:
- Use visual aids to represent systems of equations.
- Give your child a system of equations to solve graphically.
- Encourage them to find the intersection point(s) as solutions.
- Discuss the benefits of using visual representations to solve equations.
- Reflect on real-life applications of algebra and equations.

Objective 4: Explore mathematical concepts using the art of M.C. Escher as a visual and creative tool.

Activity 4:
This lesson introduces mathematical concepts and encourages your SS learner to express their creativity through art inspired by M.C. Escher. It fosters an appreciation for the intersection of mathematics and art while engaging with Escher's captivating visuals. Who was M.C. Escher? M.C. Escher, whose full name was Maurits Cornelis Escher, was a Dutch graphic artist known for his intricate and mind-bending works of art. He was born on June 17, 1898, in Leeuwarden, Netherlands, and passed away on March 27, 1972, in Laren, Netherlands. Escher is renowned for exploring mathematical and optical illusions within his artwork. He often combined mathematics, geometry, and visual perception to create stunning and perplexing images that challenged viewers to see the world from new and unexpected perspectives. Some of his most famous works include "Relativity," "Waterfall," and "Drawing Hands." Throughout his career, Escher gained international recognition for his unique style and contributions to the field of graphic art. His work has had a lasting influence on art, mathematics, and visual perception, and it continues to captivate and inspire audiences around the world.

Two fish (No 41) by MC Escher

- You can google or visit my website www.innovativehomeschoolsolutions.com to find M.C. Escher print books, pencils, paper, geometric drawing tools (rulers, protractors), and access to the internet (optional).
- Show examples of Escher's work, such as "Relativity," "Waterfall," and "Drawing Hands."
- Engage your child in a discussion about the mathematical concepts present in Escher's art, including tessellations, symmetry, perspective, and optical illusions.
- Use visuals and Escher's artwork to illustrate these concepts.
- Teach your child how to create tessellations, which are repeating patterns of shapes that fit together without gaps.
- Provide them with paper and geometric drawing tools to design their tessellation.

- Encourage creativity and experimentation and create their own artwork inspired by Escher's style. They can use tessellations, symmetry, or optical illusions in their artwork.
- Provide guidance and feedback throughout the creative process.
- Explore the concept of symmetry in Escher's art.
- Discuss bilateral symmetry, rotational symmetry, and reflections.
- Ask your child to identify and sketch instances of symmetry in Escher's work.
- Explore Escher's use of optical illusions and how he manipulated perspective to create mind-bending drawings.
- Discuss the mathematical principles behind optical illusions.

 # Science for High School Students

These science lessons encompass Earth science, life science, and physical science, offering hands-on experiences and visual representations to enhance your visual-spatial learner's understanding of key scientific concepts. These engaging activities provide valuable insights into different domains of science.

Creating a Model of the Solar System
Earth Science and Astronomy

Objective: Build an understanding of the solar system through a hands-on modeling activity.

Activity:
- Begin by discussing the solar system, its components (sun, planets, moons, asteroids), and their characteristics.
- Show images and diagrams of the solar system for visual reference.
- Provide craft supplies and guide your child in creating a scale model of the solar system.
- Choose different objects and materials (colored paper cutouts) to represent the sun, planets, and moons.
- Use string to demonstrate the distances between objects.

- Encourage creativity in the design.
- Display the solar system either on a wall or across the ceiling.
- Assign the planets to your child for research. They should gather information on its size, composition, atmosphere, and unique features.
- Create visual posters or fact cards for each planet.
- Have your child present their solar system model to you, explaining the scale, relative sizes, and distances between objects.
- Encourage them to showcase the research findings for each planet.
- Engage in a discussion about the solar system's characteristics and the significance of scale models in science. Reflect on the visual representations used in the activity.

Social Studies for High School Students

These social studies and history lessons are adaptable for homeschooled high school students worldwide, allowing them to explore historical events, civilizations, and geopolitics through engaging and visually-oriented activities. These social studies and history lessons are designed for any homeschooled high school student worldwide.

Objective: Explore geopolitics through a visual simulation of diplomatic negotiations.

Materials: World map or globe, flags representing different countries (or their names written on paper), whiteboard or large paper, markers.

Activity:
- Discuss the concept of geopolitics, focusing on international relations, alliances, and conflicts.
- Introduce key regions and countries with geopolitical significance. Use a world map or globe as a visual aid.
- Assign different countries to the student, using flags or written names to represent them.
- Explain that each country has specific resources, goals, and interests.

- Encourage the student to negotiate diplomatically with other countries to achieve their goals.
- Use a whiteboard or large paper to represent negotiations, agreements, and conflicts visually.
- Present a fictional international crisis or scenario for the student to navigate diplomatic negotiations. Emphasize the importance of visual diplomacy, such as using flags, symbols, and maps to convey intentions and agreements.
- Engage in a discussion about the challenges and complexities of geopolitics. Reflect on the role of visual diplomacy in real-world international relations.

Conclusion

Super Spatialist (SS) learners' remarkable visual and spatial thinking skills enrich your homeschooling experience by offering fresh perspectives on problem-solving, creativity, and understanding complex concepts. Harnessing these strengths through tailored strategies, like visual aids, hands-on activities, and multimedia resources, creates an engaging and effective learning environment. As a homeschooling parent, you can empower your child's holistic, non-linear thinking style. By acknowledging and nurturing their spatial intelligence, you cultivate a love for learning that extends far beyond the homeschool classroom, celebrating the uniqueness of your SS learner's cognitive abilities throughout their educational journey.

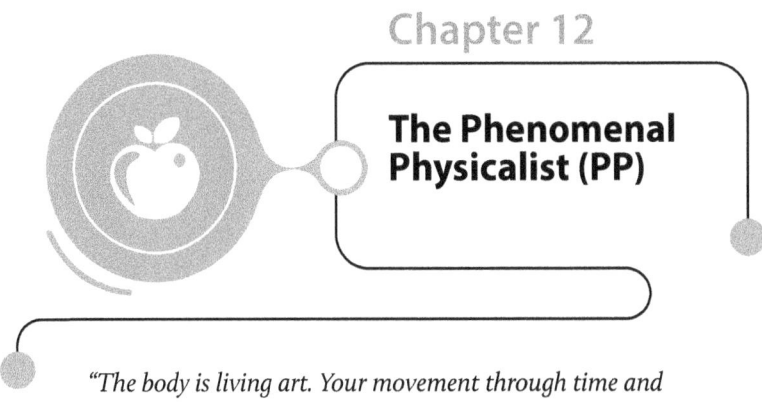

Chapter 12

The Phenomenal Physicalist (PP)

*"The body is living art. Your movement through time and
space is art. A painter has brushes. You have your body."*
—ANNA HALPRIN

I admire athletic people. The ballerina, who looks like she just came to life
from a marble statue, has graceful lines and pure strength, able to balance
her whole body on the tips of her toes of only one foot, seemingly without
effort. Then there are the Olympic sprinters who seem like they can outrun a
spirited racehorse any day, anytime. There are the Michael Jordans, Michael
Andrettis, and Tom Bradys of the world, and at one time, a child in someone's
classroom or a homeschooled child. I can say from experience these children
are not happy when they have to sit for long periods doing monotonous (to
them) activities such as reading silently, following step-by-step instructions, or
waiting for everyone else to catch up if they happen to be finished with whatever the assignment was—even if they aren't really finished. There is something
I realized many years ago about the Phenomenal Physicalist learner—if they
aren't happy, there's a possibility *no one is happy!* Let's take a few minutes and
look at the attributes of the PP learner.

Highlights:

- PP learners think by physically engaging with their environment. They often need to move, touch, or manipulate objects to understand concepts better. They may use their body as a tool for learning and problem-solving.
- These learners prefer hands-on activities and practical experiences. They learn best when actively engaging in building, crafting, or performing experiments.
- PP learners often express themselves physically. They may use gestures, body language, or physical movements to convey their thoughts and emotions. They may also excel in activities like dance, sports, or acting.
- They tend to have a heightened sense of spatial awareness and are good at visualizing and manipulating objects in space. This skill can be valuable for tasks such as solving puzzles, navigating, and understanding three-dimensional concepts.
- These learners rely on their sense of touch and bodily sensations to gather information. They may enjoy activities that involve tactile experiences, like sculpting, gardening, or cooking.
- PP learners often approach problem-solving by physically experimenting with various solutions. They may try different actions or movements to find the most effective way to solve a problem.
- They may use their body to help them remember information. For example, they might use physical gestures or movements to associate with specific facts or concepts, aiding in recall.
- PP learners may struggle in traditional classroom environments that rely heavily on passive listening and reading. They thrive when given the opportunity to engage in active, hands-on learning experiences.

Strategies:

Teaching a Phenomenal Physicalist child can be a rewarding experience, as you can harness their physical and hands-on learning style to make lessons engaging and effective. Here are some strategies to help you teach your bodily-kinesthetic child effectively. As a homeschooling mom or dad, it's essential to recognize your child's predominant intelligence and tailor your teaching methods to accommodate their learning style. Incorporating physical activities, hands-on projects, and interactive learning experiences for a PP learner can be highly effective in helping them grasp and retain information. Providing various learning opportunities that engage their body and senses will cater to their unique way of thinking and learning. So, let's examine some of the strategies you should be using to accommodate your bodily PP child.

- **Incorporate hands-on learning experiences** into your lessons whenever possible. Use manipulatives, experiments, and interactive projects to help them understand concepts better. For example, use building blocks to teach math concepts or conduct science experiments together.
- **Recognize that your child may need regular breaks** for physical movement. Allow them short breaks during lessons to stretch, jump, or engage in physical activities that can help them stay focused and energized. Utilize educational games and activities that involve physical movement. Board games, card games, and outdoor activities like scavenger hunts can be used to teach various subjects while keeping your child active and engaged. Encourage your child to engage in role-playing and drama activities. This can help them understand complex ideas, improve their communication skills, and express themselves physically.
- **Artistic activities like drawing, painting, and sculpture** can be valuable for PP learners. These activities allow them to express their creativity and understand abstract concepts. Encourage your child to demonstrate their understanding of a topic physically. They can create presentations, skits, or demonstrations to showcase their learning. Engage multiple senses in the learning process. Combine visual, auditory, and tactile elements to make lessons more immersive and memorable.
- **Show them how the subjects they are learning are applicable** in real life. Take field trips, visit museums, and explore nature to provide concrete examples of the concepts they are studying. Allow your child to choose

their learning environment within your homeschool setup. Some may prefer to sit on a yoga ball, stand at a desk, or work outdoors. Being physically comfortable can enhance their learning experience.

- **Arrange opportunities for group projects and collaborative learning experiences** within your homeschool environment, co-ops, and other families who homeschool. These interactions can provide social interaction and allow them to work together with others, which can be motivating.
- **Create a structured daily routine with clear objectives and expectations**. Knowing what to expect can help your child stay focused and organized. Allow your child to explore their interests and passions through physical activities. Offer a variety of resources and let them choose topics or projects that resonate with them. Praise your child's efforts and accomplishments. Celebrate their achievements, no matter how small, to boost their confidence and motivation.

ELEMENTARY CHILDREN

 **Books for Elementary Students**

Knowing your child must have physical activity to engage their mental activity is important for learning. Sitting and reading for a long period of time is more challenging for this type of learner *unless* they can engage with the characters in the book. The following is a list of books that your elementary bodily-kinesthetic learner may enjoy:

"The Adventures of Tintin" series by Hergé
> *Join Tintin, a young journalist, and his loyal dog, Snowy, on thrilling adventures around the world, solving mysteries, and encountering exciting challenges.*

"Diary of a Wimpy Kid" series by Jeff Kinney
Follow the humorous diary entries of Greg Heffley as he navigates the ups and downs of middle school life, filled with amusing mishaps and relatable experiences.

"The Magic Tree House" series by Mary Pope Osborne
Travel through time and space with siblings Jack and Annie as they embark on magical adventures from their treehouse, exploring history and encountering intriguing characters.

"Captain Underpants" series by Dav Pilkey
Join George and Harold as they transform their principal into the superhero Captain Underpants, resulting in hilarious escapades and misadventures.

"Cam Jansen" series by David A. Adler
Follow the adventures of Jennifer "Cam" Jansen, a girl with a photographic memory, as she solves mysteries and puzzles using her remarkable ability.

"The Berenstain Bears" series by Stan and Jan Berenstain
Join the lovable bear family, the Berenstain Bears, in their everyday adventures and life lessons as they navigate various family and community situations.

"I Survived" series by Lauren Tarshis
Dive into historical events through the eyes of young protagonists who face incredible challenges and survive against the odds in these gripping, action-packed stories.

"Junie B. Jones" series by Barbara Park
Meet the spunky and outspoken Junie B. Jones as she shares her hilarious and endearing misadventures while navigating the challenges of kindergarten and beyond.

"Nate the Great" series by Marjorie Weinman Sharmat
Follow the detective skills of young Nate the Great as he solves mysteries with the help of his trusty dog, Sludge, in these engaging and interactive stories.

"A Series of Unfortunate Events" series by Lemony Snicket (Daniel Handler)
Join the Baudelaire siblings as they unravel dark family secrets and face a series of unfortunate events in this intriguing and darkly humorous series.

"Geronimo Stilton" series by Geronimo Stilton (pseudonym)
Join the adventurous mouse journalist Geronimo Stilton on thrilling journeys full of humor, excitement, and learning experiences.

"The Boxcar Children" series by Gertrude Chandler Warner
Follow the four orphaned Alden siblings as they create a home for themselves in an abandoned boxcar and embark on heartwarming adventures.

 **Reading and Language Arts for Elementary Students**

The following unit is based on the book "Miss Rumphius" by Barbara Cooney, centered around the theme of Earth Day. This unit incorporates movement and language arts activities to engage your PP elementary-aged child. As an aside, this unit is also a dead-ringer for the EE learner.

Summary:
"Miss Rumphius" is a story about a woman named Alice Rumphius, who everyone fondly calls "The Lupine Lady." As a young girl, she dreams of traveling to far-off places, living by the sea, and making the world more beautiful. As she grows up, she accomplishes her dreams one by one, but the most important dream is to make the world more beautiful.

She achieves this by scattering lupine seeds wherever she goes, spreading colorful wildflowers, and bringing joy to everyone who sees them. The story teaches us that even small actions, such as planting seeds, can make a big difference in making the world a beautiful place.

The book is filled with beautiful illustrations that show the transformation of fields into vibrant lupine-filled landscapes, which can inspire bodily-kinesthetic learners to explore the natural world around them, plant their own seeds, and actively participate in making their environment more beautiful. It's a heartwarming tale that encourages children to dream big and take action to create beauty in the world.

Objective 1: Introduce the theme of 'Creating a Better World' and engage your child in discussing what "a better world" means.

Activity 1:
- Start by reading "Miss Rumphius" aloud to your child.
- Encourage them to act out Miss Rumphius's physical movements as she explores different places.
- Have them mimic her actions like walking, climbing, and observing nature.
- After reading, ask your child to draw or write about their favorite part of the story and why they liked it.

Objective 2: Researching Lupine Flowers.

Activity 2:
- Discuss lupine flowers, which are a central element in the story.
- Learn about their characteristics, colors, and where they grow.
- Take a nature walk or go to a local park. Allow your child to pick wild-flowers or lupines if available (ensure it's allowed and legal in your area).
- Have your child create a simple nature journal entry describing the flowers they picked and any observations they made during the walk.

Objective 3: Learn about how plants contribute to the environment.

Activity 3:
- Explore the concept of planting and growing flowers.
- Discuss how plants contribute to the environment and Earth Day.
- Provide your child with lupine seeds and a small pot of soil. Demonstrate how to plant the seeds.
- Ask your child to write or draw a step-by-step guide on planting lupine seeds. This can be a simple how-to booklet that your child can publish for the family.

Objective 4: Learn about Earth Day and how it relates to the theme.

Activity 4:
- Talk about Earth Day and its importance.
- Discuss ways in which people can care for the Earth.
- Engage in a cleanup activity in your neighborhood or local park.
- Encourage your child to pick up litter anytime and discuss how this helps the environment.
- After the cleanup, have your child write a short paragraph or draw a picture about their experience and what they did to help the Earth.

Objective 5: Finding ways to make the world a better place.

Activity 5:
- Revisit the book "Miss Rumphius" and discuss the message of making the world more beautiful.
- Encourage your child to think of ways to make the world more beautiful, just like Miss Rumphius. This could involve planting more flowers, helping wildlife, or being kind to others.
- Have your child write a short pledge or create a poster with their ideas for making the world more beautiful and environmentally friendly.

Continue to nurture your child's interest in nature and environmental conservation. Encourage them to care for the lupine seeds they planted and observe their growth over time. This reading unit combines the themes of "Miss Rumphius," Earth Day, and physical movement to create an engaging and educational experience for your Phenomenal Physicalist learner.

 **Math for Elementary School Students**

Objective 1: To use physical activity to find objects related to math.

Activity 1:
- Create a list of math-related items or concepts for your child to find around your home or in your backyard. For example, you can include

items like a ruler, a clock, a calendar, a certain number of coins, or shapes.

- Give your child a basket or bag to collect the items as they find them.
- Encourage them to measure, count, or identify the properties of the objects on the list.
- Once they've collected all the items, review their findings together and discuss the mathematical concepts behind each item. For example, talk about how a clock represents time or how different coins have different values.

Objective 2: Practice math problems using an obstacle course.

Activity 2:
- Set up a mini obstacle course in your backyard or living room using simple household items like cushions, hula hoops, or cones.
- Assign math problems or challenges to each obstacle. For example, they might need to solve addition or subtraction problems before moving to the next station.
- Your child can physically move through the obstacle course, completing math challenges at each stop. This combines physical movement with math practice.

Objective 3: Perform physical activities to complete a bingo math card game.

Activity 3:
- Create a math bingo card with various math problems or questions in each square. For example, you can include addition, subtraction, multiplication, or division problems.
- Instead of simply marking the answers on the card, assign a physical action or movement to each answer. For example, hopping for addition, spinning for subtraction, jumping jacks for multiplication, and skipping for division.
- Call out math problems; your child must solve them and perform the corresponding physical action before marking the answer on their bingo card.

- The goal is to complete a row or column on their bingo card by solving math problems and performing the associated actions.

These math activities combine physical movement with mathematical concepts, making learning math more engaging and interactive for your PP learner. They also provide an opportunity for hands-on, kinesthetic exploration of math concepts.

 ## Science for Elementary School Students

Objective 1: Identify living and nonliving items in a specified ecosystem.

Activity 1:
- Begin by discussing the concept of ecosystems and biodiversity with your child.
- Explain how different plants and animals coexist in various environments.
- Take your child on a nature scavenger hunt in a nearby park, nature reserve, or backyard.
- Provide a checklist of items to find, such as specific types of leaves, rocks, insects, or animal tracks.
- Encourage them to use their senses to explore and identify these items.
- After the scavenger hunt, discuss what they discovered and how different elements are interconnected in nature.

Objective 2: Learn how density is related to buoyancy.

Activity 2:
- Introduce the concept of buoyancy and density to your child.
- Explain that some objects are denser than water and sink, while others are less dense and float. (You will probably have to give examples or pose a question, such as *"Why doesn't a ship sink in the ocean?"*)
- Gather various objects from around your home, such as coins, small toys, fruits, and craft materials.

- Fill a large container with water and have your child predict whether each item will sink or float.
- Then, let them test each item by placing it in the water.
- As they conduct the experiment, encourage them to observe, record their findings, and discuss the reasons behind the outcomes. They can use language like "heavy" and "light" to describe the objects.

Objective 3: Learn the stages a flower goes through from seed to adult plant.

Activity 3:
- Discuss the life cycle of plants with your child, emphasizing the stages of seed germination and plant growth.
- Start a simple gardening project together, such as the 'planting lupines' from "Miss Rumphius." Provide your child with small pots, potting soil, and a variety of seeds (e.g., sunflowers, beans, or radishes).
- Have your child plant the seeds and water them regularly. (They can also decorate their plant pots).
- As the plants grow, encourage your child to measure their height, draw or take photos of the different stages, and keep a journal to document the changes they observe.
- Discuss the importance of sunlight, water, and nutrients in plant growth and how plants contribute to the environment.

These science lessons engage your PP learner by involving physical activities like scavenger hunts, hands-on experiments, and gardening. They provide opportunities for exploration, observation, and active participation in scientific concepts, making learning about the natural world enjoyable and memorable.

 **Social Studies for Elementary School Students**

These social studies lessons engage your PP learner by incorporating physical movement, role-playing, and hands-on activities. They provide a fun and interactive way to explore geography, history, and culture while allowing your child to participate in the learning process actively.

Objective 1: Learn the location of continents, countries, and oceans.

Activity 1:
- Introduce basic geography concepts to your child, including continents, countries, and major landmarks.
- Create a treasure hunt-style activity where your child has to "travel" around the world to find hidden treasures (small items or treats).
- Set up different stations or "countries" around your home or yard, each representing a continent or region. At each station, provide clues or facts about the location and a small treasure to discover.
- Your child can physically move from one station to another, using a map or globe to guide them. This activity combines physical movement with geography knowledge.

Objective 2: Explore different cultures and countries through their cuisines.

Activity 2:
- Choose a country or culture to focus on for the lesson. Research and learn about that culture's traditional foods, customs, and dining etiquette.
- Invite your child to participate in a cooking activity where they prepare a simple dish or snack from the chosen culture. This could involve making sushi, tacos, or pasta, for example.
- While cooking, discuss the cultural significance of the food, the ingredients used, and any associated traditions.
- You can also explore the country's geography and its place in the world.

Objective 3: Learn about a historical event or period in history.

Activity 3:
- Choose a historical event or period your child is interested in (e.g., the American Revolution, Ancient Egypt, or the Silk Road.)
- Encourage your child to dress up as a historical figure from that era, whether it's a famous person or a character from that time.
- Create a simple script or scenario related to that historical period. Your child can act out scenes or dialogues to bring history to life.

- After the role-playing, discuss the historical context and the significance of the event or period, helping your child understand the broader social studies concepts.

When I used this activity in my classroom, the children had to be totally still, like a life-sized doll. When I pushed the 'magic button' beside them, they came to life and told me about their era. When they were finished, they had to stop and become life-sized dolls again.

MIDDLE SCHOOL CHILDREN

 **Books for Middle School Learners**

The following is a list of books your middle school PP child might enjoy. These books offer a mix of adventure, mystery, and fantasy elements that should captivate your middle school child's imagination while providing engaging stories to cater to their PP learning style. There are a diverse range of genres and themes, from dystopian futures and Greek mythology to heartwarming tales of resilience and classic fantasy adventures. They should provide your middle school child with plenty of engaging reading material to cater to their PP learning style.

"Percy Jackson & the Olympians" series by Rick Riordan
Follow the adventures of Percy Jackson, a demigod, as he navigates the world of Greek mythology, battles monsters, and encounters ancient gods.

"The Maze Runner" series by James Dashner
Join Thomas as he wakes up in a mysterious maze with no memory of how he got there. The series follows his journey to escape and uncover the truth.

"Hatchet" by Gary Paulsen

Follow the story of Brian Robeson, a young boy stranded in the Canadian wilderness after a plane crash, as he learns to survive using his wits and resourcefulness.

"Artemis Fowl" series by Eoin Colfer

Enter the world of Artemis Fowl, a teenage genius and criminal mastermind, as he engages in adventures involving fairies, technology, and magic.

"The Giver" by Lois Lowry

Explore a dystopian society where emotions and memories are controlled, and follow Jonas as he discovers the truth about his world.

"Ender's Game" by Orson Scott Card

Follow Ender Wiggin, a young boy with exceptional strategic skills, as he trains at a military school to prepare for an alien invasion.

"The City of Ember" by Jeanne DuPrau

Dive into an underground city with Lina and Doon, two young residents who discover secrets about their decaying world and seek a way to save it.

"The Westing Game" by Ellen Raskin

Join a diverse group of characters as they attempt to solve the mystery of Samuel W. Westing's death and the hidden inheritance in a complex and engaging puzzle.

"The Alchemyst" by Michael Scott (Book 1 of "The Secrets of the Immortal Nicholas Flamel" series)

Follow twins, Sophie and Josh, as they become entangled in a world of magic and mythical creatures when they encounter the immortal alchemist Nicholas Flamel.

"The Hunger Games" series by Suzanne Collins

Enter the dystopian world of Panem, where Katniss Everdeen fights for her survival in a televised battle to the death known as the Hunger Games.

"The Tale of Despereaux" by Kate DiCamillo
> *Follow the adventures of Despereaux, a small mouse with a big heart, as he embarks on a quest to rescue a princess and confronts the world of humans and rats.*

"The War That Saved My Life" by Kimberly Brubaker Bradley
> *Set during World War II, this story follows Ada, a girl with a clubfoot, who escapes an abusive home and discovers her own strength and resilience.*

"The Hobbit" by J.R.R. Tolkien
> *Join Bilbo Baggins on a grand adventure as he accompanies a group of dwarves to reclaim their homeland from the dragon, Smaug. This classic fantasy tale is filled with action and excitement.*

 ## Reading and Language Arts for Middle School Students

I have created a comprehensive book unit centered around the novel "Holes," by Louis Sachar, for your middle school PP learners. It is an excellent way to engage them with the story and enhance their understanding.

"Holes" is a gripping novel that follows the story of Stanley Yelnats, a young boy who has been unjustly sent to a juvenile detention camp called Camp Green Lake. At Camp Green Lake, the boys are forced to dig holes in the dry lakebed under the scorching sun as a form of punishment.

As Stanley and his fellow inmates dig these deep holes day after day, they uncover a mysterious and complex web of family curses, buried treasure, and historical secrets. The book weaves together two parallel narratives: one set in the present-day camp and the other set in the past, revealing the history of the cursed Yelnats family and the hidden treasure.

Throughout the story, Stanley and his friends face challenges, forge friendships, and discover the true nature of the camp's warden and the purpose behind the seemingly pointless hole-digging. As the mysteries unravel, the novel explores themes of justice, fate, and the interconnectedness of past and present.

"Holes" is an engaging and thought-provoking book that keeps readers on the edge of their seats, blending humor, adventure, and suspense in a way that appeals to all ages.

Objective 1: Introduction to "Holes" Chapters 1-17.

Activity 1:
- Begin by introducing the novel "Holes" and discussing the importance of the title.
- Have your child create a visual representation of what they think the book might be about based on the title.

Objective 2: Create vocabulary from "Holes."

Activity 2:
- Select a list of challenging vocabulary words from the first few chapters. As you read together, have your child keep an eye out for these words in the text.
- When encountering a vocabulary word, they should write down the sentence it appears in and try to guess its meaning based on the context.
- After reading, look up the words in a dictionary and compare their definitions with your child's guesses.

Objective 3: Find grammatical errors from "Holes."

Activity 3:
- Create a set of sentence cards, each with a sentence from the book that contains a grammatical error (e.g., subject-verb agreement, punctuation, or verb tense).
- Place the cards around the room or in your backyard. Have your child run to each card, identify the grammatical error, and correct it on the card.
- Time your child to see how quickly they can correct all the sentences. Make it a fun relay race!

Objective 4: Complete a character chart for "Holes" listing all protagonists and antagonists.

Activity 4:
- Start reading the book together. Focus on character development.
- As you read, have your child create a character chart that includes details about the main characters, physical descriptions, and personality traits.
- For PP learning, encourage your child to act out scenes or gestures representing each character's traits.

Objective 5: Determine the setting by creating a geographic map of "Holes."

Activity 5:
- Discuss the story's setting, including Camp Green Lake and its geographical features.
- Use maps and geographical resources to explore deserts and lakes, and have your child create a map of Camp Green Lake.
- Consider taking a nature walk or a visit to a local lake to connect the setting to real-life experiences.

Objective 6: Determine the plot by analysis of Chapters 18–34.

Activity 6:
- Explore the novel's plot, discussing the different events and their significance.
- Create a plot diagram together, marking key events and turning points.
- Engage your child in dramatic reenactments of significant scenes from the book.

Objective 7: Learn new vocabulary.

Activity 7:
- Choose several vocabulary words from the chapters you've read. Write each word on a separate index card and place them face down.
- Your child should pick a card, read the word silently, and act it out without speaking.
- The family members can guess the word's meaning based on their actions.

Objective 8: Determine parts of speech.

Activity 8:
- Select a passage from the book with various sentences. Provide your child with a highlighter or colored pencils.
- Ask your child to identify specific grammar elements within the passage, such as verbs, adjectives, adverbs, or prepositions.
- Have them underline or highlight these elements in different colors.
- Discuss how each part of speech contributes to the overall meaning of the passage.

Objective 9: Determine the theme through character analysis of justice and friendship.

Activity 9:
- Discuss the themes of justice and friendship as they relate to the characters and their actions in the story.
- Have your child write journal entries from the perspective of one of the characters, expressing their thoughts and emotions about these themes.
- Encourage discussions about fairness, consequences, and the importance of supporting friends.

Objective 10: Determine the symbolism of onions in "Holes."

Activity 10:
- Connect the story to the physical labor of digging holes.
- Provide onions and paint, and have your child create artistic representations of onions, which are significant in the book.
- Discuss the symbolism of onions and how they relate to the story.

Objective 11: Explore literary devices and analyze them in "Holes." Chapters 35–50— Foreshadowing and Flashbacks.

Activity 11:
- Explore the literary devices used in the novel, such as foreshadowing and flashbacks.

- Have your child identify instances of foreshadowing and flashbacks in the text and discuss their significance.
- Create a timeline or visual representation of the events using flashcards or a storyboard.

Objective 12: Create a short story using vocabulary from "Holes."

Activity 12:
- Choose a few vocabulary words from the later chapters.
- Have your child create a short story or narrative using these words. Encourage them to incorporate the words seamlessly into the story.
- Afterward, they can share their stories with you, emphasizing the context in which they used the vocabulary words.
- Another variation is encouraging your child to tell their story but act it out as they read it to you and the family.

Objective 13: Identify grammar mistakes in "Holes."

Activity 13:
- Select a variety of sentences from different parts of the book. Write these sentences on large poster paper and place them around the room or in your backyard.
- Provide your child with sticky notes or small cards. Ask your child to visit each sentence and identify a specific grammar element (e.g., subject-verb agreement, punctuation, or verb tense) that is correct or incorrect.
- They should write their observations on sticky notes or cards and place them next to the sentences.

Objective 14: Compare and contrast the book "Holes" to the movie "Holes."

Activity 14:
- After finishing the book, watch the movie adaptation of "Holes" as a family.
- Discuss the similarities and differences between the book and the movie.
- Encourage your child to compare their initial visualizations from day one with how the movie portrayed the story.

Objective 15: Identify the theme, characters, and plot.

Activity 15:
- Reflect on the themes, character development, and plot of the book.
- Engage in a discussion about the life lessons and morals learned from "Holes."
- Encourage your child to write a letter to the author, Louis Sachar, expressing their thoughts about the book.

Incorporate movement and kinesthetic activities as much as possible to keep your Phenomenal Physicalist learner engaged and to enhance their understanding of the book "Holes." This unit plan combines reading comprehension with hands-on activities and discussions, making the learning experience both enjoyable and educational.

 ## Math for Middle School Students

These math lessons combine physical activity, exploration, and games to engage your middle school PP learner while reinforcing important math concepts.

Objective 1: To reinforce the order of operations (PEMDAS/BODMAS) through physical movement and teamwork.
> *For more than one player. Encourage everyone in the family to participate. If younger children in the family understand these concepts, it's great to include them, neighborhood kids, co-op groups, etc.*

Activity 1:
- Create a race track with numbered sections using chalk or tape in your backyard or a large open space. Divide the track into teams and assign each team a starting point.
- Place index cards with math expressions at various points along the track.
- When you say, "Go!" the first player from each team runs to the first math expression card, solves it using the correct order of operations, and runs to the next card.
- Continue this relay race, with each player solving one expression at a time. Time each team to see which one completes the race first.

PEMDAS and BODMAS are acronyms used to remember the order of operations in mathematics. They help us solve mathematical expressions with multiple operations like addition, subtraction, multiplication, and division.

PEMDAS *(used in the United States and some other countries):*
- **P:** *Parentheses (Solve what's inside parentheses first)*
- **E:** *Exponents (Solve expressions with exponents or powers)*
- **MD:** *Multiplication and Division (Work from left to right, performing multiplication and division as they appear)*
- **AS:** *Addition and Subtraction (Work from left to right, performing addition and subtraction as they appear)*

BODMAS *(used in the United Kingdom and some other countries):*
- **B:** *Brackets (Solve what's inside brackets first)*
- **O:** *Orders (Solve expressions with exponents or powers)*
- **DM:** *Division and Multiplication (Work from left to right, performing division and multiplication as they appear)*
- **AS:** *Addition and Subtraction (Work from left to right, performing addition and subtraction as they appear)*

So, in a nutshell, PEMDAS and BODMAS are guidelines to help you remember the order in which you should carry out mathematical operations in an expression to ensure you get the correct answer. Start with what's inside parentheses or brackets, then work on exponents or orders, multiplication and division (from left to right), and addition and subtraction (from left to right). This sequence ensures consistency and accuracy in solving mathematical problems.

Objective 2: To practice identifying and working with fractions and decimals through a fun and interactive bingo game.

Activity 2:
- Create bingo cards with a 5x5 grid, leaving the center square free for a "free space."
- Write fractions and decimals on the bingo cards, mixing them randomly.
- Prepare a set of fraction and decimal cards for the bingo caller to use.

- Distribute bingo cards and markers to your child and any other participants.
- Start the game by having the bingo caller draw cards from the deck and call out the fractions or decimals. Players should mark the corresponding fractions or decimals on their bingo cards.
- The first player to complete a row, column, or diagonal shouts "Bingo!" and wins the round.
- Discuss the concepts of fractions and decimals as you play, and encourage your child to perform mental calculations when marking their cards.

Objective 3: To practice working with fractions and percentages through a fun basketball-themed activity for one or two participants.

Activity 3:
- Set up the basketball hoop in a suitable location.
- Create a list of math problems related to fractions and percentages. For example, "What is 3/4 as a percentage?" or "Add 1/3 and 1/4."
- Take turns shooting the ball into the hoop. Each time you make a shot, you get to choose a math problem from the list. Solve the problem correctly to earn points (e.g., one point for an easy problem, two points for a moderate one, and three points for difficult problems).
- Keep track of the points on the whiteboard or paper. Play until a certain score is reached or for a set amount of time.
- For just one child, record the score each time they play this activity to compare time.

 # Science for Middle School Students

These science lessons offer hands-on experiences that engage both you and your middle school-aged PP learner in exploring meteorology and physics concepts interactively and enjoyably.

Objective 1: To learn about weather patterns and the importance of weather observation.

Activity 1:
- You will need a weather journal (a notebook or printable templates), a thermometer, a rain gauge (or improvised one), a barometer (or improvised one), and a windsock (or create one using a plastic bag).
- Start by discussing the importance of understanding and predicting weather patterns.
- Set up your weather observation station with the thermometer, rain gauge, barometer, and windsock.
- Each day, go outside together to observe and record the current weather conditions in the weather journal. Note temperature, wind direction, wind speed, cloud cover, and precipitation.
- Over time, discuss the patterns you observe and how changes in weather impact daily life.
- Encourage your child to predict the weather based on their observations.

Objective 2: To introduce the concept of simple machines and their applications through a scavenger hunt.

Activity 2:
- Discuss the following simple machines—inclined plane, lever, pulley, wheel and axle, screw, wedge—and how they make tasks easier.
- Then, search for them in your home, backyard, or community. As you go on the scavenger hunt together, encourage your child to identify and record examples of each type of simple machine they find.
- Discuss how each machine works and its purpose in everyday life.
- After the scavenger hunt, have your child reflect on the importance of simple machines and how they make work more efficient.

 ## Social Studies for Middle School Students

Objective: To learn about archaeology and history by conducting a simulated archaeological excavation.

Activity:
- You will need a sandbox or dirt area, small items (relics or objects from around the house), brushes, containers, and labels.
- Explain the basics of archaeology and its importance in uncovering history.
- Set up a designated "archaeological site" in your backyard or a sandbox. Bury small items (relics) in the soil or sand and create a map or grid for reference.
- Equip your child with brushes and containers for collecting artifacts. Have your child excavate the site, carefully brushing away dirt and collecting artifacts.
- As they find artifacts, discuss their potential historical significance and what they reveal about the past.
- Encourage your child to label and document their findings.
- Conclude by discussing how archaeologists piece together history through artifacts and why preserving historical sites is essential.

HIGH SCHOOL STUDENTS

The high school student is more focused now that they have slightly matured, but they still need to get up and move more often than others. It isn't because they are less studious than other children with other intelligences. Remember that, according to Howard Gardner, children *gain intelligence as they mature and that everyone has a mixture of all of the intelligences* of his theory. They are not only Phenomenal Physicalists but have increased their make-up of the others as they have gotten older.

 **Books for High School Students**

When it comes to reading books, your high schooler is still interested in active and exciting characters. These books offer a mix of genres and themes, from dystopian futures and adventure to coming-of-age stories and real-life survival tales. They should engage your high school-aged PP learner while providing thought-provoking content.

"The Hunger Games" by Suzanne Collins
In a dystopian society, Katniss Everdeen must use her physical and mental strength to survive a televised fight to the death while challenging an oppressive government.

"Ender's Game" by Orson Scott Card
Ender Wiggin, a brilliant young strategist, is recruited to attend a military school in space and prepares to lead humanity in a battle against an alien race.

"Divergent" by Veronica Roth
In a divided future society, Tris Prior must harness her physical and mental abilities to navigate a dangerous initiation process and uncover a world-changing secret.

"The Maze Runner" by James Dashner
Thomas wakes up in a mysterious maze with no memory and must lead a group of other teenagers in solving the puzzle of their existence.

"The Giver" by Lois Lowry
In a seemingly perfect society, Jonas discovers the dark truths hidden behind the facade and embarks on a journey to restore humanity's emotions and memories.

"The Alchemist" by Paulo Coelho
Santiago, a shepherd, embarks on a journey in search of his personal legend, encountering physical and spiritual challenges along the way.

"The Perks of Being a Wallflower" by Stephen Chbosky
Charlie, an introverted high school freshman, navigates the challenges of adolescence, friendships, and mental health in this coming-of-age story.

"Life of Pi" by Yann Martel

> *After surviving a shipwreck, Pi Patel must use his wits and physical resilience to survive on a lifeboat with a Bengal tiger in the middle of the ocean.*

"Into the Wild" by Jon Krakauer

> *This non-fiction account tells the story of Christopher McCandless, a young man who leaves everything behind to explore the wilderness and test his physical and philosophical limits.*

"Unbroken" by Laura Hillenbrand

> *This true story follows Louis Zamperini, an Olympic athlete and World War II soldier, as he endures unimaginable physical and mental challenges while stranded at sea and in Japanese POW camps.*

 ## Reading and Language Arts for High School Students

I remember some of the best times we had as a family were when everyone participated in a project. It sometimes got loud, and sometimes everyone had the giggles, but mostly, everyone in the family became closer and made memories that have lasted a lifetime. That's why I have chosen to highlight a family project that will bring a lot of creativity and fun to everyone in yours. Even the younger children can participate! There are several Shakespearean plays that a high school-aged PP learner might enjoy due to their engaging plots and opportunities for physical and dramatic activities. One such play is "Macbeth."

Objective: To engage in-depth exploration of "Macbeth" by William Shakespeare through reading, analysis, and family-based physical performance.

Summary: "Macbeth" is a tragedy that follows the ambitious Scottish general, Macbeth, who becomes consumed by greed and power after encountering three witches who prophesy his rise to the throne. The play explores themes of ambition, guilt, and the consequences of unchecked ambition. There are several reasons a PP learner might enjoy "Macbeth."

"Macbeth" offers many physically demanding and dramatic scenes, including battles, sword fights, and moments of intense emotion. Performing these scenes can be physically engaging and exciting. The play features complex characters, and your high school-aged child can immerse themselves in the roles, exploring the psychological and emotional aspects of the characters through physical expression. Shakespeare's plays contain rich and memorable speeches and dialogues. Your child can enjoy performing these monologues or scenes, honing their acting and public speaking skills.

Shakespearean plays often allow for creative interpretations regarding set design, costumes, and staging. Your child can actively participate in these aspects, adding their creative touch to the production.

"Macbeth" delves into themes like ambition, morality, and the consequences of one's actions. Engaging in discussions and physical activities related to these themes can deepen understanding.

This comprehensive unit allows your high school-aged bodily-kinesthetic learner or learners, your spouse, and others in the family to join in the immersive learning experience, deepening your understanding of "Macbeth" while fostering creativity and bonding as a family.

Objective 1: Introduction to "Macbeth."

Activity 1:
- Introduce the play, "Macbeth," and its historical context as a family.
- Discuss the importance of Shakespearean drama and its relevance.
- Provide an overview of the plot and characters.

Objective 2: Explore characterization.

Activity 2:
- Begin reading Act 1 of the play as a family. Encourage each family member to explore a character of interest from the play, such as Macbeth, Lady Macbeth, or one of the witches.
- Assign roles for a family reading of the act, allowing each family member to embody their chosen character.

Objective 3: Continue to explore characterization.

Activity 3:
- As a family, select a character from the play and create visual character portraits. This can be done through drawing, collage, or any visual art medium.
- Discuss physical details, expressions, and symbols associated with each character.

Objective 4: Explore theme.

Activity 4:
- Continue reading and discussing key scenes from Act 2 as a family.
- Focus on the development of Macbeth's character and the themes of ambition and guilt.
- Share thoughts and insights in a family journal.

Objective 5: Identify key scenes that promote the theme and characterization.

Activity 5:
- Collaborate to create "tableaux vivants" (frozen scenes) representing key moments from Act 2.
- Physically embody characters and poses to convey the essence of the scenes.
- Present the tableaux to each other, explaining your chosen moments.

Objective 6: Continue to explore theme.

Activity 6:
- Discuss the themes of ambition, power, and fate in "Macbeth" as a family.
- Work together to create posters or visual representations of these themes using physical objects and images.

Objective 7: Identify speech and vocabulary through action and word usage.

Activity 7:
- Explore Shakespearean language and vocabulary together. Analyze specific passages from the play, deciphering the meaning of unfamiliar words or phrases as a team.
- Collaborate to create modern translations or summaries of these passages.

Objective 8: Characterization through words and actions.

Activity 8:
- Assign monologues from the play to each family member. Take turns performing these monologues in front of each other, emphasizing physical expression and emotional depth.

Objective 9: Rewriting "Macbeth" into modern language.

Activity 9:
- As a family, select a scene from "Macbeth" to adapt into a modern setting or context.
- Rewrite the scene collaboratively and perform it with contemporary language and costumes.
- Discuss how the themes remain relevant in today's world as a family.

Objective 10: Interpretation of "Macbeth."

Activity 10:
- Organize a family performance night.
- Each family member selects a scene or monologue to perform.
- Encourage creative interpretations and physical engagement in the performances.

Objective 11: Summary of "Macbeth" to gain insight and growth of human behavior.

Activity 11:
- Reflect on the unit as a family, discussing the impact of physically engaging with the text.
- Analyze how performance enhanced comprehension and emotional connection to the play.
- Share personal insights and growth throughout the unit.

Exploring Shakespeare's works can be a rewarding experience for a PP learner as they bring the text to life through physical engagement and dramatic expression.

 ## Math for High School Students

These math lessons combine physical activities, real-world applications, and interactive learning to engage your high school-aged Phenomenal Physicalist learner in math concepts. They promote a deeper understanding of geometry, statistics, and financial literacy in a hands-on and enjoyable way. These math lessons explore higher levels of thinking for your PP learner while incorporating their need for activity.

Objective 1: To reinforce geometry concepts by physically constructing and measuring angles and polygons.

Activity 1:
- Begin by discussing the basics of angles and polygons.
- Challenge your child to create a set of different polygons (e.g., triangles, quadrilaterals) using large sheets of paper.
- Have them measure and label the angles in each polygon using protractors.
- Encourage them to be creative and explore the properties of various polygons.
- Discuss the relationship between the number of sides and the sum of angles in each polygon. For instance, the sum of the interior angles of a triangle is *always* 180 degrees, the sum of the interior angles of a quadrilateral is *always* 360 degrees, etc.

Objective 2: To apply statistical concepts to sports data and analyze athletic performance.

Activity 2:
- Select a sport or multiple sports that interest your child (e.g., baseball, basketball, soccer).
- Collect statistical data for players or teams in the chosen sport(s).
- Create bar graphs, line graphs, or scatterplots to represent the data visually on graph paper.
- Discuss and analyze trends in the data, such as batting averages, field goal percentages, or goals scored.
- Encourage your child to draw conclusions and make predictions based on the graphs.
- Challenge them to create their own sports-related statistical questions and graphs.

Objective 3: To teach financial literacy and budgeting skills through a hands-on activity.

Activity 3:
- Provide your child with a monthly income (allowance, part-time job earnings) and a list of expenses (e.g., rent, groceries, entertainment).
- Have them create a budget by listing income sources and allocating funds to cover expenses.
- Encourage them to calculate and adjust the budget to ensure that income exceeds expenses.
- Discuss the importance of saving and planning for future financial goals.
- Challenge your child to visually represent their budget, such as a pie chart or bar graph.
- Reflect on the budgeting exercise and discuss strategies for managing finances effectively.

 ## Science for High School Students

Objective: To explore principles of physics, specifically projectile motion, through the construction and launch of a model rocket.

Activity:

- You will need a model rocket kit (including rocket, engines, launch pad), safety goggles, and open outdoor space.
- Introduce the concept of projectile motion and its relevance in rocketry.
- Assemble a model rocket together, following the instructions carefully.
- Discuss the science behind rocket propulsion and aerodynamics.
- Choose a safe outdoor location for rocket launching. Launch the rocket and observe its flight path, acceleration, and descent.
- Discuss the forces at play during the rocket's flight, including thrust, drag, and gravity.
- Encourage your child to make adjustments and launch the rocket multiple times for experimentation. As a culminating activity, watch the movie, "October Sky."

 ## Social Studies for High School Students

Objective: To delve into a specific decade of the past and understand the historical, social, and cultural context.

Activity:

- Choose a particular decade from the past (e.g., the 1960s, 1980s, etc.).
- Research and discuss the significant events, social movements, and cultural phenomena of that decade.
- Encourage the child to read books, watch documentaries, and explore primary sources from that time.
- Have them create a historical time capsule by collecting items, news clippings, and memorabilia that represent the chosen decade.
- Write a reflection on what life might have been like during that time, considering music, fashion, politics, and major historical events.
- Discuss how historical events can shape the present and future.

Conclusion

In the homeschooling journey, one of the most enriching and rewarding experiences has been catering to the needs of our PP learners. As parents, we've delved into the world of education with a desire to make learning an engaging and interactive adventure for our children.

In this chapter, we've explored many strategies and activities that align with the PP child's unique learning style and celebrate the joy of movement and hands-on experiences. We've witnessed the transformation of traditional subjects into lively, dynamic lessons that tap into our child's innate curiosity and physicality.

The essence of homeschooling lies in the freedom to tailor education to each child's unique strengths and preferences. We've embraced this freedom wholeheartedly and harnessed it to create a vibrant learning environment where our PP learners thrive.

As we conclude this chapter on nurturing Phenomenal Physicalist learners, let us reflect on the growth we've witnessed in our children. They've become not just learners but enthusiastic explorers who thrive on the physicality of knowledge acquisition. Their confidence has soared, and their love for learning has blossomed.

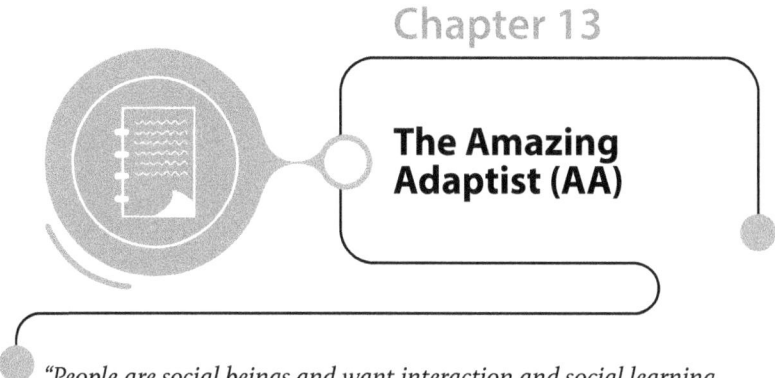

Chapter 13

The Amazing Adaptist (AA)

*"People are social beings and want interaction and social learning
is the primary form of learning, just as word of mouth
advertising is the highest form of advertising."*
—STEPHEN R. COVEY

O f all the children I have taught over the years, the Amazing Adaptist learners were perhaps some of the most fascinating children to observe. They are the charismatic ones who seem to be able to control the rest of the class with just a raised eyebrow. The trick was to make sure they were on *my* side when it came to doing things the others may not like to do. The only time I ever worried was if I had identical interpersonal twins in the same classroom. They each had their own posse of friends, and because of their magnetic draw to the others, they could easily control the whole class! That's why it was imperative to convince the AA learners to go with me; then, everyone else would follow. The trick was never letting them know they were being convinced into *my* way of thinking! The same goes with your own AA child.

We will first delve into the Amazing Adaptist's characteristics, skills, and implications, shedding light on the profound ways they shape our lives and relationships. As you examine the lessons I have designed, you will notice how I weave into their rich tapestry of interpersonal intelligence, using their mind to guide their social and emotional interactions. In the following lessons, your AA's own curiosity will not be able to resist 'what's next!' Get ready to embark on a thought-provoking exploration of the mind and heart, where human connections take center stage.

An AA child, according to Howard Gardner's Theory of Multiple Intelligences, tends to think and engage with the world in ways that emphasize their strengths in interpersonal intelligence. Here are some ways in which an interpersonal child may think and approach various aspects of life:

Highlights:
- Amazing Adaptist children often have a strong ability to empathize with others. They can think from another person's perspective and understand their emotions and feelings.
- These children are highly attuned to social cues and the emotions of those around them. They may intuitively pick up on nonverbal signals and respond accordingly.
- AA children excel in verbal and nonverbal communication. They are skilled at expressing themselves clearly and effectively and may enjoy engaging in conversations and discussions with others.
- They tend to be adept at resolving conflicts and disputes. They can think critically about interpersonal conflicts, find common ground, and facilitate peaceful resolutions.
- AA children thrive in group settings. They enjoy working with others, sharing ideas, and collaborating on projects or activities.
- They have a natural talent for building and maintaining relationships. They may be inclined to make friends easily and connect with people on a deep level.
- AA children are emotionally intelligent and able to recognize and manage their own emotions as well as those of others. They may use this emotional insight to navigate social situations effectively.
- They often rely on their intuitive understanding of people and situations. Their gut feelings and hunches about others' intentions or feelings can be remarkably accurate.
- Amazing Adaptist children may find themselves in leadership roles or positions of influence, as they can inspire and motivate others through their AA skills.
- They may naturally be inclined to teach and mentor others, as they enjoy helping people grow and develop through guidance and support.

Strategies:

Teaching your AA child can be a rewarding experience in a homeschooling environment. Since homeschooling allows you to tailor your child's education to their individual strengths and needs, you can be as flexible as you want and adapt your teaching strategies to align with your child's AA while also addressing other areas of their development. You can help your AA child thrive academically and socially by providing a supportive and nurturing environment. Here are some strategies you can employ to effectively educate and support your child's development:

- **Provide opportunities for your child to engage in social interactions** with peers, siblings, and other individuals. Organize playdates, join homeschooling groups, or participate in community activities to foster social skills and cooperation. When possible, incorporate cooperative learning activities into your curriculum. Group projects, team challenges, and collaborative problem-solving exercises with other family members can help your child develop their teamwork and communication skills.

- **Encourage discussions about emotions and feelings**. Use literature, movies, and real-life situations to help your child understand different perspectives and empathize with others' experiences. Engage in role-playing activities to practice social skills and conflict resolution. Create scenarios that mimic real-life situations, allowing your child to navigate interpersonal challenges in a safe and controlled environment.

- **Teach your child the importance of active listening skills,** including maintaining eye contact, nodding, and asking clarifying questions. These skills will enhance their ability to connect with others on a deeper level. Provide opportunities for your child to work on their verbal and nonverbal communication skills. Encourage them to express themselves clearly and effectively through conversations, presentations, and public speaking exercises.

- **Allow your child to take on leadership roles** in group projects or activities. Leadership experiences can help them build confidence and develop their ability to influence and inspire others positively. Teach your child strategies for resolving conflicts peacefully and constructively. Encourage open communication, active listening, and compromise.

- **Engage your child in volunteer work** or community service projects. These experiences can help them develop a sense of social responsibility and a deeper understanding of the needs of others. Help your child develop self-awareness by encouraging regular self-reflection. Discuss their feelings, experiences, and interactions with others, and guide them in identifying areas for personal growth.

In today's digital age, it's essential to teach your child appropriate online communication and digital etiquette. Discuss the importance of being respectful and responsible when using social media and other online platforms. Instill strong values of honesty, integrity, and empathy in your child. Teach them the importance of using their interpersonal skills for positive and ethical purposes.

THE ELEMENTARY STUDENT

 **Books for Elementary Students**

The following is a list of books that your elementary-aged, Amazing Adaptist child may enjoy reading, either by themselves or with you and others. They offer engaging stories with relatable characters and themes that can resonate with your interpersonal child, promoting empathy, social understanding, and emotional growth while fostering a love for reading.

"Wonder" by R.J. Palacio
Follow the heartwarming journey of Auggie, a boy with a facial deformity, as he navigates the challenges of fitting in and finding true friendship in a world that can be unkind.

"The One and Only Ivan" by Katherine Applegate
Join Ivan, a gentle gorilla, on his quest to protect his animal friends and find a better life outside of the Big Top Mall.

"Matilda" by Roald Dahl
Delve into the magical world of Matilda, a brilliant young girl with tele-kinetic powers, as she outwits her neglectful parents and a tyrannical headmistress.

"Charlotte's Web" by E.B. White
Experience the enduring friendship between Wilbur the pig and Charlotte the spider as they work together to save Wilbur's life.

"The Lemonade War" by Jacqueline Davies
Follow the story of Evan and his younger sister, Jessie, as they engage in a friendly competition to see who can run the best lemonade stand, learning important lessons about sibling bonds and teamwork.

"The Tale of Despereaux" by Kate DiCamillo
Meet Despereaux, a small mouse with big dreams, as he embarks on a heroic quest to rescue a princess and defy the conventions of mouse society.

"Ramona Quimby, Age 8" by Beverly Cleary
Join the adventures of Ramona Quimby, a spirited and imaginative eight-year-old, as she navigates the challenges of growing up and the ups and downs of family life.

"The Penderwicks" by Jeanne Birdsall
Follow the delightful Penderwick sisters as they spend a summer vacation full of adventure and friendship in the beautiful Arundel estate.

"The Miraculous Journey of Edward Tulane" by Kate DiCamillo
Accompany Edward Tulane, a china rabbit, on an extraordinary jour-ney of self-discovery and love as he learns the importance of human connections.

 ## Reading and Language Arts for Elementary School Students

For this elementary literature unit, I've chosen the theme, 'Empathy and Kindness,' and the book "Each Kindness" by Jacqueline Woodson.

Summary: "Each Kindness" tells the story of a young girl named Maya who joins a new school. She is initially ignored and excluded by the other students, including the story's narrator. When the teacher talks about the power of kindness, it prompts the narrator to reflect on her actions and missed opportunities to befriend Maya. The book explores themes of empathy, regret, and the importance of showing kindness to others.

This book is an excellent choice for an Amazing Adaptist child as it encourages discussions about empathy, inclusivity, and the impact of our actions on others. It can help your child develop a deeper understanding of the importance of treating others with kindness and compassion, which aligns well with the AA intelligence trait. It combines reading comprehension, vocabulary development, and creative activities to engage your child in exploring the themes of empathy and kindness found in "Each Kindness."

Objective 1: To develop interpersonal skills of empathy and kindness.

Activity 1:
- Read the book's title and author.
- Discuss the importance of kindness and empathy. Identify and define key vocabulary words from the book, such as "empathy," "regret," and "inclusivity."
- Peruse the book to find other vocabularies you want your child to recognize and understand.

Objective 2: Continue to develop interpersonal skills of empathy and kindness.

Activity 2:
- Read the first part of "Each Kindness" together.
- Pause at key moments and ask comprehension questions, such as, *"How did Maya feel when she first joined the class?"*

- Have your child draw a picture representing an act of kindness they have experienced or witnessed.

Objective 3: To develop key vocabulary from the story.

Activity 3:
- Review the vocabulary words from the first activity from this section.
- Encourage your child to use and write the vocabulary words in sentences.
- Have your child create a short comic strip or storyboard illustrating a kind and empathetic action.

Objective 4: Continue to develop interpersonal skills of empathy and kindness.

Activity 4:
- Complete reading "Each Kindness."
- Engage in a reflective discussion about the story and its themes.
- Challenge your child to perform a random act of kindness for someone in the family or community and share their experience, especially the reaction of others.

Objective 5: Continue to develop vocabulary and the themes of empathy and kindness.

Activity 5:
- Review the vocabulary words again.
- Engage in a culminating activity: Write a thank-you letter to someone in your child's life who has shown them kindness.
- Encourage your child to share their letter and the lessons learned about empathy and kindness from the book.

 # Math for Elementary School Students

These math lessons combine hands-on activities, real-life applications, and creative exploration to engage your AA child in learning math while emphasizing.

Objective 1: Develop a budget around a set amount of money.

Activity 1:
- Give your child a set budget (e.g., $20) and create a shopping list with prices for items.
- Have them practice addition and subtraction while choosing what to purchase, staying within their budget.
- Discuss the importance of making financial decisions and sticking to a budget.

Objective 2: Use building supplies to create structures with given specific attributes.

Activity 2:
- Provide your child with building materials like wooden blocks or LEGO® bricks.
- Challenge them to build structures with specific attributes, such as "Build a tower with ten blocks" or "Create a symmetrical design."
- Encourage them to measure and count the blocks they use.

Objective 3: Record time spent on real-time activities to create graphs.

Activity 3:
- Create a simple graph on paper or using a computer. Have your child list their favorite activities (e.g., reading, playing outside, drawing).
- For a week, record how much time they spend on each activity and create a bar graph to visualize the data.

Objective 4: Use puzzles and logic to develop critical thinking and problem-solving.

Activity 4:
- Introduce your child to Sudoku puzzles or logic puzzles appropriate for their age.
- Work on solving the puzzles together and discussing strategies and patterns.
- Encourage critical thinking and problem-solving skills.

 Science for Elementary School Students

These science lessons incorporate hands-on activities, outdoor exploration, and opportunities for your Amazing Adaptist learner to engage with the natural world and others.

Objective 1: Encourage discussions, questions, and observations to foster a deeper understanding of scientific concepts and promote social interaction.

Activity 1:
- Choose a simple baking experiment, such as making bread or cookies.
- Explore the chemical reactions during baking, like yeast fermentation or the effect of heat on chocolate chips or the cookie dough.
- Document the process and outcomes together, discussing the science behind it.

Objective 2: Develop a recycling and waste reduction station.

Activity 2:
- Teach your child about recycling and waste reduction practices.
- Create a recycling station at home and involve them in sorting recyclables.
- Discuss the environmental impact of recycling and reducing waste.

 Social Studies for Elementary School Students

These social studies lessons provide opportunities for your interpersonal child to connect with others and encourage them to explore diverse cultures, historical events, and community involvement.

Objective 1: Emphasizing communication, collaboration, and a deeper understanding of the world.

Activity 1:
- Encourage your child to interview family members about their life stories and experiences.
- Create a family history timeline or scrapbook, including photos, stories, and mementos.
- Discuss the importance of preserving family traditions and heritage.

Objective 2: Develop the concepts of supply and demand, pricing, budgeting, and profit through entrepreneurial strategies.

Activity 2:
- Help your child start a small business or entrepreneurial project (e.g., lemonade stand, handmade crafts).
- Discuss concepts like supply and demand, pricing, budgeting, and profit.
- Allow them to interact with customers and manage their earnings.

THE MIDDLE SCHOOL STUDENT

 **Books for Middle School Learners**

These books offer a variety of genres and themes, ensuring that your middle school Amazing Adaptist child has several engaging options to choose from for their reading pleasure and personal interests. They offer unique and imaginative stories, encompassing various genres and themes, to captivate the imagination of middle school-aged children. While the books listed above may appeal to a wide range of middle school-aged children, including those with AA intelligence, it's essential to recognize that individual preferences can vary. However, many of these books feature engaging characters, diverse interactions, and themes that can resonate with AA learners. They often explore relationships, teamwork, and the dynamics between characters. To determine which books might best fit your specific interpersonal middle school child, consider their unique interests within the realm of AA intelligence.

"Wonder" by R.J. Palacio
> *Join Auggie Pullman, a boy with a facial deformity, as he navigates the challenges of fitting in and finding true friendship.*

"Bridge to Terabithia" by Katherine Paterson
> *Follow the friendship between Jess and Leslie as they create an imaginary kingdom in the woods, facing both magical and real-world trials.*

"The Outsiders" by S.E. Hinton
> *Delve into the world of Ponyboy and his gang of "Greasers" as they confront class differences and societal expectations in this classic novel.*

"The Chronicles of Narnia" series by C.S. Lewis
> *Step through the wardrobe into the magical land of Narnia, where children embark on epic adventures and confront evil forces.*

"The Westing Game" by Ellen Raskin
> *A diverse group of individuals is brought together to solve the mysterious death of eccentric millionaire Samuel Westing in a thrilling puzzle-filled mystery. *The game of 'Clue' was devised after this book.*

"The Girl Who Drank the Moon" by Kelly Barnhill
> *Explore a world of magic and wonder as a young girl named Luna, raised by a witch, discovers her extraordinary abilities and sets out to uncover her true past.*

"The Inquisitor's Tale: Or, The Three Magical Children and Their Holy Dog" by Adam Gidwitz
> *Journey alongside three unique children with extraordinary abilities in medieval France as they become unlikely heroes and defenders of a sacred book.*

"Escape from Mr. Lemoncello's Library" by Chris Grabenstein
> *Join a group of children as they participate in a library-themed puzzle competition designed by the eccentric game maker, Mr. Lemoncello.*

"The House with Chicken Legs" by Sophie Anderson
> *Journey with Marinka, a young girl with a house that has chicken legs and the power to transport to different places, as she seeks her own destiny.*

"The 13-Story Treehouse" by Andy Griffiths
> *Explore the zany and imaginative world of Andy and Terry, who live in an ever-expanding treehouse filled with absurdities and unexpected adventures.*

 ## Reading and Language Arts for Middle School Students

This unit will guide your child through the novel "Maniac Magee" by Jerry Spinelli, incorporating reading comprehension, language arts, and AA activities. Throughout this unit, engage in meaningful discussions, encourage your child to express their opinions, and provide opportunities for social interaction. It enhances reading and language arts skills and fosters interpersonal intelligence by promoting dialogue, empathy, and collaboration through the shared reading experience.

Summary: "Maniac Magee" is a novel that tells the story of Jeffrey Lionel Magee, a young boy who becomes a legend in the racially divided town of Two Mills. After a tragic family incident, Maniac runs away and embarks on a journey that leads him to Two Mills, where he defies racial boundaries, brings people together, and performs extraordinary feats of athleticism. Maniac's ability to bridge divides and spread kindness makes him a hero and a symbol of hope in a community struggling with prejudice and segregation. The book explores themes of friendship, belonging, and the power of human connection in the face of adversity.

Objective 1: Introduction to Maniac Magee and prediction of what to expect in the book.

Activity 1:
- Discuss the author, setting, and initial impressions. Ask your child to predict the story based on the cover and title.

Objective 2: To create a character analysis of the main character, Maniac Magee.

Activity 2:
- Read the first few chapters of the book together.
- Discuss the main character, Jeffrey "Maniac" Magee, and his unique qualities.
- Have your child create a character profile, including Maniac's traits, actions, and motivations.

Objective 3: To develop vocabulary and figurative language using similes and metaphors.

Activity 3:
- Identify and define vocabulary words from the text.
- Encourage your child to use these words in sentences.
- Explore the use of figurative language (similes, metaphors) in the book.
- Practice identifying and explaining them.

Objective 4: To develop theme and conflict through discussion of the story.

Activity 4:
- Engage in a discussion about the themes and conflicts in the story.
- Ask open-ended questions to encourage critical thinking and perspective-sharing.
- Encourage your child to express their thoughts and opinions about the characters and events.

Objective 5: Develop character analysis by writing in the voice of a chosen character.

Activity 5:
- Have your child write a letter or journal entry from the perspective of one of the characters in the book.
- Organize a "book club" discussion with friends or family members who have also read "Maniac Magee."
- Encourage them to share their thoughts and insights about the story.

Objective 6: Develop the story elements of rising action and climax through key events.

Activity 6:
- Continue reading the book, focusing on significant plot developments.
- Ask your child to identify key events, rising action, and the climax.
- Discuss the impact of these events on the characters and the story.

Objective 7: Write a story analysis and book review of "Maniac Magee."

Activity 7:
- Finish reading "Maniac Magee."
- Have your child write a book review that includes a summary of the plot, their favorite character, and their overall thoughts on the book.
- Encourage them to share their review with family and friends.

 ## Math for Middle School Students

The following math lessons incorporate hands-on activities, problem-solving, teamwork, and discussions to engage your interpersonal middle school child while strengthening their mathematical skills. Tailoring math lessons to their interests and strengths can make learning more enjoyable and meaningful.

Play board games. Board games often require decision-making skills and depend on chance and probability. Others, such as "Monopoly," require making money and dabbling with overspending, risk, buying and selling, and probability outcomes.

Objective 1: Plan a family event using a given budget to work with.

Activity 1:
- Give your child a fictional budget and have them plan a family outing or event.
- Discuss concepts like income, expenses, and making financial decisions.

Objective 2: Use ratio and proportion to cook or bake to adjust the recipe for the amount of servings needed.

Activity 2:
- Choose a favorite recipe and ask your child to scale it up or down to serve a different number of people.
- Encourage them to adjust ingredient quantities and cooking times accordingly using their math skills. For instance, doubling a recipe or scaling it down for just two people.

Objective 3: Develop problem-solving strategies through logic and jigsaw puzzles.

Activity 3:
- Solve logic puzzles, Sudoku, or other brain teasers as a family.
- Encourage discussions about strategies and problem-solving approaches. Spend time constructing a jigsaw puzzle.
- Time your progress.

 ## Science for High School Students

These science investigations offer hands-on learning experiences, encourage problem-solving, and provide opportunities for your middle school child to explore scientific concepts while fostering their AA skills through collaboration and communication. Enjoy the learning journey!

Objective 1: Build a bridge using toothpicks or craft sticks to determine the structure's ability to hold weight.

Activity 1:

- Challenge your child to design and build a bridge using toothpicks or craft sticks.
- Explore the concepts of structure, stability, and weight distribution.
- Test the bridge's strength by gradually adding weight (e.g., coins or small objects) to determine how much it can hold before collapsing.

Objective 2: Explore force, momentum, and impact by constructing a device to keep a raw egg from breaking.

Activity 2:

- Task your child with designing a contraption to protect a raw egg from breaking when dropped from a specific height.
- Discuss concepts related to force, momentum, and impact.
- Conduct controlled drops from different heights and analyze the effectiveness of their designs.

 ## Social Studies for Middle School Students

These social studies projects capitalize on your child's Amazing Adaptist intelligence by involving them in activities requiring interaction, communication, and collaboration. They also provide opportunities for in-depth research, presentation skills, and a deeper understanding of historical and cultural topics.

Objective 1: Create a documentary video of the child's local community.

Activity 1:

- Suggest your child create a documentary or video project focusing on a particular aspect of their local community.
- Guide them to interview community members, such as local leaders, business owners, or residents.
- Have them research the history and development of the community, emphasizing its unique characteristics and contributions.
- Encourage your child to edit the footage and present their documentary to an audience, fostering communication and storytelling skills.

Objective 2: Debate or hold a mock trial related to a significant event from history.

Activity 2:
- Challenge your child to organize a historical debate or mock trial related to a significant event or issue from history.
- Assign roles to participants who will represent different historical figures or viewpoints.
- Encourage research and preparation as they develop arguments and counterarguments.
- Host the debate or trial, inviting grandparents, aunts, uncles, and neighbors to the event, allowing your child to moderate and facilitate discussions, and promoting critical thinking and public speaking skills.

THE HIGH SCHOOL STUDENT

 **Books for High School Students**

The following books I have recommended for high school Amazing Adaptist learners are excellent choices because they tend to feature strong character development, complex relationships, and thought-provoking themes—all of which can resonate with individuals who thrive on social interactions and connections. They foster rich character relationships, explore emotions, have complex themes, the characters are relatable, the narratives are dialogue-driven, and give many opportunities for discussion. Overall, I chose these books for their ability to foster social interaction, empathy, and deep discussions, making them ideal choices for high school interpersonal learners who thrive on interpersonal connections and exploring human relationships and emotions. They offer a mix of contemporary and classic literature, each with its own unique narrative and themes that can resonate with a high school-aged AA learner.

"To Kill a Mockingbird" by Harper Lee
> *This classic novel explores themes of racial injustice, empathy, and compassion as seen through the eyes of a young girl named Scout Finch.*

"The Catcher in the Rye" by J.D. Salinger
> *Follow the adventures of Holden Caulfield, a disenchanted teenager who navigates the complexities of adolescence and adulthood.*

"The Giver" by Lois Lowry
> *Venture into a seemingly utopian society that conceals dark secrets, as Jonas discovers the true cost of conformity and sameness.*

"The Book Thief" by Markus Zusak
> *Set in Nazi Germany, this novel tells the story of Liesel Meminger, a young girl who finds solace in stealing books during a time of turmoil and war.*

"1984" by George Orwell
> *Explore a dystopian future where the government exercises absolute control over citizens' lives and thoughts, raising questions about freedom and surveillance.*

"The Perks of Being a Wallflower" by Stephen Chbosky
> *Dive into the world of Charlie, an introverted high school freshman, as he navigates friendship, mental health, and self-discovery.*

"Brave New World" by Aldous Huxley
> *Explore a world where science and technology have eliminated pain and suffering but also suppressed individuality and freedom.*

"The Road" by Cormac McCarthy
> *Embark on a harrowing journey with a father and son as they navigate a post-apocalyptic world in search of safety and survival.*

"The Absolutely True Diary of a Part-Time Indian" by Sherman Alexie
> *Join Junior, a Native American teenager, as he navigates life on a reservation and explores identity and cultural heritage.*

"One Flew Over the Cuckoo's Nest" by Ken Kesey
Witness the rebellion of patients in a mental institution against an oppressive system, led by the charismatic Randle P. McMurphy.

"The Night Circus" by Erin Morgenstern
Immerse yourself in a magical competition between two young illusionists, Celia and Marco, whose destinies become intertwined in a surreal and enchanting world.

"All the Bright Places" by Jennifer Niven
Follow Violet and Finch's emotional journey as they form an unlikely bond while dealing with personal struggles and discovering the beauty in life's small moments.

"The Alchemist" by Paulo Coelho
Join Santiago, a young shepherd, as he embarks on a quest to discover his personal legend and fulfill his dreams, exploring themes of destiny and self-discovery.

"Eleanor & Park" by Rainbow Rowell
Experience the heartwarming love story of two misfit teenagers, Eleanor and Park, as they navigate the challenges of family, friendship, and first love.

"The Handmaid's Tale" by Margaret Atwood
Enter a dystopian world where women's rights have been stripped away, and follow the story of Offred as she resists oppression and seeks freedom.

"The Secret History" by Donna Tartt
Delve into the dark and mysterious world of a group of classics students at an elite college, where secrets, betrayal, and murder unravel their lives.

 **Reading and Language Arts for High School Students**

<u>**Literature Unit Title: Exploring "The Fault in Our Stars" by John Green**</u>

"The Fault in Our Stars" by John Green is a contemporary young adult novel about Hazel Grace Lancaster, a sixteen-year-old girl living with cancer. Hazel's life takes an unexpected turn when she meets Augustus Waters at a cancer support group. Augustus is a charismatic and charming young man who has also battled cancer.

As Hazel and Augustus spend time together, they form a deep and passionate bond. Their relationship is filled with humor, love, and a shared understanding of the fragility of life. Together, they embark on a journey to meet their favorite author and seek answers to life's big questions.

The novel explores themes of love, mortality, the pursuit of meaning, and the impact of illness on young lives. It is a poignant and emotionally charged story that delves into the complexities of living with a terminal illness while celebrating the power of love and human connection. "The Fault in Our Stars" has touched the hearts of readers around the world and has become a beloved modern classic in young adult literature.

Unit Objectives:
- **Analyze** and interpret complex themes and character development.
- **Develop** critical thinking and literary analysis skills.
- **Strengthen** writing, speaking, and listening skills.
- **Prepare** for college-level discussions and essay writing.

This literature unit plan provides a structured approach to studying "The Fault in Our Stars" while reinforcing critical thinking, writing, and analysis skills needed for college-level language arts. It also encourages discussions and reflections on profound themes, making it a valuable educational experience.

Objective 1: Explore the author's style of John Green and create a vocabulary list.

Activity 1:
- Read the first few chapters of "The Fault in Our Stars."
- Discuss the author, John Green, his style, and the context in which the book was written.
- Begin building a vocabulary list from the text. Add to the list as you find more words, making sure you understand the meaning of each.

Objective 2: Begin character analysis of Hazel and Gus while analyzing the various themes presented in the story.

Activity 2:
- Explore the main characters, Hazel and Gus, and their development throughout the novel.
- Analyze the novel's themes, including love, loss, mortality, and the pursuit of meaning.
- Discuss how the characters' personalities and actions reflect these themes.

Objective 3: Explore the literary elements of symbolism, foreshadowing, and irony.

Activity 3:
- Discuss the book's literary elements, such as symbolism, foreshadowing, and irony.
- Encourage critical thinking and close reading through discussions and journal entries.
- Present and defend their interpretations of key passages.

Objective 4: Write a literary essay of the book focusing on theme and characterization.

Activity 4:
- Teach essay writing skills, including thesis development, evidence selection, and proper citation.
- Instruct how to structure a literary analysis essay.
- Assign a literary analysis essay focusing on a theme, character, or element from the novel.

Objective 5: Review and edit the essay from Objective 4 above.

Activity 5:
- Have someone else in the family review the essay and provide constructive feedback.
- Encourage revisions based on feedback.
- Discuss the importance of revision and editing in the writing process.

Objective 6: Create a final project of the child's choice to emphasize the broader implications of real-life issues.

Activity 6:
- Let your child choose a final project, like creating a book trailer, writing a character's diary, or composing a creative response to the novel.
- Discuss the novel's broader implications and connections to real-life issues.
- Reflect on the unit's objectives and the college-level skills developed throughout.
- Explore related poetry and literature to enhance understanding of themes. Compare and contrast the novel with its film adaptation.

 **Math for High School Students**

These math lessons are designed to provide your high school Amazing Adaptist learner with practical math skills and knowledge that can be applied to real-life situations, from personal finance to home improvement and decision-making. They emphasize the relevance of mathematics in everyday contexts while accommodating your child's interests and educational goals.

Objective 1: Create a monthly budget that reflects savings, investing, and spending.

Activity 1:

- Introduce budgeting principles and the importance of financial planning.
- Teach your child how to create a monthly budget, track expenses, and set financial goals.
- Discuss topics such as saving, investing, and managing debt.

Objective 2: Use real-world data to analyze and interpret data using mean, median, and mode.

Activity 2:

- Explore the basics of statistics, including mean, median, and mode.
- Use real-world data sets to analyze and interpret data.
- Discuss the relevance of statistics in everyday life, from sports to marketing.

 ## Science for Middle School Students

These science lessons incorporate hands-on experiments, interactive activities, and discussions to make learning engaging and enjoyable for your high school AA learner. They cover a wide range of science topics and provide opportunities for exploration, experimentation, and real-world application.

Objective 1: Create a model of the human body that includes structure and organ systems.

Activity 1:

- Explore human anatomy and physiology by creating a model of the human body using household materials.
- Learn about organ systems, their functions, and how they work together.
- Discuss the importance of a healthy lifestyle for overall well-being.

Objective 2: Explore the behavior of light and lenses using various prisms.

Activity 2:

- Explore the behavior of light and lenses through experiments with prisms, mirrors, and lenses. Learn about reflection, refraction, and how lenses affect the path of light.
- Discuss the applications of optics in technology and science.

 ## Social Studies for High School Students

These social studies lessons offer unique and interactive opportunities for your high school AA learner to explore diverse cultures, engage with global perspectives, and make real-world connections. They emphasize communication, empathy, and a deeper understanding of the world.

Objective 1: Create a family tree that reflects the family's cultural heritage and traditions.

Activity 1:

- Explore your family's history and genealogy.
- Create a family tree and gather stories and anecdotes from relatives. Investigate your family's cultural heritage and traditions.
- Reflect on how your family's history has shaped your identity and values.

Objective 2: Explore food from history to discover cultural significances; prepare a family meal using recipes from history; create a cookbook from researched recipes.

Activity 2:

- Explore history through the lens of food and cuisine.
- Research the historical context of dishes from different time periods or regions.
- Cook and taste historical recipes, discussing their cultural significance and evolution.
- Serve them for a family meal.
- Create a cookbook or culinary presentation featuring the researched recipes.

Conclusion

In this chapter, we've explored the unique qualities and needs of the AA child, emphasizing their ability to connect deeply with others and thrive in social environments. For parents, it's essential to create environments that allow these individuals to flourish.

From tailored literature units to hands-on math lessons, we've seen how education can captivate interpersonal learners. Engaging in science investigations and social studies projects fosters empathy and appreciation for diversity.

Nurturing the Amazing Adaptist child involves recognizing their gifts and empowering them to utilize their talents fully. This journey celebrates connections, empathy, and the beauty of human relationships. These individuals have the potential to make a lasting impact rooted in collaboration and a profound understanding of the human experience.

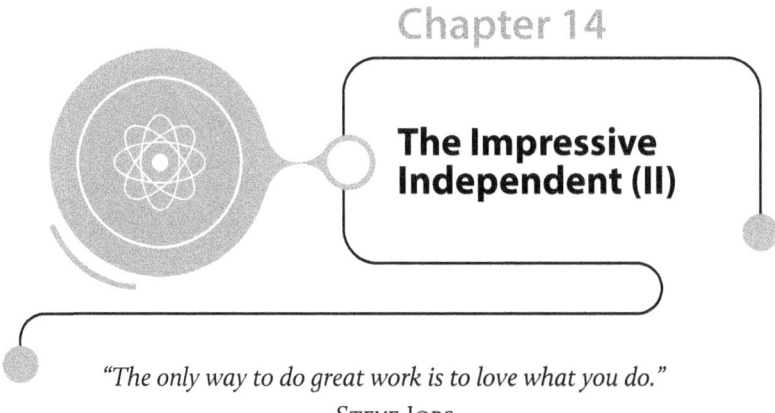

Chapter 14

The Impressive Independent (II)

"The only way to do great work is to love what you do."
—STEVE JOBS

Impressive Independent children are probably the least understood people in the world–until you learn what makes them 'tick.' Their unique ability to navigate the intricate landscapes of their inner thoughts and emotions can be a source of strength and wisdom. As parents, educators, and family members, taking the time to appreciate and nurture their introspective nature can open the door to a deeper understanding of their rich inner worlds, fostering a sense of self-acceptance and encouraging them to shine in their own distinctive ways. With patience, empathy, and support, II children can flourish, sharing their unique insights and gifts with those who take the time to understand and connect with them truly.

Let me introduce you to "Barry." Barry looked like every other third grader, but he didn't act like every other third grader. From the moment he walked into the classroom, it was clear that Barry possessed a remarkable sense of self-awareness and an innate curiosity about the world within him. While his peers often chatted and played together, Barry could often be found quietly absorbed in his own thoughts. I guess he could have been described as 'an old soul,' someone who is described as an individual who seems to possess wisdom, maturity, and a deep understanding of life beyond their years.

Barry had a way of observing the classroom dynamics and his classmates' emotions with an uncanny sensitivity. He could sense when a friend was upset, even if they hadn't uttered a word. His ability to empathize and offer solace made him a trusted confidant among his peers.

While he participated willingly in group activities, he would rather work independently, taking the time to explore his own ideas and solutions. His introspective nature allowed him to see connections and patterns that others might have missed, often leading to innovative solutions to problems. When he participated in discussions, he often offered ideas that the other children would not have thought about, such as adding a parachute to the rocket to allow it to slow its descent, keeping it from crashing and allowing it to travel farther.

Barry's love for reading was apparent. Books were not just a source of entertainment for him; they were windows into different worlds, allowing him to delve even deeper into his thoughts and emotions. He found solace in the pages of books, and his book choices often reflected his desire to understand the human experience from various angles.

I encountered many Impressive Independents during the many years I taught in public schools. Homeschooling II children is a great way to keep them involved in their education because they flourish in a quiet setting, unlike a classroom where collaboration and cooperative learning are the norm, not the exception.

Impressive Independent intelligence refers to a person's ability to understand and effectively manage their own thoughts, feelings, and behaviors. Here are some characteristics associated with individuals with strong Impressive Independent intelligence.

Highlights:

- People with II have a deep understanding of themselves. They are in tune with their emotions, values, beliefs, and strengths and weaknesses.
- They are skilled at introspection and regularly reflect on their thoughts and feelings. They often engage in self-examination and contemplation to gain insight into their own lives.
- Individuals who are II learners tend to have high emotional intelligence. They can identify, label, and regulate their emotions effectively. They are also empathetic and understanding of the emotions of others.
- They are typically self-motivated and have a strong sense of purpose and inner drive. They set personal goals and work diligently to achieve them.
- Impressive Independents are often independent thinkers and do not rely heavily on external validation or guidance. They trust their own judgment and intuition.
- They have well-defined values and beliefs that guide their decisions and actions. They are often principled and clearly understand what is important to them.
- They can control their impulses and emotions, which helps them make rational decisions and stay focused on their goals.
- IIs are skilled at setting realistic and achievable goals for themselves. They have a clear sense of where they want to go in life.
- They are committed to personal growth and self-improvement. They are open to learning from their experiences and are willing to adapt and change as needed.
- They often value and seek out moments of solitude and quiet reflection, as it allows them to connect with their inner thoughts and emotions.

Strategies:

Teaching an intrapersonal child at home can be a rewarding experience, as you have the flexibility to tailor your approach to their unique learning style. Here are some strategies to consider when homeschooling an intrapersonal child:

- **Encourage your child to journal** or keep a diary to help them reflect on their thoughts and feelings. Provide opportunities for them to discuss and analyze their thoughts with you, helping them better understand their own thinking processes. Involve your child in setting their own learning goals and objectives. This can help them feel more in control of their education. Break larger goals into smaller, manageable tasks, allowing your child to track their progress and celebrate achievements.

- **Designate a peaceful and quiet space** for your child to study and reflect. Minimize distractions in this space. Consider using tools like noise-canceling headphones if there are external distractions.

- **Provide resources** and materials that cater to your child's interests and passions, allowing them to pursue topics they are passionate about independently. Encourage self-directed research and exploration and give them the autonomy to choose their own learning materials. Give your child choices in their daily learning activities. This helps them feel a sense of control and ownership over their education. Allow them to choose the order in which they tackle subjects or projects.

- **Utilize online resources** and educational platforms that align with your child's interests and learning style. Interactive, self-paced online courses and educational games can be effective for intrapersonal learners. Support your child in pursuing long-term personal projects or hobbies that interest them. These projects can provide valuable learning experiences. Allow them to set their own goals and timelines for these projects.

- **Motivate** your child to question and analyze information critically. Teach them how to evaluate sources and form their own opinions. Engage in discussions and debates to stimulate their intellectual growth. Schedule regular periods for your child to engage in self-reflection and introspection. This can be done through activities like mindfulness exercises or meditation.

While II learners often value solitude, it's important to strike a balance by providing opportunities for social interaction with peers through homeschooling groups, clubs, or extracurricular activities. Be flexible and adapt your homeschooling approach based on your child's changing needs and interests. Be open to modifying your curriculum and methods as necessary.

 ## Books for Elementary Students

The following list of books is a great library for your elementary-aged Impressive Independent child. Since they are self-motivated, they tend to read higher-level reading material at a younger age. I've listed more books than usual because of the independence of II children and their love of books.

"Brown Bear, Brown Bear, What Do You See?" by Bill Martin Jr. and Eric Carle
A classic with repetitive text and vibrant illustrations, perfect for early readers.

"The Very Hungry Caterpillar" by Eric Carle
A beautifully illustrated book that introduces days of the week and numbers.

"Frog and Toad Are Friends" by Arnold Lobel
Follow the adventures of two best friends, Frog and Toad, in these heartwarming stories.

"Pete the Cat" series by James Dean and Eric Litwin
The series combines repetitive phrases and catchy tunes, making it accessible and enjoyable for young readers.

"Elephant and Piggie" series by Mo Willems
Humorous and relatable stories featuring Elephant and Piggie, with simple text and expressive illustrations.

"If You Give a Mouse a Cookie" by Laura Numeroff
A delightful story about cause and effect with engaging text.

"Llama Llama" series by Anna Dewdney
> *These books address common childhood experiences with easy-to-read text.*

"Corduroy" by Don Freeman
> *Follow the adventures of Corduroy, a lovable teddy bear, in this classic tale.*

"Little Bear" series by Else Holmelund Minarik
> *Simple and gentle stories about Little Bear's adventures.*

"Fancy Nancy" series by Jane O'Connor
> *Join Nancy, a young girl with a vivid imagination, in her fancy adventures.*

"Magic Tree House" series by Mary Pope Osborne
> *These books take young readers on exciting adventures through time and around the world.*

"Amelia Bedelia" series by Peggy Parish
> *Follow the hilarious misadventures of Amelia Bedelia with fun wordplay.*

"Junie B. Jones" series by Barbara Park
Join the spirited Junie B. Jones in her humorous escapades.

"Stellaluna" by Janell Cannon
> *A heartwarming tale of a baby fruit bat named Stellaluna who learns about friendship, identity, and acceptance while navigating the world of birds.*

"Ramona Quimby" series by Beverly Cleary
> *Join Ramona in her relatable and humorous everyday adventures.*

"Charlotte's Web" by E.B. White
> *A timeless classic about the friendship between a pig named Wilbur and a spider named Charlotte.*

"The Boxcar Children" series by Gertrude Chandler Warner
> *Follow the adventures of the resourceful Alden siblings.*

"The BFG" by Roald Dahl
A delightful story about the Big Friendly Giant and his young friend Sophie.

"The Wind in the Willows" by Kenneth Grahame
Join the adventures of Mole, Rat, Toad, and Badger in the English countryside in this timeless classic.

"The Neverending Story" by Michael Ende
Dive into the enchanting world of Fantastica through the eyes of Bastian, a boy who becomes part of the story.

"The Secret of the Old Clock" (Nancy Drew Mysteries) by Carolyn Keene
The first book in the classic Nancy Drew series, This mystery novel features a young detective who solves puzzles and uncovers secrets.

"The Mouse and the Motorcycle" by Beverly Cleary
Join Ralph, a mouse with a love for adventure, as he embarks on thrilling escapades using a miniature motorcycle.

"The Mysterious Benedict Society" by Trenton Lee Stewart
This book follows four gifted children who form a secret society to thwart a mysterious plot to take over the world.

"The Miraculous Journey of Edward Tulane" by Kate DiCamillo
Follow the journey of Edward Tulane, a porcelain rabbit, as he learns about love, loss, and self-discovery.

"The One and Only Ivan" by Katherine Applegate
Told from the perspective of a captive gorilla named Ivan, this book delves into themes of friendship, freedom, and self-awareness.

"Anne of Green Gables" by L.M. Montgomery
The story of Anne Shirley, an imaginative and introspective orphan who comes to live with an elderly couple, is a tale of self-discovery and the joys of nature.

 **Reading and Language Arts for Elementary Students**

I have chosen "Flat Stanley" by Jeff Brown for a reading unit with the theme, 'Flat Stanley—World Explorer.' This unit is different from other units in this book because it is an all-inclusive unit that takes more time to complete. Some parts of this unit cannot be completed until Stanley is returned to you from wherever your child mailed him.

Summary: "Flat Stanley" tells the story of Stanley Lambchop, an ordinary boy who becomes extraordinary when a bulletin board falls on him during the night, flattening him to the width of a sheet of paper. Embracing his newfound flatness, Stanley embarks on a series of whimsical adventures, sliding under doors, flying like a kite, and even mailing himself to far-off destinations. Along the way, he learns that being different can be a source of fun and excitement. With humor and heart, "Flat Stanley" encourages readers to embrace their unique qualities and imaginations, making it a timeless classic that captivates young minds and sparks their creativity.

Objective: Learn about other regions of the world by writing a letter to a friend or relative for the purpose of sharing a time period of their life with "Flat Stanley" using pictures and anecdotes.

Activities:
- Read the book "Flat Stanley" by Jeff Brown with your child. Discuss the main character, Stanley Lambchop, and his unique adventure after becoming flat. Explore key vocabulary words related to the story, such as "adventure," "flat," "envelope," "journey," and "destination."
- Have your child create their own "Flat Stanley" character by drawing and coloring a picture of themselves or a fictional character. You can use plain paper, print a template, or trace Stanley from the book. Encourage your child to think about the details of their character's appearance and personality.
- Teach your child the mechanics of writing a friendly letter and addressing an envelope. Help your child write a letter from their "Flat Stanley"

character, introducing themselves and explaining their flattened state. Encourage the use of descriptive language, proper grammar, and a friendly tone in the letter.

- Think of a friend or relative in another state, country, or region of the world to send this letter. Ask that person to take 'Stanley' with them wherever they go, including adventures, work, shopping, or entertainment, like movies, concerts, and ball games. Take pictures with their phone to show where Stanley has been, including Stanley in each. At the end of a week, ask the person to please send Stanley back to you with a letter describing where Stanley has gone with them, using a blank flash drive that you included in your original letter to this person.
- While waiting for Stanley to return to you, select a few vocabulary words from the story and have your child create sentences using these words. Encourage them to write sentences that describe their "Flat Stanley" character's adventure or personality.
- Ask your child to write a short adventure story for their "Flat Stanley" character. This story should describe their journey to another specific destination. Focus on storytelling elements like a beginning, middle, and end. Incorporate descriptive language and dialogue to make the story engaging.
- When Stanley returns to you, use a poster board to place the letter, messages, and pictures your friend included. Then, share Stanley's adventures with other family members. Leave it in a prominent spot so that when visitors come to the house, you can share Stanley's adventures with them.
- Make sure you write a thank you letter to your friend who took great care of Stanley while visiting them.

Finally, discuss the entire "Flat Stanley'" project with your child, including what they learned and enjoyed most. Reflect on how writing, vocabulary, grammar, geography, and communication skills were integrated into the project. The Flat Stanley project provides an excellent opportunity to enhance reading, writing, vocabulary, and grammar skills while engaging in a fun and interactive adventure with "Flat Stanley'" as the central character.

 **Math for Elementary School Students**

The following math activities are extensions of the Flat Stanley project from above and can be included in this unit. Since this is an all-inclusive unit over a specific period of time, this unit can be completed in separate chunks of time instead of a day-to-day lesson plan.

Objective 1: Explore linear measurement using customary metric units of measure.

Activity 1:
- Have your child measure the height of their Flat Stanley character before sending it on its adventure.
- Ask the recipient to measure Flat Stanley's height when he arrives.
- Compare the two measurements and calculate the difference. This can be a fun way to introduce basic subtraction.

Objective 2: Create a budget for Flat Stanley while on his adventure.

Activity 2:
- Assign a fictional budget to Flat Stanley's adventures.
- Determine how much "money" Flat Stanley has for each trip.
- Research the costs of transportation, accommodation, and activities at each destination.
- Have your child calculate and keep a running total of expenses, practicing addition and subtraction.

Objective 3: Identify geometric shapes from Flat Stanley's adventures.

Activity 3:
- While Flat Stanley is on his adventures, encourage your child to look for and identify different geometric shapes in the environment.
- Create a "shape log" or journal where your child can sketch and label the shapes they encounter, such as rectangles, circles, and triangles.

Objective 4: Explore time zones around the world.

Activity 4:
- If Flat Stanley travels to locations with different time zones, discuss the concept of time differences.
- Use a world map to show the time zones and calculate the time difference between the locations.
- Practice telling time in both the home and destination time zones.

Objective 5: Explore map scale for distance; design graphs; practice rounding skills.

Activity 5:
- Research the distance between your home and that location for each destination Flat Stanley visits.
- Use a map or an online mapping tool to measure and calculate the distances.
- Encourage your child to record the distances in both miles and kilometers. Graph the distance on graph paper both in miles and kilometers.
- Use rounding skills to make it approximate miles or kilometers.

 ## Science for Elementary School Students

Objective: To incorporate weather and ecosystems into the Flat Stanley project in the area he is visiting.

Activities:
- Keep track of the weather at each destination Flat Stanley visits.
- Record temperature data in Fahrenheit and Celsius and create a weather log.
- Make a line graph to show how the temperature changes from day to day.
- Research the ecosystems that are in the area where Stanley is visiting and include pictures of animals and plants that Stanley might encounter.
- Compare and contrast the temperatures and weather conditions in different locations.

 **Social Studies for Elementary School Students**

Objective: To incorporate geography and maps into the Flat Stanley project.

Activities:
- Explore geography concepts by discussing the location of your home on a map. Introduce terms like "city," "state," "country," and "continent."
- Have your child mark the location of their home on a map.
- Find where you sent Stanley on a map.
- Research all the uniqueness of where Stanley is visiting and write a report on that area to include in this project.

MIDDLE SCHOOL STUDENTS

As middle school parents, we witness our children's growth, not just academically but as unique individuals with distinct thinking and learning styles. Some students in this transformative phase demonstrate exceptional self-awareness and independence, showcasing 'Impressive Independent intelligence.' These students are fine-tuning their understanding of their inner selves and forging deep connections with their thoughts and emotions. Their ability to self-guide and navigate personal journeys with purpose sets them apart. As homeschooling parents, our role extends beyond academics; we have the privilege of nurturing environments where our middle schoolers can harness their II intelligence, fostering self-motivation, self-reflection, and decision-making skills. In addressing the needs of these students, we'll explore empowering strategies to create a space where they can truly thrive as students and individuals.

 **Books for Middle School Learners**

Since the Impressive Independent child loves to read, especially about exploring human characteristics and emotional needs, I recommend the following books to have on hand for your child. These books offer a range of genres and themes that can captivate middle school students, fostering their love for reading and self-discovery.

"Peak" by Roland Smith
> *This thrilling novel follows a teen climber as he attempts to conquer Mount Everest, blending adventure, survival, and self-discovery.*

"The Outsiders" by S.E. Hinton
> *Explore themes of identity and class struggle through the eyes of Ponyboy and his friends in this classic novel.*

"The 57 Bus" by Dashka Slater
> *Based on a true story, this book explores themes of identity, empathy, and justice as it follows the lives of two teenagers from different backgrounds.*

"I Am Malala: The Girl Who Stood Up for Education and Was Shot by the Taliban" by Malala Yousafzai
> *A powerful memoir of a young girl's fight for education and her unwavering determination to make a difference.*

"The Miscalculations of Lightning Girl" by Stacy McAnulty
> *Follow Lucy, a math genius with obsessive-compulsive disorder, as she navigates middle school while grappling with her unique talents.*

"The House of Scorpion" by Nancy Farmer
> *Set in a dystopian future, this novel explores themes of identity and ethics through the life of Matteo Alacrán, a young clone.*

"Ungifted" by Gordon Korman
> *When a prank gone wrong places Donovan Curtis in a gifted program, he discovers the power of unconventional thinking and unique talents.*

"The Thing About Jellyfish" by Ali Benjamin
> *After her friend's death, Suzy sets out on a quest to prove that a rare jellyfish sting caused it, examining grief and self-discovery along the way.*

"The Terrible Two" by Mac Barnett and Jory John
> *A hilarious tale of pranks and wit as two middle school students engage in a prank war that turns into an unexpected friendship.*

"Refugee" by Alan Gratz
> *This historical novel weaves together the stories of three refugees from different time periods and backgrounds, offering a unique perspective on the refugee experience.*

"The Name of this Book Is Secret" by Pseudonymous Bosch
> *A mysterious adventure involving secret societies, codes, and puzzles that draws readers into an enigmatic world of intrigue.*

"Fish in a Tree" by Lynda Mullaly Hunt
> *Follow the journey of Ally, a dyslexic middle school student, as she learns to embrace her unique learning style and discovers her strengths.*

"Serafina and the Black Cloak" by Robert Beatty
> *In this historical mystery, Serafina, a young girl who secretly lives in the basement of the Biltmore Estate, must solve a series of dark mysteries.*

"The Girl Who Could Silence the Wind" by Meg Medina
> *Set in a magical-realism world, this novel tells the story of Sonia, a girl with the power to predict death, as she embarks on a journey to save her village.*

"The Nest" by Kenneth Oppel
> *A unique and eerie story about a boy named Steve who believes a wasp's nest will help his baby brother, leading to unexpected consequences.*

"The Evolution of Calpurnia Tate" by Jacqueline Kelly
> *Set in the early 1900s, this novel follows Calpurnia Tate as she explores her love for science, nature, and the world around her.*

"The Night Diary" by Veera Hiranandani
> *Told through the diary of Nisha, a young girl during the partition of India, this book offers a unique perspective on history and identity.*

"The Penderwicks: A Summer Tale of Four Sisters, Two Rabbits, and a Very Interesting Boy" by Jeanne Birdsall

> *Follow the adventures of the Penderwick sisters during their summer vacation, filled with humor and heart.*

"The Dreamer" by Pam Muñoz Ryan

> *This novel explores the life of Pablo Neruda, the Nobel Prize-winning poet, through the eyes of a young boy with a unique gift for words.*

 ## Reading and Language Arts for Middle School Students

I created this language arts unit based on "Island of the Blue Dolphins" by Scott O'Dell. It will engage your Impressive Independent child's interests in survival and self-reliance. Below, I've outlined the unit, which incorporates various reading and writing skills, as well as vocabulary practice, centered around the book's themes. Overall, this unit combines reading, writing, critical thinking, and research skills while nurturing independence and self-reflection—all of which are valuable preparations for the academic demands of high school. As you continue to adapt and expand your child's curriculum, consider incorporating a variety of literary genres and texts to broaden their reading and analytical capabilities further.

Unit Theme: Survival and Self-Reliance

Objective: To develop reading comprehension, critical thinking, and writing skills while exploring the theme of survival through the novel "Island of the Blue Dolphins."

Pre-Reading Activities:
Begin with a discussion about survival skills and what it means to be self-reliant. Introduce the book, its author, and the story's historical context.
Set reading goals and expectations.

Objective 1: To gain an understanding of survival when faced with the challenges of being alone; to gain empathy for the natural world.

Activity 1:

- Read the novel together, either aloud or independently, depending on your child's reading level.
- Encourage your child to take notes or create a reading journal to record their thoughts, questions, and reflections as they progress through the story.

Objective 2: To gain vocabulary related to survival; to understand meaning through context clues and dictionary skills.

Activity 2:

- Identify and discuss key vocabulary related to survival, island life, and Native American culture.
- Use context clues and dictionary skills.
- Create a vocabulary notebook with definitions, sentences, and illustrations.

Objective 3: To create a character analysis of the main character, Karana.

Activity 3:

- Explore the main character, Karana (also known as Won-a-pa-lei), and her journey towards self-reliance.
- Discuss character traits, motivations, and how she evolves throughout the story.
- Encourage your child to keep a character journal to track Karana's development.

Objective 4: To gain writing fluency through the use of journal entries, persuasive essays, book reviews, and letters.

Activity 4:

- Creative Writing: Have your child write journal entries or letters from Karana's perspective, describing her daily life, challenges, and feelings.
- Persuasive Writing: Ask your child to write a persuasive essay on the importance of self-reliance and survival skills.

- Book Review: After completing the novel, guide your child in writing a book review, discussing their thoughts on the story, characters, and themes.

Objective 5: Promote critical thinking skills through discussion of themes and open-ended questions.

Activity 5:
- Engage in discussions about the themes of isolation, resilience, and cultural preservation presented in the book.
- Encourage your child to ask and answer open-ended questions that promote critical thinking.

Objective 6: Create a survival guide written by Karana to pass on to others who might get stranded on an island.

Activity 6:
- Create a survival guide: Have your child develop a "Survival Guide for Island Life" based on lessons learned from the novel. This can include tips, illustrations, and explanations.
- Present their survival guide to you or a small group, explaining the importance of each skill.

Extension Activities:
- Watch a documentary or video about Native American culture or survival skills and compare them to the book.
- Research the real-life story of the Lone Woman of San Nicolas Island, upon whom Karana's character is based.
- Watch the movie, "Island of the Blue Dolphin," and compare and contrast the movie to the book.

By structuring the unit this way, you can provide your Impressive Independent child with a comprehensive and engaging language arts experience while exploring the themes of survival and self-reliance in "Island of the Blue Dolphins." Tailor the activities to your child's interests and abilities to make the learning experience more enjoyable and meaningful.

 **Math for Middle School Students**

The Impressive Independent middle schooler is more concerned with getting to the point on how to do certain processes. They do not need a lot of flash and flair. Therefore, I've designed these lessons to show the steps of teaching these concepts. It is up to you to review the processes either from math textbooks or online videos. There are tons of websites with the information you need to arm yourself with! These lessons cover a range of middle school math topics and provide opportunities for your child to practice, apply, and understand each concept independently while receiving guidance as needed.

Objective 1: To understand the relationship between fractions and percents.

Activity 1:
- Discuss why understanding fractions and percents is essential in real-life situations, such as discounts or interest rates.
- Explain how to convert fractions to percents and vice versa, but teach those processes separately. For example, show how to convert 1/4 to 25%. Provide several fractions for your child to convert into percentages. Start with simple fractions like 1/2 and progress to more complex ones.
- Discuss real-world scenarios where knowing fractions as percentages is useful, such as calculating discounts or tips.
- Encourage your child to create their own fraction-to-percent conversion problems for you to solve.

Objective 2: To understand and calculate measures of central tendency.

Activity 2:
- Start with a discussion about why understanding measures of central tendency is important in data analysis and interpretation.
- Introduce the concepts of mean (average), median (middle value), and mode (most frequent value) using a simple data set.
- Provide your child with data sets and ask them to independently calculate the mean, median, and mode.

- Discuss scenarios where each measure is most useful. For example, the mean for finding the average test score, the median for determining a fair middle price, and the mode for identifying the most common color in a survey.
- Encourage your child to create their own data sets and calculate these measures.

Objective 3: To introduce the concept of probability.

Activity 3:
- Begin with a discussion about why understanding probability is important in decision-making and games of chance.
- Introduce the concept of probability as the likelihood of an event happening. Use examples like coin tosses (heads or tails) or rolling a dice (1 to 6).
- Demonstrate how to calculate probability by using the number of favorable outcomes divided by the total possible outcomes.
- Provide scenarios or experiments (e.g., rolling dice, flipping coins) for your child to calculate probabilities independently.
- Discuss real-life examples where probability plays a role, such as weather forecasts or sports outcomes.
- Encourage your child to create their own probability experiments and calculate probabilities.

 ## Science for Middle School Students

The following science project will fill the needs of the Impressive Independent child to use their own discovery and intuition and to work independently. Remember, when your II child needs help, they will not hesitate to ask you.

Objective: To understand the water cycle and natural water filtration.

Activity:
- Begin by exploring the earth's water cycle and hone in on groundwater and how wells are formed.

- Explore the earth's natural water filtration system and why well water is safe to drink.
- Then, set up an experiment to purify dirty water. Have your child design a filtration system using materials like sand, gravel, and cotton.
- Test the effectiveness of the filtration system by passing contaminated water through it and measuring the clarity of the filtered water.
- Allow your child to use other materials as they think of them, such as charcoal or coffee filters.
- Research other ways people get safe drinking water in other parts of the world, such as desalination plants.

 Social Studies for Middle School Students

An enigma is a mystery or puzzle, often characterized by something that is difficult to understand, explain, or solve. Enigmas can manifest in various forms, such as unsolved mysteries, riddles, perplexing situations, or complex and cryptic challenges that require careful thought and investigation to unravel. Enigmas often spark curiosity and intrigue because they defy easy explanations, inviting people to explore and decipher the hidden meanings or solutions behind them. A social studies unit focused on enigmas can be a fascinating and intellectually stimulating experience for your middle school II child. This unit will encourage critical thinking, research skills, and exploration of historical and contemporary mysteries.

Objective: To explore historical and contemporary enigmas, encouraging critical thinking and research skills.

*You will need books, internet access, research tools, notebooks, presentation materials, and the list of enigmas below.

Activity:
- Discuss what an enigma is and why they are intriguing.
- Encourage your child to choose one enigma that interests them the most. Instruct your child to research the chosen enigma using both books and online resources.

- Have them create a research journal where they document key information, theories, and sources.
- Explore the historical context of the enigma, if applicable. Dive deeper into the various theories and explanations surrounding the chosen enigma.
- Encourage critical thinking by evaluating the credibility and evidence behind each theory. Have your child identify the most plausible theories.
- Instruct your child to organize their research and findings into a well-structured presentation. Emphasize the importance of clear communication and storytelling. Allow them to choose a format that suits their style (e.g., oral presentation, multimedia presentation, or written report).
- Have your child present their findings to the family, explaining the enigma, its historical context, theories, and conclusions.
- Encourage family members to ask questions and engage in discussions about the enigma.
- Explore the significance of enigmas in history and contemporary culture.

Conclude the unit with a reflection activity where your child discusses what they've learned, what fascinated them most, and whether they believe there are satisfactory explanations for the enigma they studied. Encourage them to consider future exploration of enigmas or mysteries that pique their interest.

This "Enigmas of the World" unit allows your middle school intrapersonal child to explore their intellectual curiosity while honing research, presentation, and critical thinking skills. It also allows one to delve into history and cultural mysteries, fostering a deeper understanding of the world's enigmatic phenomena. Here is a list of some famous historical and contemporary enigmas and mysteries from around the world:

- **Voynich Manuscript:** An ancient, undecipherable book filled with strange illustrations and an unknown script.
- **Bermuda Triangle:** An area in the western North Atlantic Ocean known for the unexplained disappearances of ships and aircraft.
- **Nazca Lines:** Giant geoglyphs etched into the Nazca Desert in Peru, the purpose of which remains a mystery.

- **Stonehenge:** A prehistoric monument in England, the construction and purpose of which are still debated.
- **The Lost City of Atlantis**: A legendary island or city that supposedly sank beneath the ocean, mentioned in Plato's dialogues.
- **Oak Island Money Pit:** A supposed buried treasure on Oak Island in Nova Scotia, Canada, that has eluded treasure hunters for centuries.
- **Crop Circles:** Complex geometric patterns that appear mysteriously in fields, with no clear explanation for their origin.
- **The Mary Celeste:** An abandoned ship discovered in the Atlantic Ocean in 1872 with its crew missing.
- **The Loch Ness Monster**: A cryptid creature said to inhabit Loch Ness in Scotland.
- **Roanoke Colony**: The disappearance of the settlers of Roanoke Island in the late 16th century, leaving behind only the word "Croatoan."
- **The Taos Hum:** A low-frequency humming sound heard by residents of Taos, New Mexico, with no known source.
- **DB Cooper:** The alias of a man who hijacked a plane in 1971, received a ransom, and parachuted into obscurity, never to be found.
- **Wow! Signal:** A strong, unexplained radio signal detected from space in 1977.
- **The Shroud of Turin:** A linen cloth bearing the image of a man, believed by some to be the burial shroud of Jesus Christ.
- **The Dyatlov Pass Incident:** The mysterious deaths of nine hikers in the Ural Mountains of Russia in 1959, with unusual injuries and circumstances.
- **The Marfa Lights:** Unexplained lights that appear in the night sky near Marfa, Texas.
- **The Disappearance of Flight MH370:** The disappearance of Malaysia Airlines Flight MH370 in 2014, with no definitive explanation for its fate.

These enigmas and mysteries have captured the imagination of people for generations, and each one presents a unique puzzle waiting to be solved or at least explored. Your child can choose one of these enigmas for their social studies project or delve into any other that piques their interest.

THE HIGH SCHOOL STUDENT

The distinction between a high school Impressive Independent student and a middle school Impressive Independent student can vary depending on individual characteristics and development. However, there are some general differences that you may have observed:

High school students are typically older and more mature than middle school students. With age often comes increased self-awareness and a deeper understanding of one's own thoughts, feelings, and abilities. High school students may have a more developed sense of self than their younger middle school counterparts. They may engage in more complex and nuanced self-reflection. They may think deeply about their values, beliefs, and goals and have a better grasp of their strengths and weaknesses. Middle school students may be less experienced in introspection and self-analysis.

High school students often focus on setting and working towards long-term goals, such as college or career aspirations. They may better understand how their personal traits and interests align with these goals. Middle school students, on the other hand, may be more focused on short-term goals and immediate concerns related to academics and social interactions. They may have more autonomy and independence in deciding about their education and extracurricular activities. They may be more able to advocate for their needs and preferences. Middle school students may rely more on parental guidance and support.

High school II students may have developed better emotional regulation skills to manage stress and difficult emotions more effectively. Middle school students may still be learning and developing these skills, which can lead to more pronounced emotional ups and downs. These students may have a clearer sense of their interests and passions, which can influence their extracurricular activities and career aspirations. Middle school students may be exploring a wider range of interests and may not have yet discovered their true passions.

Remember that these differences are generalizations, and there can be a wide range of individual variations within both middle and high school students. Additionally, developmental stages are not rigid, and some middle school students may exhibit traits associated with high school II students, while some high school students may still be working on self-awareness and personal development. Effective education and support should be tailored to a student's specific needs and characteristics at their respective stages of development.

 **Books for High School Students**

The following books offer diverse perspectives and themes that can resonate with a high school Impressive Independent student, encouraging reflection and personal growth. Your homeschooled high school student may find these books valuable for exploring their own thoughts, emotions, and identity. Your II high schooler will want to read:

"The Perks of Being a Wallflower" by Stephen Chbosky
> *A coming-of-age novel that delves into the emotional struggles of a high school student named Charlie as he navigates friendship, love, and mental health issues.*

"Man's Search for Meaning" by Viktor E. Frankl
> *A powerful memoir by a Holocaust survivor that explores the quest for meaning and purpose in life.*

"The Road" by Cormac McCarthy
> *A post-apocalyptic novel that follows a father and son as they journey through a desolate landscape, raising questions about survival, morality, and the human spirit.*

"Educated" by Tara Westover
> *A memoir that recounts the author's journey from a strict, isolated upbringing in rural Idaho to achieving higher education and self-discovery.*

"The Hate U Give" by Angie Thomas
> *This contemporary novel explores the life of Starr Carter, a teenager who grapples with issues of race, identity, and finding her voice after witnessing a police shooting.*

"Everything I Never Told You" by Celeste Ng
A family drama that explores the secrets, expectations, and inner lives of the Lee family members in 1970s Ohio.

"Circe" by Madeline Miller
A retelling of the story of Circe, the enchantress from Greek mythology, that explores themes of identity, power, and transformation.

"Born a Crime: Stories from a South African Childhood" by Trevor Noah
The memoir of comedian Trevor Noah, detailing his experiences growing up in apartheid-era South Africa and his path to becoming a successful entertainer.

"The Nightingale" by Kristin Hannah
A historical fiction novel set during World War II, focusing on the lives of two sisters in Nazi-occupied France and their struggles for survival and resistance.

"Braiding Sweetgrass: Indigenous Wisdom, Scientific Knowledge, and the Teachings of Plants" by Robin Wall Kimmerer
A blend of indigenous wisdom and scientific knowledge, this book explores our connection to nature, offering a unique perspective on personal and environmental well-being.

"The Name of the Wind" by Patrick Rothfuss
The first book in "The Kingkiller Chronicle" series follows the life and adventures of Kvothe, a gifted young musician and magician, as he seeks knowledge and unravels the mysteries of his world.

"Graceling" by Kristin Cashore
In a world where some individuals are born with special powers, the protagonist, Katsa, has a killing grace. She embarks on a journey of self-discovery and resistance against a corrupt king.

"The Wheel of Time" series by Robert Jordan (completed by Brandon Sanderson)
A massive and epic fantasy series that spans multiple books, following the adventures of a group of young people destined to save the world from a dark force.

"The Magicians" by Lev Grossman
A contemporary fantasy series that follows Quentin Coldwater as he enters Brakebills University for Magical Pedagogy, exploring themes of magic, identity, and adulthood.

"The Inheritance Trilogy" by N.K. Jemisin
This trilogy explores themes of power, gods, and humanity in a world where mortals and gods are intertwined. The series begins with "The Hundred Thousand Kingdoms."

 ## Reading and Language Arts for High School Students

The following is an integrated unit that combines all of the major subject areas and will take several weeks to complete. This unit could fit any of Gardner's intelligences, but the Impressive Independent student will love it because they can do a lot of it independently. This child will strive for perfection as he learns about not only the aesthetic contributions to your yard but also about budgeting, flowering plants, geometric and algebraic use, the history of gardening, and soil attributes that are needed for the choices he makes, plus a whole lot more!

The book choice I am using is an internationally best-selling anthology of many writers who shared a story about their lives. They talk about where they began on the journey of their story and how they changed. They each give back by giving the reader heartfelt and simple 'things to do' to help the reader move from one place in their psyche to a better place. The name of this book is *"Ignite Forgiveness,"* and I am proud that I am one of the authors of this book. Lady JB Owen, the publisher of Ignite Forgiveness, is also the publisher of this book, *"Learning Outside the Line."* You can get this book on Amazon or get an autographed copy directly from me, along with a personal message to you.

Exploring Forgiveness and Personal Growth through "Ignite Forgiveness"

Throughout the unit, emphasize the importance of self-reflection and Impressive Independent growth, encouraging your student to apply the book's lessons to their own life. By the end of the unit, they should have a deeper understanding of forgiveness and personal development and have grown as individuals.

Objectives:
- Analyze the themes and messages in "Ignite Forgiveness."
- Develop critical thinking skills through discussions and reflections.
- Improve writing skills through essays and journaling.
- Foster intrapersonal growth and self-awareness.

Activities:
- Read the book's introduction and preface. Discuss the authors' backgrounds and motivations for writing the book. Identify the central theme of forgiveness and personal growth.
- Select one or more authors from the book. Create a character profile, including traits, motivations, and changes throughout the story. Discuss how their journeys related to the theme of forgiveness.
- Read and analyze specific chapters or passages that highlight forgiveness. Discuss the concept of forgiveness and its importance. Have your child write a reflective essay on forgiveness, citing examples from the book.
- Identify moments in the book where the characters experience personal growth.
- Discuss the importance of self-awareness and personal development. Encourage your child to write a personal growth journal, reflecting on their own experiences.
- Choose specific chapters or quotes for in-depth analysis. Have your child write a critical analysis essay on the book's themes using textual evidence. Reach out to some of the authors that your child connected with and schedule a Zoom interview with them.

- Encourage your child to express their understanding of forgiveness and personal growth through a creative project. This could be a poem, artwork, or a short story inspired by the book. Share and discuss the creative projects, connecting them to the book's themes.
- Host a "book club" discussion with other homeschooling families if possible, allowing students to share their thoughts and insights on the book. Allow your child to express their personal growth and what they've learned from reading "Ignite Forgiveness."

 # Math for High School Students

This unit expands the literature unit from above by creating a lesson plan for your child to design a flower garden in the shape of a pentagon while staying within a budget. It is an excellent way to combine and integrate geometry, budgeting, and gardening. This project engages your child in a hands-on learning experience incorporating various skills and knowledge. It also allows them to apply mathematical concepts in a real-world context while enjoying the rewards of gardening.

Designing a Pentagonal Flower Garden within a Budget

Subject Areas: Math (Geometry, Algebra), Budgeting, Planning, Gardening.

Objectives:
- Apply geometric concepts to design a pentagonal flower garden.
- Create a detailed budget for the garden project, considering the costs of materials and flowers.
- Develop practical skills in planning and executing a garden project.

Materials Needed: Paper and pencil for sketches and calculations, gardening tools (shovel, rake, gloves, etc.), flower seeds or young plants, soil and compost, mulch, garden markers or labels, measuring tape, price lists from local garden centers or online source, calculator.

Activities:

- Introduce the project and explain the goal of designing a pentagonal flower garden with varying flower heights.
- Discuss the importance of budgeting and planning in real-life projects. Provide an overview of the project's requirements and constraints.
- Review the geometric concept of a pentagon and its properties. Have your child draw and label a pentagon on paper.
- Discuss how to divide the pentagon into rows or sections for planting flowers. Using this drawing, start sketching ideas for the garden layout, considering the placement of the tallest flowers.
- Research different types of flowers that vary in height and are suitable for your climate. Create a list of flowers, including their names, heights when fully grown, and prices.
- Discuss the budget constraints and set an initial limit (e.g., $150). Introduce the concept of budgeting.
- Have your child create a detailed budget that includes costs for flowers, soil, mulch, and any necessary gardening tools.
- Calculate the cost per flower and square foot of garden space. Make adjustments to the flower selection and layout to stay within the budget.
- Finalize the flower selection based on the budget.
- Create a detailed garden layout plan specifying where each type of flower will be planted.
- Recalculate the total area of the garden and the space allocated to each type of flower for accuracy.

Purchase all necessary materials and flowers within the budget. Follow the garden layout plan and plant the flowers accordingly. Use a measuring tape to ensure proper spacing and alignment. Label each section or row with the flower type and expected height. Discuss basic garden care and maintenance, including watering and weeding. Keep a garden journal to record growth and any adjustments made. Track expenses and compare them to the budget to ensure it stays on track. Reflect on the project, discussing the challenges and successes. Evaluate the garden's progress in terms of design and budget. Discuss lessons learned about budgeting, planning, and gardening.

Incorporating science into the garden project can enhance the learning experience and give your child a well-rounded understanding of how various disciplines intersect. Here's a science project that complements the math project of designing a pentagonal flower garden:

 ## Science for High School Students

By combining the math project with this science project, your child will not only learn about plant growth and ecosystems but also gain a deeper understanding of the intricate relationship between math and science in real-life projects. This integrated approach promotes critical thinking, observation skills, and a holistic view of the natural world. In this unit, it is necessary to arrange the steps as 'phases' rather than activities since each step is dependent on outside factors such as temperature, amount of rainfall, and rate of growth of each species of flower.

Objectives:
- Observe and document the growth of plants in the pentagonal flower garden.
- Investigate the interactions between plants and the local ecosystem.
- Analyze the impact of environmental factors on plant growth.

Materials: Garden journal or notebook, measuring tools (ruler, measuring tape), camera or smartphone for photos, soil testing kits (optional), weather station (optional).

Phase 1: Baseline Observations
Start with baseline measurements of each type of flower planted in the garden, including height, leaf size, and flower color. Document the date and weather conditions during this initial observation. Review the concept of 'hypotheses' and have your child predict how the plants will grow.

Phase 2: Growth Monitoring (Ongoing)
Regularly measure and document the growth of each type of flower in the garden (e.g., weekly or bi-weekly). Encourage your child to take photographs to visually track the changes over time. Record any observations related to pest damage, changes in leaf color, or other signs of plant health.

Phase 3: Soil and Environmental Testing (Optional)
Collect soil samples from different garden areas and test them for pH, moisture content, and nutrient levels. Set up a weather station to monitor the garden's temperature, humidity, and sunlight. Discuss how these environmental factors may affect plant growth.

Phase 4: Ecosystem Observations (Ongoing)
Keep a record of any wildlife or insects that visit the garden, such as pollinators (bees, butterflies) or herbivores (caterpillars, aphids). Explore the concept of plant-pollinator interactions and discuss their importance in ecosystems.

Phase 5: Data Analysis and Conclusion (Ongoing)
Analyze the growth data collected over time, comparing the growth rates of different types of flowers. Investigate any correlations between environmental factors (e.g., sunlight, temperature) and plant growth. Formulate conclusions based on the data and observations, including whether the hypotheses were supported.

Phase 6: Presentation and Reflection
Prepare a presentation summarizing the project, including the garden design, budget, and scientific observations. Reflect on the connections between math, gardening, and science. Share the findings and insights with family, friends, or a local gardening club.

Incorporating social studies into your ongoing gardening, math, and science project can provide a well-rounded educational experience for your child. Here are ways to include social studies concepts into the project:

 **Social Studies for High School Students**

Gardening and agriculture have played a pivotal role in shaping the course of human history, leaving an indelible mark on different cultures and time periods worldwide. This multifaceted exploration aims to delve into the historical significance of gardening and agriculture, uncovering their profound influence on civilizations throughout the ages. By examining the unique practices and traditions of various cultures, from the herbal gardens of ancient Egypt to the formal gardens of Europe, we will unravel the intricate tapestry of knowledge and innovation that has contributed to the development of gardening techniques. Additionally, we will scrutinize the evolution of gardening practices and their multifaceted roles in providing sustenance, medicinal resources, and aesthetic beauty to societies, offering valuable insights into the interplay between humanity and horticulture across the ages.

- **Research** and discuss the historical significance of gardening and agriculture in different cultures and time periods.
- **Explore** how various civilizations have influenced gardening practices, such as the use of herbal gardens in ancient Egypt or the concept of formal gardens in European history.
- **Investigate** how gardening has evolved over time and its role in providing food, medicine, and aesthetics to societies.

Objective: Compare and contrast different gardens around the world

Activities:
- Study different types of gardens from around the world, such as Japanese Zen gardens, English cottage gardens, or Native American three-sisters gardens.
- Examine the cultural and historical aspects of these gardens, including their symbolism, purpose, and design principles.
- Have your child choose a cultural or regional garden style to incorporate elements into their own pentagonal flower garden.

Objective: Explore the economic aspects of gardening

Activities:
- Explore the economic aspects of gardening, including the historical role of gardens in providing sustenance during economic hardships.
- Discuss the economic impact of gardening today, such as the agricultural industry, local farmers' markets, and the sustainability movement.
- Calculate the potential economic benefits of your child's flower garden, considering factors like the cost of flowers, soil, and tools compared to the value of the flowers when fully grown.

Objective: To discuss gardening and its relationship to environmental and social impact on society

Activities:
- Investigate the environmental impact of gardening, including issues related to pesticide use, water conservation, and soil health.
- Discuss the importance of sustainable gardening practices and their contribution to environmental conservation.
- Explore the history of environmental movements and their connection to gardening, such as the organic gardening movement.

Conclusion

Understanding and embracing the Impressive Independent learner is not only essential but immensely rewarding. These individuals possess a profound connection with their inner selves, offering a unique perspective that enriches our world. As parents, educators, and caregivers, we have the privilege of nurturing their introspective nature, providing them with the tools and support they need to thrive. By recognizing The II''s exceptional qualities, fostering self-acceptance, and allowing them to shine in their distinctive ways, we empower Impressive Independents to become confident, self-motivated individuals who contribute their valuable insights and gifts to the world. With patience, empathy, and an unwavering belief in their potential, we can help II"s navigate their educational journey with purpose and fulfillment. As we celebrate their high emotional intelligence, self-awareness, and commitment to personal growth, let us be inspired by the remarkable journey of these learners and the profound impact they can make on our lives and society as a whole.

Section 3

Other Considerations Of Homeschooling

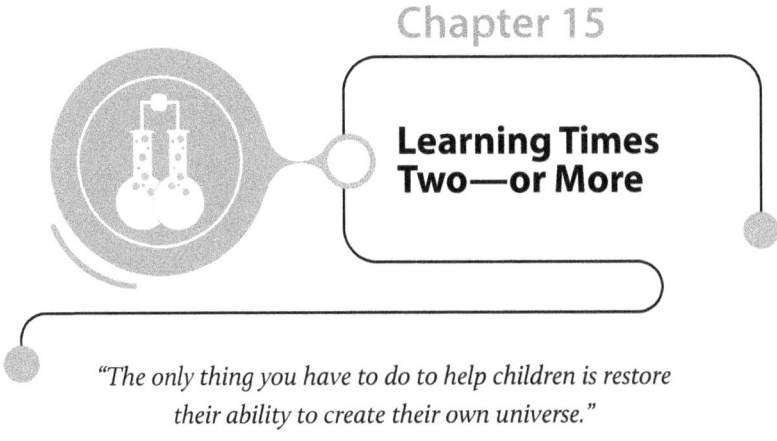

Chapter 15

Learning Times Two—or More

"The only thing you have to do to help children is restore their ability to create their own universe."
–Meir Ezra

Earlier in this book, I introduced you to my adapted theory of multiple intelligences that I used in my classroom of twenty-five-plus children. My weekly test scores immediately increased by twenty-five percent. As time went on during the year, that percentage increased to around forty percent. In addition, everyone in the classroom became more responsible for themselves and supported their classmates so that no one ever failed. My classroom became a learning machine; the kids were smiling and happy. At the end of the year, they left my classroom as confident, curious learners. Other teachers in the next grade often told me, "We can spot your students immediately, just by their level of confidence, preparedness, and what they already know." You can do the same thing with your children now that you know this powerful technique!

Let's talk about what you already have at your fingertips, either at home, in the community, or on the World Wide Web. Many programs on the internet offer ideas, worksheets, and even whole units of study around specific topics, such as animal behaviors. Don't spend a lot of money until you've taken the time to research all the freebies you can find on the World Wide Web. Take the time to look around your home, neighborhood, and community to locate ways to teach your kids. For instance, while fixing meals, a measuring cup can teach fractions as well as units of measure, and the playground has all sorts of equipment to teach simple machines, forces, and energy. Depending on the region you live in, walking to the park and comparing the differences in trees, from their leaves to the type of bark they have, is a great science adventure.

Below is a list of ways to teach your kids that will support your new *Outside the Line* teaching style. Not everything has to be conventional learning, i.e., from a workbook or worksheet.

 ## Movie Night

Many things can be taught using family outings and family activities. Dozens of things can be taught at family movie night, and I recommend one every week. Watch a historically-accurate movie like "Hidden Figures." Following the movie, have a family discussion about cultures, prejudice and racism, assumptions, heroes and heroines, NASA, women throughout history who have changed the world, and so on. You can highlight how people dressed back then, family culture, car styles, and how they've changed. Implement creative and technical writing lessons the following day. Research the characters in the movie to discover their personal histories and how they changed the world. Ask, *"How do you think history would have been different if these women had not existed?"* Using a film, documentary, short film, or even an animated program can enhance your child's learning experience with relevant information that is factual. These modalities use the five senses, not just reading and writing, which brings your child into the information in a subtle yet powerful way. Using videos allows your child to see and hear what they were studying from the video. They can connect emotionally with feelings of joy or sadness. Sometimes, watching a movie with scenes surrounding a picnic brings subconscious memories of certain smells and tastes.

 ## Field Trips

Field trips are a great way to foster experiential learning and play a pivotal role in homeschooling by providing hands-on, real-world experiences that can forge deeper learning for children. Field trips provide homeschooling children with rich, diverse, and immersive learning experiences that go beyond traditional classroom settings. These experiences contribute to a holistic and profound understanding of the world, fostering a love for learning that extends well beyond textbooks.

Here's an example of using the area around your home in your community. Let's say you are taking the family to the zoo. This is a day you should either shorten the morning subjects by at least fifteen minutes or cut out formal lessons altogether and leave for the zoo. While at the zoo, you discuss science by identifying different species and genomes—insects, birds, reptiles, fish, mammals—and reinforcing what traits make a mammal, those traits that make a fish, and so on. At the same time, you identify where each animal lives in its natural environment, such as the giraffes living in the wild in Africa, i.e., geography. Reinforce that Africa is a continent, and oceans surround continents.

When you get home, you have a plethora of writing starters: *What was your favorite animal and why? Describe the difference between the Bengal tigers and the lions. What is the difference between spiders and beetles, and how are they alike or different?* You also have science and social studies/geography for the rest of the week because now you can explore all sorts of topics—*maps, social attributes of various animals, names of continents and oceans and where they are located on earth, how people depend on animals in different parts of the world and in different ways.* You can do hundreds of things just by going to the zoo!

In another example, I helped a family with three teenagers design a whole unit around a snow-skiing trip. They explored the mechanics of the ski lift, the dynamics of skis, gravity, acceleration, how body movement aided in getting from the top to the bottom of the ski run, potential energy, and much more. They also had two distinct types of writing: technical writing about all of the above topics and descriptive writing, talking about the trip itself, the look and feel of the adventure, describing their surroundings, and so on. This was a great way to incorporate schooling and fun time. Another way they increased the experience and enhanced their learning was by taking videos of their outing, along with pictures and keeping journals or written work about their field trip. You are documenting learning and providing evidence to save in digital form or a portfolio. This documentation is necessary for homeschooled children who intend to attend post-secondary education, providing proof that grades and mastery of content in various subjects have been acquired.

 ## Pet Care

Taking care of pets is a great way to enhance learning. During my teaching career, I often had animals in the classroom. I had aquariums full of fish, iguanas, frogs, and toads, even mice and hamsters! Caring for animals instills responsibility for another creature and promotes self-esteem and bonding between the animal and the child. At the same time, your child will learn about habitats and ecosystems, the life cycles of different animals, how adaptations in each animal species have fostered their survival, and the animal behavior of different species.

 ## Amusement Park

Taking a trip to an amusement park is one of the best ways to teach Physics and Einstein's Laws of Relativity, also known as the "Three Laws of Motion," forces, simple and complex machines, and energy. I recommend you teach these first in the weeks prior to the field trip. While at the amusement park, you and your child will not only be able to point these various science concepts out but you and your child will have fun experiencing them. When you get home, you have two ready-made Language Arts writing activities—technical writing and descriptive writing. On the one hand, you can have your child pick one science topic, such as simple and complex machines, to compare and contrast, and on the other hand, ask your child to describe how they felt while riding the roller coaster, such as the first hill where the roller coaster stopped at the top awaiting the release of potential energy!

 ## Local Library

Every town has a local library, and it is here you can find a plethora of resources, all free and primed for learning. The library has tons of reading materials, from the books I recommended previously to research materials. Besides books, many libraries offer some, if not all, of the following: digital media, recording rooms, study rooms, computers, scanners, artwork, telescopes, museum passes, and even musical instruments you can rent. Some even give away museum passes and free seeds to plant.

Libraries always have lecture series, guest speakers, or author readings that will benefit your child by meeting writers of their favorite books and engaging in conversations with them. Interacting with speakers and acquiring first-hand information that these people share is something that most children never get the chance to encounter. Meeting an author at the public library is a remarkable experience for your child, providing them with the invaluable opportunity to interact with someone who has contributed to the world of literature, thereby developing insight into topics from first-hand points of view.

 ## Museums, Art Galleries, and Planetariums

Depending on where you live, many communities have various museums, art galleries, and even planetariums. Some of these places are free or have a small entry fee. For instance, if you live near a capital city, take advantage of museums that house that country's historical pieces, such as the Vatican in Italy, Egyptian antiquities in Cairo, The Great Wall of China, or Neuschwanstein Castle in Bavaria. Almost all towns have art galleries to celebrate local artists. If you happen to live in Japan, Argentina, Spain, or England, they have some of the largest planetariums in the world outside of the dozens in the United States.

The EE, SS, and VV child will thrive on a trip to a planetarium because of the order of the universe and the significance of the well-being of space. In contrast, the MM child will love the structure and organization of all of these adventures and the scientific and historical significance of each. The CC and SS child will adore the artistic relevance of ancient artifacts as well as the creations of modern artists. The PP child will love the physical activity involved, while the AA child will adore getting out and meeting new people and experiencing different cultures. The II will take the time to internalize the art and its significance to humanity, self-reflecting on how it fits into the course of life. All in all, different children will take away what naturally is significant to each individual learner and capitalize on what is important to their holistic cognitive development.

 **Historical Forts, Landmarks, or Look Out Points**

You might be surprised that history is right in your backyard when you take the time to discover what is right outside your door. Many towns and cities have historical settlements, battlefields, or famous people who may have grown up or lived in that town. Visiting battlefields, historic sites, and places of interest in your hometown can be an enriching and educational experience for budding historians. Here are some suggestions to make the most out of these visits:

Preparation and Research:
- Before the visit, engage your children in research about the site's historical significance. This can include watching documentaries, reading books, or exploring online resources.
- Encourage them to create a list of questions or topics they want to explore during their visit.

Guided Tours and Programs:
- Many historic sites offer guided tours or educational programs. Check if these are available and consider participating to gain deeper insights into the historical context. Some places may also have educational workshops or hands-on activities for students. Living history museums are excellent sources of information that immerse your child into the era and ways of life from the past.

Interactive Learning:
- Create a scavenger hunt or a quiz based on the historical facts related to the site. This adds an element of fun and engagement to the visit.
- Bring along maps, historical documents, or reference material to refer to during the trip.

Documenting the Experience:
- Encourage your children to take photos, make sketches, or keep a journal. This helps them document their experiences and observations.
- Later, use these materials as part of a bigger project or end-of-unit presentation.

Role-Playing:
- Have your children research historical figures associated with the site and engage in role-playing activities. This helps them understand different perspectives and historical events. Dressing up in period costumes can add an extra layer of immersion and emotional awareness.

Post-Visit Discussions:
- After the visit, facilitate discussions about what was learned, any favorite information, and how the experience added to their overall knowledge.
- Encourage critical thinking by asking open-ended questions that make your child use more than yes or no responses.

Follow-Up Projects:
- Assign follow-up projects such as writing essays, creating presentations, or building dioramas based on what was learned during the visit.
- Display the projects at home or in your home classroom space.

Remember that these visits can provide not only historical knowledge but also valuable life skills such as observation, analysis, and critical thinking. Tailor the experience to your child's interests and learning style for a more meaningful homeschooling adventure.

Finding the Right Stuff

The internet has a wealth of information. Using it as a powerful teaching tool, your kids learn how to ask specific questions to get specific answers. They must then read and deduce to find the answers! If they need to be sure they are doing a science problem correctly, Google™ can even assist them by providing details, background, and explanations of how to work out the problems with them. Let's remember YouTube™, also. For example, you may need to remember different math algorithms, so go to YouTube for instructions on solving that particular math lesson. There is even a version of YouTube just for students, where they can find videos of teachers explaining different concepts in all the major subject areas, such as all the domains of math, how to write a friendly letter, how to solve technical science equations, or the significance of archeological finds.

Different subscription sites, such as BrainPOP™ and Khan Academy™, entertain kids as they teach them specific skills and topics in under five minutes and then quiz them to see if they got the information from the lesson. These sites often include other activities to continue to explore that specific topic. They are FUN and help provide interest in the subject matter they are learning. They will engage your child digitally and offer assistance if they have difficulty answering questions. When the child has gained mastery, they even offer testing materials that can be downloaded. After taking the tests you will print and file in their portfolio. Using learning sites such as this will help bring clarity of subjects into focus while allowing your child to learn while using different modalities of learning other than a worksheet or workbook.

Finally, join as many homeschooling groups as you see fit. You can always unjoin them if you think a particular group doesn't agree with your ideas. Try them all, just as if they were a buffet. Eat what you like and enjoy what suits you. Leave the things you don't care for. There are groups and co-ops where people meet regularly in and around their communities. Some even work with other families to have play dates and excursions together. Some share the teaching of subjects and materials. For example, if you are great with science but not reading, find someone great with reading but not science—Why not share knowledge, especially if what you are doing is similar to what they are doing? Some groups meet on Zoom™-type platforms and use them to share ideas, teach the group something that is needed or of added value, or acquire knowledge to teach something to *your* child. Plenty of social media groups can support you in finding the materials you are seeking, offering ideas for enhancing and engaging your child, validating your concerns, and even helping you find groups outside your home to help facilitate learning or socialization. There are even national organizations such as NHSA—the National HomeSchool Association, HSLDA—Home School Legal Defense Association, and the Coalition for Responsible Home Education that fill the needs of homeschooling parents. Look in your areas, state, or country to find what is available to help you along your homeschooling journeys.

 ## Books

If you are homeschooling, it means that you may also need to do a bit of schooling for yourself. Some books, such as this one, provide guidance and suggestions to get you started and offer support as you homeschool through the years. There are many books on the market that share similar information, from various points of view. When it comes to books, be willing to find the pieces that fit you and trust that every book you read has some redeeming value and something to teach you. Books are a huge resource for homeschooling parents and offer teaching and parenting tips, educational support, and information that is critical for a successful homeschooling experience. I would recommend a few books that caught my eye, such as "Busy Homeschool Mom's Guide" by Heidi St. John and "Homeschooling the Early Years" by Linda Dobson.

 ## International Travel

Something like seeing a Broadway play, swimming with the sharks, or climbing the pyramids may be on your child's bucket list. Planning big family trips like this is a great way to foster your child's enthusiasm for the arts, history, ecology, and other interests outside of their community. It calls to their adventurous nature and offers educational experiences that create lasting memories, allowing them to communicate and have versatile conversations throughout their lives.

Travel also allows for skills in math as you calculate currency conversions, measure conversions to metric in driving distances or food consumption, and even time zones. Saving for such an experience can develop skills in budgeting for all the expenses for the trip—food, car expenses, airline tickets, shopping for appropriate shoes and clothing, and fees for admissions tickets or tour guides.

One of the greatest things about homeschooling is you get to choose what your kids are learning, so be sure to listen to what they are most interested in and support them in their big ideas and dreams. Your kids have the best ideas when it comes to what they enjoy. When children take the reins of their education, they steer their learning journey towards subjects and interests that ignite their passion. The greatness of kids directing their own homeschooling experience lies in the beautiful tapestry of discovery, creativity, and self-motivation. Here are just a few of the advantages of letting your child be involved in directing their learning:

- Unleashes Inherent Curiosity
- Fosters Lifelong Love for Learning
- Cultivates Independence and Responsibility
- Embraces Diverse Talents
- Nurtures Critical Thinking
- Sparks Creativity and Innovation
- Tailors Education to Personal Needs
- Builds Intrinsic Motivation
- Supports a Growth Mindset
- Builds Lifelong Learners

In the wondrous world of child-directed homeschooling, every subject chosen, every question asked, and every project undertaken becomes a brushstroke in the masterpiece of a child's education—a testament to the incredible potential that lies within each young mind.

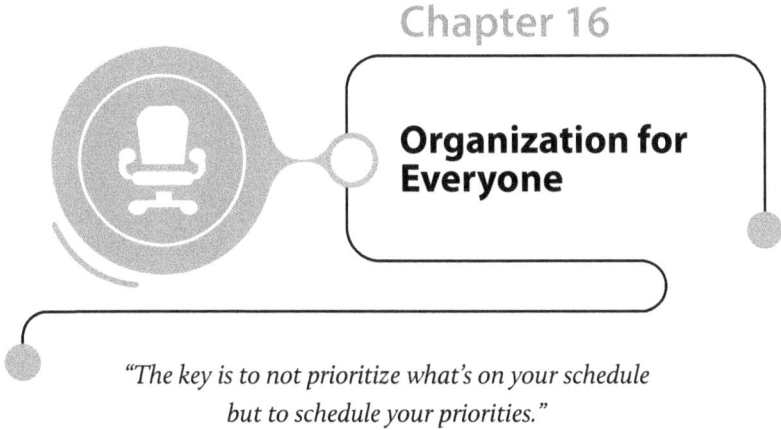

Chapter 16

Organization for Everyone

"The key is to not prioritize what's on your schedule but to schedule your priorities."
–Stephen R. Covey

There are many concepts to explore and learn in educating children. Although homeschooling families do not have to be as stringent in time management, it is a good idea to establish some daily routine, especially if you have more than one child you are homeschooling.

As a homeschooling parent, you are responsible for what your children learn. Guess what? You can't just say, "Okay, kids! Go learn something!" It would be best if you had a plan.

 ## Establishing Schedules

I suggest everyone in the house have a posted routine or a schedule because that gets the expectations for the day started, and everyone knows where everyone is and what they are doing. A schedule doesn't mean you and your kids can't have fun while learning, go to places on the spur of the moment, or even have a serendipitous idea and do something other than what you planned. If what you planned only takes twenty minutes, but you planned for an hour, do you move on to tomorrow's expectations, or do you shorten the day? *That's up to you.* A homeschool schedule indicates what you want to accomplish and the order you want to get it done. If you have more than one child teaching different levels, having a schedule will help you navigate time and deliverables immensely. Ideally, by using a schedule, each person in the household knows what the other is doing at certain times of the day and can help the other be accountable for what has to be done. It also keeps each person focused on what they must do by a certain time.

A schedule tells each other if someone has an appointment outside the home that will require modifications to the lesson plan. Finally, a schedule lets you organize your day so everyone gets their teaching time. For instance, with a schedule, while working with one child teaching long division, another can memorize multiplication facts, while another is taking a quiz on what you taught yesterday or working in an online program or printed worksheet. A schedule for each child, each day, will determine the amount of success you will attain as a homeschooling unit.

Schedules can also be dependent on the type of learner each child identifies with. Some children will learn well in the early mornings with sunlight and a view of the outdoors. Others will enjoy learning after playtime when things are more creative and less structured, activating the more creative side of the brain. A Magical Mathematician will want to study in a quiet and tidy place, whereas an Exceptional Ecologist might need to be near a window, open the door, or have lots of plants in the room. Making sure the schedule adheres to where your child learns best according to their type of learning will be a part of planning a successful day.

 ## Creating a Great Schedule

Homeschooling can begin the moment everyone wakes up. Using morning chores and getting ready is a great way to start. Begin with having your children make and clean their beds. It has often been said, "A messy bed is a messy head." Have them start their day off right. You can support your child by assigning chores, such as sweeping the kitchen floor or vacuuming, taking out the garbage, and washing their clothes—or at least separating them into appropriate loads to wash, folding, and putting them away. Requiring dishes to be cleaned and loaded in the dishwasher or folding towels can be fun with music playing or a timer on; turning it into a race or game! If you have pets, someone should be assigned to feed and water them, brush or comb them, clean their tank, or give them some cuddle time. These chores should be completed by the time 'school' begins.

Your entire home routine can be made into learning opportunities and great ways to build family bonding time. You can think of other things, such as meal preparation, sorting things for charity, organizing the garage, or lawn and garden care. Involving your children in the responsibility of the home will help them establish lifelong positive routines and habits they will carry to college and into adulthood and eventually use to prepare their own children for life.

 ## Learning While Doing Chores

Chores are a topic that no one likes to talk about. Children don't like to do them and, if not corrected, will put them off or not do them. Parents don't like to listen to the excuses and whining that goes with assigning chores or nagging their kids to complete them. However, a successful homeschool structure will have assigned chores for each family member, including the parents.

Not everyone has the same chores, and it's imperative not to assign younger children to do things they could not do or require to be perfectly done. Older children can be overseers of younger children once they have completed their assignments. Think about everything you, as the mom and dad, do every day that can be divided up between everyone:

- Making beds
- Picking up toys
- Taking out the garbage
- Picking up and putting away breakfast or lunch items
- Feeding pets
- Sweeping the floor
- Sorting laundry
- Putting clothes in the washing machine
- Folding clothes/towels

- Walking pets
- Dusting furniture
- Getting food out of the freezer
- Straightening family rooms—bathroom, living room, TV room, dining room, etc.
- Taking out recycling
- Getting the mail
- Watering plants

These are just a few chores in a household, but your family might have other things considered as chores. You will notice that I allotted forty-five minutes for chores in the sample schedules I provided below. Now think about how long it takes one person to do the above. Even a five-year-old can pick up toys and help straighten things out of place in family rooms, and it doesn't take a lot of time! They can also assist older kids with a family pet. All of the above can be done in a short amount of time, especially when more than one child assists you in the home.

Chores are important because they teach a lot of characteristics you want for your children. They learn to be responsible for their actions and self-discipline because they learn to complete tasks independently and on time. This will allow them to develop a sense of independence and ownership of their actions. If something presents a challenge, they learn how to solve problems that might arise. Completing a job well done provides a way to build self-confidence. When assisting others, they learn teamwork and respect for one another. They learn accountability, and if things don't go the way they want, they learn patience.

Depending on your family's beliefs, you may or may not agree with an allowance for doing their chores well, but if you give your children an allowance, it gives you a chance to teach money management and saving for something they want. Chores can also be used to get to a family outing. For instance, when everyone has completed all their specified chores for the week, the family has a fun excursion to someplace everyone has agreed to, such as that day trip to the zoo, an amusement park, or even a current movie the family wants to see. In conclusion, chores are a useful and necessary concept in developing a successful homeschooling experience!

A Sample Schedule for One Child Including Chores:

Feel free to tweak it to fit your family or develop your own:

JAYLA'S SCHEDULE _____ / _____ / _____

7:00 AM – Rise and shine!
7:15 AM – Breakfast
7:45 AM – Today's Chores—clean room, start your laundry, load dishwasher
8:30 AM – Math
9:30 AM – Reading
10:30 AM – Writing and Language Arts
11:30 AM – Lunch/chores—sweep floor/load dishwasher/put clothes in the dryer
12:30 PM – Science and/or Social Studies
1:30 PM – Exploring My Interests
3:00 PM – Dance class

 **Make the Schedule Successful**

Post everyone's schedule somewhere convenient and allow your kids to check off the jobs as they are completed. Don't forget to post your schedule alongside everyone else's so it is apparent you are doing things and an indicator of where you might be at a given time! One of the best ways to maintain expectations is to make the schedule clear and identifiable. Therefore, build checking in on the schedule into the day's activities to ensure accuracy, completion, and effective timeline habits.

Since there isn't any competition between you and thirty other children, you should not need several hours per day per subject matter. Children learn best between eight and noon, so I recommend you start school at 8:30 AM or before if possible. I also suggest you teach Math or Reading and Language Arts first. Language Arts takes longer to instruct and practice because it includes reading, grammar, writing, and writing mechanics, such as handwriting and listening skills. My suggestion is both Math and Language Arts should be finished by lunch.

To keep your daily running smoothly, everyone should have a job that gets lunch prepared and eaten and the kitchen cleaned as quickly as possible. Science and History should follow after lunch, as well as extra review for an upcoming exam, completing an assignment, or just reading a book of choice. Getting your children back on task toward their afternoon school work can be done by doing something as simple as turning on some music and having a short 'dance party' or singing a song in different ways, such as whispering the lyrics, then singing at the top of their voices! Make it a short time frame and something that quickly gets their attention with fun in mind!

To give you and your children non-cognitive learning time, teaching should be finished by 2:30 PM *or earlier* so that each person can play or do something fun, personal projects, read a book, go outside, or even participate in community classes or groups. The afternoon is when your children have time to take that dance, karate, or swim class. Since it's difficult to get multiple children to multiple places, consider carpooling with another child's parents or scheduling your children at the same or different activities at once within a few minute's drive to various locations. Once they get old enough to drive, they can take themselves to activities or drive other siblings.

 ## Non-Cognitive Learning

Non-cognitive learning is an important part of homeschooling and refers to aspects of learning that go beyond traditional cognitive skills, which involve acquiring knowledge, understanding concepts, and problem-solving. Non-cognitive skills encompass a range of personal, social, and emotional abilities that contribute to overall development and success in various aspects of life. These skills are often referred to as "soft skills" or "life skills." Some examples of non-cognitive skills include:

- **Emotional Intelligence:** The ability to recognize, understand, manage, and express one's own emotions, as well as understand and influence the emotions of others.
- **Social Skills:** The capacity to interact effectively with others, including communication, teamwork, collaboration, and conflict resolution.

- **Adaptability:** The ability to adjust to new situations, learn from experiences, and respond positively to change.
- **Resilience:** The capacity to bounce back from setbacks, overcome challenges, and persevere in the face of difficulties.
- **Motivation:** Intrinsic motivation and a sense of purpose drive individuals to set and achieve goals, sustaining a commitment to learning and personal growth.
- **Self-Regulation:** The ability to control and manage one's thoughts, emotions, and behaviors, leading to better decision-making and impulse control.
- **Grit:** A combination of passion and perseverance, allowing individuals to maintain long-term goals despite obstacles and setbacks.
- **Time Management:** Effectively planning and organizing one's time to maximize productivity and meet deadlines.
- **Communication Skills:** The ability to convey ideas clearly, listen actively, and engage in meaningful conversations.
- **Critical Thinking**: Evaluating information, analyzing situations, and making informed decisions based on evidence and reasoning.

As you include these skills into your teaching program you enhance the overall experience and quality of your teaching skills, leading to a well-developed whole-brain student—your child—who is ready to take on the challenges you give them every day.

 ## Bloom's Taxonomy

I had never heard of Bloom's Taxonomy when I was studying in college. It was not mentioned even in student teaching or any of my senior Education classes. I learned about Bloom's taxonomy at a teacher's workshop nearly four years after my first day of teaching in August of 1976. Now you might be asking, *"What is Bloom's taxonomy, and why is it important?"* Answer: Taxonomy refers to the science or practice of classification. Blooms Taxonomy is a hierarchy of how to ask questions and examine the answers, using ready-made worksheets, to develop the thinking mind of your child.

Benjamin Bloom developed a taxonomy for education in 1956 and it is still used today, worldwide, to develop lessons and textbooks. It is known simply as 'Bloom's Taxonomy' and it uses categories arranged in a hierarchy from lower-order to higher-level thinking skills. These categories are, in order from lower to higher order thinking: *Knowledge, Comprehension, Application, Analysis, Synthesis*, and *Evaluation*. It was revised in 2001 to reflect more modern expectations of what kids need to know in today's worldwide community.

How Bloom's Taxonomy helps homeschooling parents is that it allows you to develop your questioning tactics to challenge your child to think 'outside the box.' You task your child to move beyond remembering facts to applying them to new situations and analyzing the outcome. That leads to reflecting on the outcome and evaluating that outcome as to its success. If your child can take the lesson and create another way to express it, sometimes more creatively, then your child has moved to the highest level of understanding. You can begin to use Bloom's Taxonomy as soon as your child understands simple stories by beginning with simple remembering and understanding. For instance, if you read "The Three Little Pigs" to your three-year-old, instead of only asking, "What did the Big Bad Wolf do to the house of straw?" ask questions like, *"What would you have done when The Big Bad Wolf blew down the first Little Pig's house of straw?"* You have gone from 'remembering' to 'analyzing' with how you frame the question.

The following lists the updated Bloom's Taxonomy with a short description of what each category corresponds to in the hierarchy of thinking skills. I have highlighted what these categories mean:

- **Remembering:** This corresponds to the 'Knowledge' category in the original taxonomy. Remembering involves *recalling or recognizing facts, information, and concepts.* Learners at this level *focus on remembering and retrieving information.*
- **Understanding:** This corresponds to the 'Comprehension' category in the original taxonomy. Understanding involves *grasping the meaning of information and being able to explain ideas, concepts, or principles in one's own words.* It includes tasks related to comprehension and interpretation.
- **Applying:** Applying corresponds to the 'Application' category in the original taxonomy. At this level, learners can *take the knowledge and understanding they have acquired and use it to solve problems, perform tasks, or apply information in practical situations.*

- **Analyzing:** Analyzing corresponds to the 'Analysis' category in the original taxonomy. Analytical thinking at this level involves *breaking down complex information into component parts, identifying relationships, and understanding the underlying structure. It includes tasks like comparing, contrasting, and organizing information.*
- **Evaluating:** Evaluating corresponds to the 'Evaluation' category in the original taxonomy. At this level, learners *make judgments, assess the quality of information or arguments, and make informed decisions. It involves critical thinking, critique, and the ability to justify one's opinions.*
- **Creating:** Creating corresponds to the 'Synthesis' category in the original taxonomy. This is the highest level of cognitive complexity in the revised taxonomy. Learners at this level *are able to combine different elements or ideas to generate new and original solutions, designs, or products. It involves creative thinking and innovation.*

The categories move from regurgitating information to using ideas to create new and original thought processes. The untrained eye does not know how to evaluate whether a worksheet has a good sample of higher-level thinking skills; however, when you engage your child in researching topics to develop a stance on those topics, creating new inventions, or finding solutions that may not have been thought about, then orally and in writing put those thoughts into words, you are engaging all of the taxonomy—you are developing your child's whole brain.Thinking skills are not developed overnight. It is a process that takes time. Sometimes, you have to let information marinate; other times, you use it immediately. As you teach your child, you may discover you are learning by trial and error how to incorporate your child's whole brain in the course of the day, but that's okay!

 ## Eliminating Homework

When you homeschool, there should not be any homework. If you are using your time effectively and planning your lessons according to a doable schedule, children should be able to finish their work in the time you have allotted. Homework was designed in school to allow children to practice new skills to reinforce what was learned that day, to allow parents to see what their children were learning at school, and, in some cases, to improve their grades. Since you are the teacher, know what your child is learning, and have a bird's eye view of your child's mastery of the material you are teaching; there is no need for homework.

Remember, a schedule is just a guide to when to start different activities. It is not chiseled in stone; no one will shake their finger at you and tell you messed up. You create your schedule based on your family's needs and requirements. The most important thing about the schedule is that your child is completing their work and able to move on to what is fun and enjoyable for them, explore what piques their individual interests, and develop skills that will foster their lifelong love of learning.

 ## Managing Homeschooling for Multiple Children

Teaching multiple children at once may seem daunting because there will be times when each child needs your attention immediately, but there's only one of you and more than one of them. This is where the older kids come in handy. Let's say you have three children. Robert is the oldest, Julie is the middle child, and Joey is the youngest. Since Robert has already mastered what Julie and Joey are doing, Robert can answer Julie's questions while you are working with Joey. Then Julie sits beside Joey, and they both work on their lessons while you work with Robert. I call it *divide and conquer.*

I realize you might not think it's fair to have your children 'doing your job,' but it's a win-win situation. Because Robert works with Julie, he gets to review his understanding of the subject as he assists Julie. It's the same with Julie when she sits beside Joey as she helps answer any questions he may have when needed. If you work your children's schedules right, there won't be many instances where one child has to work with another for more than a few minutes. Below is an example of scheduling so that each child gets maximum time with you without interrupting or interfering with another of the children. Remember, though, these are only examples and represent a regular day when no outings are scheduled. Your children may not need an hour for each subject, so you would adjust the schedules to accommodate your family's needs.

Sample Schedule For Multiple Children

Joey:
7:00 AM – Rise and shine!
7:15 AM – Breakfast
7:45 AM – Chores
8:30 AM – Math
9:30 AM – Reading

10:30 AM – Writing and Language Arts
11:30 AM – Lunch/chores
12:30 PM – Science/Social Studies
1:30 PM – Exploring My Interests

Julie:
7:00 AM – Rise and shine!
7:15 AM – Breakfast
7:45 AM – Chores
8:30 AM – Reading
9:30 AM – Writing and Language Arts

10:30 AM – Math
11:30 AM – Lunch/chores
12:30 PM – Science/Social Studies
1:30 PM – Exploring My Interests

Robert:
7:00 AM – Rise and shine!
7:15 AM – Breakfast
7:45 AM – Chores
8:30 AM – Writing and Language Arts
9:30 AM – Math
10:30 AM – Reading
11:30 AM – Lunch/chores
12:30 PM – Science/Social Studies
1:30 PM – Exploring My Interests

As you can see in the above example, each child is doing something different. While you teach Joey math, Julie silently reads her book while Robert completes an essay. You rotate to Julie to discuss what she is reading. Ask questions reflecting critical thinking skills or refer to Bloom's Taxonomy, which centers around story development, new vocabulary, and characterization. When you talk with Robert, you will review grammar rules, such as punctuation and spelling, and the essay format. Teaching your kids becomes a rotation of who is doing what simultaneously!

Helping one another is second nature. If you feel conflicted over asking your children to help, remember that homeschooling families need to support one another to ensure everyone is learning equally. As part of the core family values, family unity is strengthened. Responsibilities, compassion, empathy, support, and communication skills are all heightened and improved upon.

One final note: Don't be afraid to use your phone for quick information, such as "Hey Siri" (or Ok, Google), who wrote "To Kill a Mockingbird?" or "Show me in step-by-step order, how do I write 657,000,000,000 in scientific notation?" "What is the capital of Zimbabwe?" or "What year did Columbus sail to America?" You can always check in with tools like this to get quick, factual answers to move your lessons.

 **Transcripts**

Many homeschooling parents need to be aware of the importance of a high school transcript, especially if they go to college or trade school. Since many parents don't know they can create their children's transcripts, they don't research how to develop them so their children can get into college or other schools after graduation from high school. Most parents don't know that just because their child is ten years old does not mean what they do at home can't be used on a high school transcript. Since you homeschool your child or children, you do not have to hold them back from learning content and ideas not usually taught in public schools until they reach a particular grade. That means your child could be ready to attend or even graduate by the time they celebrate their 16th birthday! There are even a few tricks to how your child can take college courses even younger than the norm by developing a transcript! The key is to ensure your child has mastered the courses required to be eligible for higher educational choices. Make sure you save examples of their work, which will document that your child successfully passed each course you put on the transcript. I suggest electronic portfolios and saving information to flash drives.

There are several formats of high school transcripts. Below are the most common types used in public education, but each can be formatted to your high school homeschool.

- **The Simple Transcript** is for families who want a straightforward transcript. It includes space for basic information, such as the student's name, date of birth, contact information, and a list of courses, grades, and credits earned.

- **Comprehensive Transcript** is more detailed and includes information about extracurricular activities, standardized test scores, and awards or honors the student has received. It has space for course descriptions, which may be helpful for college admissions.
- A **Subject-Based Transcript** organizes the transcript by subject area rather than yearly grades. This might be helpful to the student who takes more than four years to complete high school courses, as it allows them to demonstrate mastery of specific subject areas over time.
- **Portfolio-Based Transcript** is more flexible. It allows students to showcase their work in various subject areas, such as essays, research projects, and creative writing assignments. This is useful to students with unique interests or learning styles.
- A **Chronological Transcript** organizes courses and grades by year. It can also include a summary of the student's achievements or milestones each year.
- A **Narrative Transcript** uses a narrative approach to describe the student's academic achievements and growth throughout the time of high school courses. It may include stories, anecdotes, and examples of the student's work to showcase their skills and abilities.

Most states in the United States do not have specific homeschool graduation requirements. Still, following the public school-suggested courses for graduation is usually a good rule of thumb, especially if your student plans to attend college or university.

According to www.homeschool.com, "While homeschoolers are not bound by the graduation requirements of their home state, many still want to be able to compare their credits and coursework with their state department of education guidelines." The above link takes you to each state's high school homeschool graduation information. According to people outside the US, transcripts are indeed needed for graduation purposes, so making a transcript for any student is imperative. If you live outside of America, you should find out what is needed in your country for your child to graduate and keep a portfolio of their work and a digital copy of other educational choices.

 **Assigning Credits**

Public high school transcripts require a given number of credits, or classes, to finish high school, a minimum of twenty-two credits. Those credits generally mean sixteen main courses and six elective classes: four math, four English, three Social Studies, one History, three sciences, plus one lab. Depending on the school, electives include choices in such classes as music, band, art, home economics, physical education (usually two years), computer science, business sciences, and foreign languages (usually two years). If you homeschool, activities like piano, dance, and martial arts can count as electives if you track the time in these classes. For instance, your are paying for a karate course that lasts one hour, and your child practices at home for forty-five minutes four days per week, which counts as physical education. Suppose you happen to be a religious family. In that case, you can even use Bible study, or the religion of your choice, as one of the electives on their transcript, just as if your children were attending a private religious school.

To prove your child participated in an outside class, retain your receipts and ask the instructor to write an assessment of your child's progress. Most require a foreign language, but several language courses on the internet offer many languages. Babbel™ and The Rosetta Stone™ have various tests that can be printed to place in a portfolio. To determine how many total credits your child needs to finish high school requirements, call the district board of education to find out how many credits are required for graduating from high school, or www.homeschool.com has each state's high school graduation requirements.

The following is an example of a four-year high school transcript that you can begin to fill in no matter how old your child is. As you can see, it is arranged into years and semesters by the coursework completed. Hence, it is a simple transcript in chronological order that shows the grades achieved for the subjects and the credits received for completing the coursework successfully. Where it says Year 1, Year 2, Year 3, and Year 4, please provide the dates for completing this coursework.

Remember to name your transcript because it makes your school work official. For example, you might name your school "Smith Family High School" or "Smith Homeschool High School." Make sure you continue this name with each of your children. If you happen to move, you must not change the name. *How cool is that!?* You have a high school named after your family!

Year 1

Semester 1   Semester 2

Course	Grade	Credits	Grade	Credits	Total Credits
English 1		½		½	1
Algebra 1		½		½	1
Biology		½		½	1
US History		½		½	1
Spanish 1		½		½	1
PE - Karate		½		½	1

Year 2

Semester 1   Semester 2

Course	Grade	Credits	Grade	Credits	Total Credits
English II		½		½	1
Algebra II		½		½	1
Chemistry		½		½	1
Chem Lab		½		½	1
World History		½		½	1
Spanish II		½		½	1
PE Dance		½		½	1

Year 3

Semester 1   Semester 2

Course	Grade	Credits	Grade	Credits	Total Credits
English III		½		½	1
Geometry		½		½	1
Physical Sci		½		½	1
Civics		½		½	1
Driver's Ed		½		½	1
Music Piano		½		½	1
PE Dance		½		½	1

Year 4

Semester 1   Semester 2

Course	Grade	Credits	Grade	Credits	Total Credits
English IV		½		½	1
Trigonometry		½		½	1
Physics		½		½	1
Economics		½		½	1
Elective		½		½	1
		½		½	1
		½		½	1

In the above examples, each semester is worth ½ of a credit, but to a home-school parent, it represents half the material for that subject. The grade your child receives is up to your standards. Still, most homeschooling parents require the equivalent of an A because to get into colleges or universities, they will have to take either the Scholastic Aptitude Test—the SAT—or the American College Test—the ACT. Those tests are not administered at home; they are timed tests scheduled at different times of the year, usually at a local college or university. There is a fee involved with taking them. It may seem unfair, but many colleges and universities require higher scores for homeschooled children.

When deciding on what type of transcript you want to use, I recommend you use a combination of transcripts—a written one such as the example above, as well as a portfolio that includes not only written examples but also a compilation of pictures and other audio-video files on a flash drive, your paid receipts, and written observations from other qualified adults. As home-schooled students, their transcripts cannot be questioned if you prove your child deserves every "A" for every course they completed.

The beauty of a transcript is this: just because a child's age would make them a fifth grader in a traditional public school does not mean your child has to be held back in their learning—another plus for homeschooling. You do not need to take weeks and months off yearly to observe holiday breaks, federal holidays, teacher training days, etc. Everyone knows a year is three hundred and sixty-five days long, but traditional public school calendars are only written for around one hundred and eighty days. You do the math. Three hundred and sixty-five days a year, minus the traditional one hundred and eighty-day school calendar, means each public school child does not attend school for one hundred and eighty-five days a year. Look at all the time wasted that children could be learning. This is true for other countries who make room in school schedules for holidays and other breaks. Homeschool children, quite literally, do not waste any time when it comes to learning. They learn even when they take time for family field trips or vacations. All those fun activities you and your family take are prime opportunities for hands-on learning. The bonus is you and your family enjoy fun, hands-on activities while building strong relationships all year long!

My final suggestion is for parents: Prepare for tomorrow today. Make sure, in addition to the schedule, each child has a list of things they will be learning the next day written on that day's schedule. Children need to know what exactly they will be learning. For example, if you are working on Thursday's schedule, and "math" is at 8:30, tell what math concept to expect tomorrow morning, such as reducing fractions. If you teach that concept, ensure you know how to reduce fractions, the vocabulary they need to know this day, and future concepts. It's as important for you to be prepared to teach the concepts as it is for your child to know what to expect for the day.

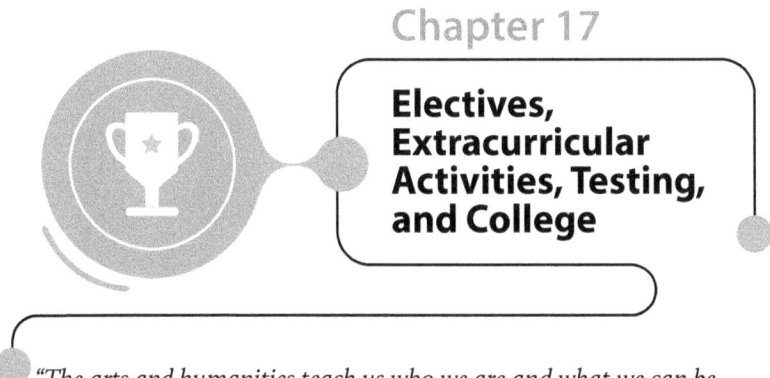

Chapter 17

Electives, Extracurricular Activities, Testing, and College

"The arts and humanities teach us who we are and what we can be.
They lie at the very core of the culture of which we're a part."
–Ronald Reagan

As a homeschool parent, you likely have unique goals and aspirations for your child, and your child likely has unique goals and desires for their future. Helping them reach those goals is probably why you chose homeschooling. Making sure they have what they need to achieve that future starts the minute you decide homeschooling is for both of you.

There are many topics that parents never think to ask about when they decide to homeschool that will ensure those goals are achieved. The topics in this chapter address four added variables that parents do not consider until their child reaches high school age and higher formal education becomes a necessary option. At this juncture of their child's education, parents assume that for their child to continue to college or other post-secondary education, they must send their child to high school for that coveted diploma. They presume this is the only way their child can obtain proof of successfully graduating with a diploma to continue their education at a higher level. This assumption is not true.

 **Extracurricular Activities**

I touched on extracurricular activities, electives in the last chapters, and a few websites that can be used, such as Babbel, for teaching foreign language and paid activities outside the home, such as karate, dance, and swimming. This is where beginning to create transcripts for your child becomes essential for their long-term goals. Mastering a foreign language by using an online site can be used as a foreign language on a high school transcript. Coordinated physical activities outside the home can count as the credits needed for Physical Education. Attending art courses can count for art, and taking piano is music. Different organizations, such as public libraries or churches, often offer classes in technology, science, or religion.

Every high school transcript has to include a minimum of six elective classes. The specific elective requirements for graduation can vary depending on the educational system, school district, and individual state regulations. In many cases, elective courses are chosen by students based on their interests and career goals. Here are some common types of electives that students might consider:

Fine Arts:
- Visual arts (drawing, painting, sculpture)
- Performing arts (music, theater, dance)

Foreign Language:
- Courses in a second language can be an elective requirement. Common choices include Spanish, French, German, Mandarin, etc.

Technology and Computer Science:
- Computer programming
- Web design
- Digital media production

Career and Technical Education (CTE):
- Courses related to specific careers, such as automotive technology, culinary arts, or graphic design.

Health and Physical Education:
- Courses related to fitness, wellness, and health education.

Business and Finance:
- Accounting
- Entrepreneurship
- Marketing

Social Studies and Humanities:
- Psychology
- Sociology
- Philosophy

Science:
- Astronomy
- Environmental science
- Anatomy and Physiology

Mathematics:
- Advanced math courses beyond the required curriculum

Literature and Writing:
- Creative writing
- Journalism
- World literature

It's important to check with the specific educational institution or home-schooling program to determine the elective requirements for graduation. Some institutions may have specific guidelines or recommendations, while others may offer more flexibility for students to choose electives based on their interests and future academic or career plans. Additionally, colleges and universities may have specific requirements or preferences when reviewing applications, so it's worth considering the academic and career goals of the student when selecting elective courses.

Tracking Extracurricular Activities

You may wonder how these activities can be used as elective classes when most people say they are extracurricular activities. This is true if your child attends public or private traditional schools because they offer choices for electives and hire teachers to teach them. That teacher decides your child's grade. Your child is expected to use what is offered. If a traditionally educated child takes an interesting class outside of school, it is rarely allowed as a credit for their high school transcript because the school district does not allow them to use it as a choice. *Why?* They do not monitor those activities or have their hired teacher give them a grade. However, suppose you, a homeschooling parent, hire a professional to instruct your child in various activities. In that case, you get to decide their "grade" with the input of the professional who is teaching your child. You must make sure your child is putting in as much time in those classes as they would be if they attended public school, and if questioned, be able to prove it. This is how.

First, purchase a simple planner for each child you are homeschooling. Then, find out the amount of time spent in high school periods or classes in the school district in which you live. Most periods range from forty-five to fifty minutes long per class. Hence, a traditional school's average high school student spends approximately 225 to 250 minutes per week in classes. Remember, a typical school year is only 180 days, making a semester ninety days or eighteen weeks.

Let's say your child, Ben, is interested in playing the piano. That qualifies as a music class. You signed Ben up for piano lessons. He is scheduled to attend class on Mondays from 3:30 to 4:30 each week, beginning January 2nd. Write that in Ben's planner. That's sixty minutes. Ben must practice an additional 165 to 190 minutes the rest of the week. Ensure it is logged in to his planner how many minutes he practices at home and on what days, as well as make digital copies of Ben practicing at home—videos and pictures—and ensure there is a time stamp on them.

At the end of eighteen documented weeks, Ben has put in the time equivalent to a traditional high school semester. If you or the piano teacher took time off, log that. Most self-employed music instructors have a recital every few months to highlight each student's progress. Ensure you video each of Ben's performance recitals for his portfolio. Using the feedback of Ben's teacher and how much time and effort he makes at home to practice, you can assign Ben a grade for a semester of music and have documentation of him completing a semester of an elective and justification for his grade. For added documentation, have the piano teacher sign his planner at the end of eighteen weeks, and keep your payment receipts.

You can follow this formula for any child and any subject that qualifies as an elective *or* a required course—English, Math, Science, or Social Studies. For instance, any physical activity would qualify as Physical Education—dance, martial arts, swimming, skiing, ice skating, and many more. As mentioned above, piano classes qualify as music, as will any other type of learning a musical instrument, such as drums, guitar, violin, voice classes, etc. If your child is interested in acting, any community musical or play can count as drama classes. As mentioned, if your child is learning a foreign language with something you purchase online, such as The Rosetta Stone or Babbel, log the hours they spend each week using that product. Plus, if your child has a strong aptitude for a required class, such as math, and has mastered Algebra 1 by the time they are twelve years old, log that in their planner, and save their tests in their portfolio. Do this for all other courses of study that qualify as high school-required classes.

 ## Supporting Your Child's Future Education

One of the biggest advantages of homeschooling is you do not have to put an age on your child to begin course study of traditional high schools. This is one of the drawbacks of traditional schools—if a child is already reading high school level material by the time they are ten years old, why does your child have to wait until they are fourteen to begin studying high school courses? *Answer: They don't!* You are the deciding factor as to when you think they are ready for higher-grade-level learning.

Once your child has fulfilled all the requirements of a traditional school, no matter their age, it's time to begin studying for the SAT (Scholastic Assessment Test) or ACT (American College Testing). Both are required for college entrance, but the ACT is more advantageous for homeschooled students because they can tailor their education to the subjects tested on it. When it's time to prepare for the test, test prep materials that suit the child's learning style and needs can be chosen. The questions on the ACT are straightforward and direct. On the other hand, the SAT does not have a dedicated Science section. The questioning is more evidence-based instead of knowledge-based, and incorrect answers to questions come with a penalty of 0.25% of a point per missed answer. However, some colleges have specific policies or guidelines for homeschooled students regarding standardized testing, so it is best to check with the institution your child wants to attend.

The SAT and ACT are both standardized tests used for college admissions in the United States, but there are some key differences between them:

Structure:
- SAT: The SAT has two main sections: Evidence-Based Reading and Writing (EBRW) and Math. There is also an optional Essay section.
- ACT: The ACT consists of four main sections: English, Math, Reading, and Science. There is an optional Writing section.

Content:
- SAT: The SAT focuses on evidence-based reading and writing, mathematical reasoning, and problem-solving. It includes vocabulary-based questions and a no-calculator math section.
- ACT: The ACT includes English, emphasizing grammar and usage; Math, focusing on algebra, geometry, and trigonometry; Reading, assessing comprehension; and Science, which tests interpretation and analysis of data.

Scoring:
- SAT: The SAT is scored on a scale of 400 to 1600, combining scores from the EBRW and Math sections. The optional Essay is scored separately.
- ACT: The ACT is scored on a scale of 1 to 36 for each of the four main sections. The composite score is the average of these section scores. The optional Writing section is scored separately.

Penalties for Wrong Answers:
- SAT: There is a penalty for incorrect answers (minus 1/4 point for each wrong answer).
- ACT: There is no penalty for guessing, so students are encouraged to answer every question.

Math Emphasis:
- SAT: The SAT places a stronger emphasis on algebra, data analysis, and problem-solving.
- ACT: The ACT covers a broader range of math topics, including trigonometry and geometry.

Science Section:
- SAT: The SAT does not have a dedicated science section, but it includes science-related questions in the reading and writing sections.
- ACT: The ACT has a separate Science section that assesses interpretation, analysis, evaluation, reasoning, and problem-solving skills.

Essay (Optional):
- Both tests have an optional essay section. The SAT essay analyzes a provided source, while the ACT essay requires students to evaluate multiple perspectives on a given issue.

Ultimately, students may choose to take either the SAT or ACT based on their strengths, preferences, and the requirements of the colleges or universities to which they plan to apply. Some students may take both tests to determine which showcases their abilities more effectively. Students should research the specific testing requirements of the institutions they are interested in. Additionally, there may be certain advantages of one college placement test, the SAT and ACT, over the other.

Homeschooled children may have an advantage with the ACT because it doesn't test for specific skills taught in traditional classroom settings. It's more of a test of what students have learned through life experiences rather than just what they learned in school. It tests English, Math, Reading, and Science with an optional writing section.

 ## Advanced Placement Tests

Advanced Placement (AP) tests are a set of standardized exams offered in the US by the accredited College Board. These exams are designed to assess a student's proficiency in college-level courses. They are often taken by high school students who wish to demonstrate their readiness for college-level learning. It is not necessary for a child to attend public school in order to take AP tests. Completing AP exams can also earn students college credit and advanced placement in college courses.

AP tests might be required to prove your child knows and has passed certain classes with college-level efficiency. The plus to taking AP tests is if they pass with the required score, they may count as college credits. Since all colleges and universities have different rules and regulations, you must check with the college your child wants to attend to see if AP courses are accepted as coursework, credits, or neither.

Key features of AP tests include:

Subject Areas:

- AP exams cover a wide range of subject areas, including but not limited to English, mathematics, sciences, history, foreign languages, and the arts.

College Credit and Placement:

- Depending on the student's performance on the AP exam, they may be eligible to receive college credit or advanced placement in certain college courses. This allows students to skip introductory courses and move directly into more advanced coursework.

Scoring:

- AP exams are scored on a scale of 1 to 5, with 5 being the highest possible score. Colleges and universities may have different policies regarding the scores they accept for credit or placement.

Exam Format:

- The format of AP exams varies by subject, but most exams consist of a combination of multiple-choice questions, free-response questions, and, in some cases, performance-based tasks.

Preparation:

- Many high schools offer AP courses to prepare students for the corresponding AP exams. However, students can also choose to self-study or seek additional preparation resources.

National Recognition:

- Success on AP exams is nationally recognized and can be a valuable addition to a student's college application. It demonstrates a commitment to challenging coursework and academic excellence.

AP Capstone Program:

- In addition to individual AP courses, the College Board offers the AP Capstone Program, which consists of two courses: AP Seminar and AP Research. Successfully completing this program provides students unique opportunities to develop research, critical thinking, and communication skills.

Global Availability:

- AP exams are not limited to students in the United States. They are available to students around the world, allowing for a global assessment of academic achievement.

It's important for students to research the AP policies of the colleges they are interested in attending, as each institution may have its own criteria for granting credit or placement based on AP exam scores. Additionally, successful performance on AP exams can provide a well-rounded academic profile.

 ## Community College Classes

The last thing I'd like to discuss is the advantages of your child taking community college classes before applying for a college or university. There are a few positives to taking community college courses early but also a few negatives. Let me point out the positives first.

Positives

- Your child can take community college courses before completing their high school transcript. This allows your child to get a head start on their college education and gain credits before "graduating" high school.
- Taking courses in community college gives your child a taste of college-level coursework.
- Taking a course in community college gives them an idea of the rigors of college-level coursework and the workload to maintain sufficient grades.
- It allows your child to get a head start on their college education.
- It could allow them to graduate from college earlier than those who do not take community college courses.

- It can help them stand out on college applications because they will already have completed college-level coursework, proving they can handle college-level coursework.
- It allows them to take courses unavailable in their homeschool environment or area.
- Colleges and universities recognize community college transcripts on their application, making it easier for the homeschooled student to be admitted.
- Community college coursework can be found many times as online courses, so they do not have to travel to a physical facility, which takes the worry out of how to get them to class.

Taking community college coursework is optional, and there may be some negatives to taking community college courses before your child is ready.

Negatives
- Community colleges may offer different resources and opportunities than four-year colleges and universities.
- Four-year colleges and universities, in particular, may offer research opportunities that community colleges do not offer.
- Four-year colleges and universities may offer study abroad programs that are advantageous to some career choices.
- Some homeschooled students may want to take more time to explore their interests and passions more earnestly before committing to a specific field of study.
- Every college and university has definitive courses that a student must pass to gain a diploma in fields of study. Some community college courses may not be accepted in some fields of study.

Taking college courses before "graduation" is ultimately up to the individual student. They must devote time to thinking about their goals, interests, and abilities. It's important to consider the pros and cons carefully and get insight and guidance from their parents and other respected family members.

Preparing your Child Post Homeschooling

As you focus on your homeschooling curriculum, it is important to factor in the long-term goals and what your child will require should they choose post-secondary education. Knowing this ahead of time is strategic to what subjects your child focuses on in more detail. Some careers, such as Medicine, require more advanced math and science courses in secondary studies—Calculus, Trigonometry, and Statistics, while other careers, such as Law, require more of the humanities—History, Literature and Language Arts, Philosophy, and the Arts, to name a few. Other careers, such as Cosmetology, may not require such an advanced curriculum and may not require either the ACT or SAT at all. Some careers also require a minimum score on either the ACT or SAT test. Deciding what your child is interested in pursuing in post-secondary education will make a huge difference in guiding their secondary coursework.

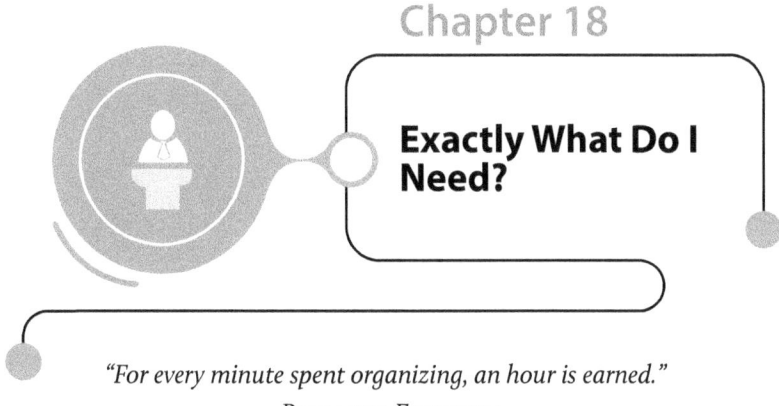

Chapter 18

Exactly What Do I Need?

"For every minute spent organizing, an hour is earned."
–BENJAMIN FRANKLIN

Deciding to homeschool one's children requires more than opening a book or signing up for an online homeschool platform for learning at home. Parents who decide to homeschool their children often dive into homeschooling without fully organizing what they need to efficiently teach, such as: where to set up learning spaces, which materials they will need, or how to make learning experiences meaningful, but at the same time, making it fun. I have seen parents go to the nearest store and purchase all sorts of things, thinking homeschooling mimics traditional public schools. Homeschooling can be very different and far more efficient when you have a good set of systems in place and are well-prepared for what you need.

 ## Tools and Supplies

To create an effective and enriching learning environment, parents may find the following tools helpful:

Curriculum Materials:
- Choose appropriate textbooks, workbooks, and educational materials that align with your child's grade level and learning style.

Lesson Planning Tools:
- Use planners, calendars, or digital tools to organize lesson plans, schedules, and educational activities. This helps maintain structure and consistency.

Learning Resources:
- Access to various learning resources, including books, online materials, educational apps, and multimedia resources, to supplement the curriculum and cater to different learning styles.

Basic School Supplies:
- Stock up on essential supplies such as notebooks, pens, pencils, rulers, markers, and other stationery items for various learning activities.

Computer and Internet Access:
- A computer or laptop with internet access is valuable for online research, educational games, and accessing digital learning platforms.

Printer/Scanner:
- Having a printer and scanner can be useful for printing worksheets, assignments, and other educational materials. Scanning capabilities can be handy for documenting and saving student work.

Educational Software and Apps:
- Explore educational software and apps that align with your child's curriculum, providing interactive and engaging learning experiences.

Arts and Crafts Supplies:
- Stock up on art supplies for creative projects and hands-on activities that enhance learning in subjects like art, science, and history.

Library Access:
- A library card provides access to a wide range of books, research materials, and educational resources. Utilize your local library to supplement your homeschooling curriculum.

Educational Games and Toys:
- Incorporate educational games and toys that promote learning through play, fostering a fun and interactive approach to education.

Storage and Organization Solutions:
- Organizational tools such as shelves, bins, and storage containers help keep materials, supplies, and resources neatly organized.

Whiteboard or Chalkboard:
- A whiteboard or chalkboard can serve as a versatile teaching tool for explaining concepts, practicing problems, and visualizing information.

Documenting Tools:
- Keep records of your child's progress with tools for documenting assignments, assessments, and achievements. This may include a grade book or a digital record-keeping system.

Online Learning Platforms:
- Explore online learning platforms and educational websites that offer supplementary lessons, interactive activities, and assessments.

Field Trip Resources:
- Plan and execute educational field trips with access to transportation, maps, and information about local museums, parks, and historical sites.

Remember that the specific tools needed can vary based on your child's age, grade level, and individual learning preferences. Adapt and customize your homeschooling environment to meet the unique needs and interests of your child.

In a traditional school, every child has a set of pencils, crayons, erasers, colored pencils, and binders. However, with homeschooling, consider buying one set of school supplies and keeping them in an organized location, such as a storage room or designated storage drawers. As your children need an item, they go to where the item is located and retrieve it, making sure to return it when finished. If you have more than one child that needs crayons simultaneously! Buy two sets. Having a supply of pencils and paper within easy reach makes sense, but you do not need *everything* up front. When starting, do not buy anything except the basics unless you need it or until you need it. For instance, don't buy colored card stock unless your child is doing a project that needs colored card stock. As you plan your lessons, you can also plan your supplies and required extra tools.

 ## Technology Tools

Earlier, I suggested you get a supply of Teachers' manuals at different levels of instruction for various subject areas. These are helpful for explanation purposes, basic information, and definitions, and they're in your home at your fingertips. If you don't want those books around the house, allow your kids to use the internet to find answers. Don't be afraid to let them use the internet to investigate and research topics. If you are willing to allow your child to investigate using Artificial Intelligence (AI) or other apps that will aid their education, please supervise them to ensure they get the benefits without allowing AI to do all the work. If you allow them to use the internet—and you should—then you need laptops or smartphones available for their use.

Regarding laptops, remember that certain models are more suitable for older children while others are more suitable for younger children. Also, if you use an online homeschooling program/school, you will need laptops for their use. Since technology is continually improving, I cannot suggest a perfect laptop, but I'm sure technicians at stores like Staples™ and Best Buy™ can give you suggestions based on your family's needs. I do suggest you purchase those tools that are fast, as well as check your Wi-Fi to ensure it accommodates the entire family.

A new technology accessible via the internet called ChatGPT: virtual AI—artificial intelligence—is also helping kids learn. This up-and-coming technology can be used for anything you or your children want to learn in the area of facts, data, and details. Some AI is free; even the search engine BING™ uses AI now. You can utilize it by typing in a specific query and asking for activities that can be done around that activity. For instance, you can type the question, *"Where are hands-on science museums for children in Montreal, Canada?"*

Then: *"What are specific hands-on activities available at the above museums?"* There are millions of things that can be asked and answered in ChatGPT™. It's like saying, "Hey, Siri," but Siri™ is now on super steroids!

There are many online resources and websites that are filled with materials you can use to teach, provide practice for your child, and even evaluate their mastery of what you are teaching. Some are free; some are fee-based. Some provide free materials but have more refined materials for a fee. The websites I include at the end of this book are geared specifically toward homeschooling families and provide free access to thousands of worksheets and materials to print, such as maps, number lines, and measurement tools like rulers. I have included a few paid sites that offer really good materials because obtaining memberships on paid sites is much more economical than paying for more expensive private education and private educational virtual schools, and they are geared to assist you in your homeschooling endeavors. I include them all so that you have plenty of materials to pick and choose from if you opt to create your curriculum rather than purchase canned curriculums.

 ## Learning Environment

Other things to consider are where your child will learn best. *The living room? Their bedroom? Around the dining room table? Do they need a desk? Filing cabinets? Do they want a bulletin board?* Remember from Chapter 5 that certain learners need certain environments regarding noise and stimuli levels. If you have an II learner, they will not pair well with a lot of noise and stimulus, so the learning environment for that child would be more suitable in the quietest part of your home. The II child will easily choose a desk in their room, away from all the hustle and bustle of family life. EE and PP learners will like working outside, around a garden, or near a window; VV's will like a reading corner or library; AAs will probably gravitate to places where there is a lot of room to work on projects and social interaction with the family. The CC child will want somewhere they won't bother others when they want to get up and dance or thrum out a beat with their fingers as they work. MMs will want somewhere conducive to their experiments with math manipulatives, strategy and logic games, and problem-solving equipment nearby. Not every child will learn best at home all of the time, so consider other locations to support your child's learning style. Homeschooled children can learn effectively in various environments, and the best learning environment often depends on the individual child's needs, preferences, and learning style.

Here are some potential places where homeschooled children may learn best:

Libraries:
- Advantages: Access to a wide range of books and resources, quiet and conducive to focused learning, potential for social interaction.
- Considerations: Observe library rules and etiquette.

Museums and Science Centers:
- Advantages: Hands-on learning experiences, exposure to real artifacts and exhibits, educational programs and workshops.
- Considerations: Plan non-peak visits and take advantage of educational programs.

Nature and Outdoor Spaces:
- Advantages: Exploration of the natural world, opportunities for hands-on science and environmental education opportunities, and physical activity.
- Considerations: Weather-dependent, be mindful of safety.

Cooperative Learning Centers or Homeschooling Groups:
- Advantages: Social interaction with peers, group activities, shared resources, and expertise.
- Considerations: Availability of local groups, compatibility with the child's learning style.

Online Learning Platforms:
- Advantages: Access to a wide range of courses and educational materials, flexibility in scheduling, and interactive and multimedia resources.
- Considerations: Monitor screen time and choose reputable platforms.

Educational Field Trips:
- Advantages: Real-world learning experiences, exposure to different cultures and environments, and hands-on activities.
- Considerations: Plan trips based on the curriculum and consider logistical aspects.

Community Centers or Recreation Facilities:
- Advantages: Physical education opportunities, social interactions, potential for organized classes or activities.
- Considerations: Check for availability, fees, and safety measures.

Local Businesses or Workplaces:
- Advantages: Exposure to real-world professions, mentorship opportunities, and practical application of skills.
- Considerations: Establish connections and ensure safety and appropriateness.

Educational Workshops and Classes:
- Advantages: Specialized instruction in specific subjects, hands-on learning opportunities.
- Considerations: Availability of local workshops, alignment with the child's interests.

Cultural Institutions (Theaters, Art Galleries, Concert Halls):
- Advantages: Exposure to the arts, cultural education, potential for performances or exhibitions.
- Considerations: Plan visits based on the child's interests and check for age-appropriate content.

Travel and Educational Trips:
- Advantages: Exposure to different cultures, history, and geography, firsthand experiences.
- Considerations: Plan trips in alignment with the curriculum and consider logistical aspects.

Ultimately, the best learning environment for homeschooled children caters to their individual needs, supports their learning styles, and provides opportunities for exploration and discovery. Flexibility and adaptability are key to creating a dynamic and effective homeschooling experience.

 ## Community Services

Other places where you can find valuable information are public libraries, where computers can be accessed, as well as books and other media. There are also virtual libraries where these same things are found.

Bookstores are your friends when finding books of interest that you and your family might want hard copies of. They will be your best friend when you need to find practice and study materials for the SAT or ACT. Don't forget there are thousands of websites for research and sites like YouTube. Local colleges and universities often allow the public to pay for membership services. There are also homeschool websites, homeschool social media sites, and rooms to discuss issues on apps such as Clubhouse™. Don't forget to take advantage of state.gov websites for education.

Many community services and resources can play a valuable role in supporting homeschooling families.

Here is a list of community services that can aid in homeschooling:

Community Centers:
- Provide spaces for physical activities, sports, and recreation.
- May offer classes or workshops in various subjects.
- Serve as meeting spaces for homeschooling groups.

Museums and Science Centers:
- Offer educational exhibits and programs.
- Host workshops and hands-on activities.
- Provide opportunities for experiential learning.

Homeschool Co-ops:
- Organize group classes or activities for homeschooled children.
- Facilitate social interaction among homeschooling families.
- Share resources and expertise.

Local Parks and Nature Centers:
- Offer outdoor spaces for physical education and nature studies.
- Host environmental education programs.
- Provide a natural setting for hands-on learning.

Tutoring Services:
- Connect homeschooling students with subject-specific tutors.
- Provide additional support in challenging subjects.

Local Businesses and Professionals:
- Collaborate with local businesses for educational field trips.
- Connect with professionals for mentorship opportunities.

Historical Societies and Heritage Centers:
- Organize historical tours and events.
- Provide access to primary sources and artifacts.

Language and Cultural Centers:
- Offer language classes or cultural immersion programs.
- Facilitate connections with native speakers.

Youth Organizations and Clubs:
- Join local youth organizations or clubs.
- Participate in scouting programs or youth groups for additional learning experiences.

Community Events and Festivals:
- Attend local events and festivals for cultural exposure.
- Participate in community service projects organized during events.

Sports Leagues and Teams:
- Join local sports leagues for physical education.
- Participate in team sports for social interaction.

Community Gardens:
- Engage in gardening projects for hands-on science learning.
- Learn about sustainability and environmental science.

Public Speaking and Debate Clubs:
- Develop communication and critical thinking skills.
- Participate in local debate or public speaking clubs.

Utilizing these community services can enhance the homeschooling experience by providing diverse learning opportunities, social interactions, and additional support for both students and parents.

 # Homeschool Plan

The following is a summarized list of materials you should obtain for home-schooling your children. I don't recommend rushing out and purchasing anything until you see what you need as you plan your children's lessons. Again, many online websites have these things available to print if and when you need them. You will also need consumables—things only used once, such as a practice worksheet, so don't forget printer paper.

- **A budget:** Homeschooling can be as simple or as elaborate as you want or can afford. A budget allows you to stay within your means, especially if you need to be more frugal. A budget will keep you accountable.
- **Curriculum Materials:** This can include textbooks, workbooks, and reading materials; Online curriculums; Websites for printing worksheets or other materials needed for teaching and practicing.
- **Office Supplies:** These materials include pencils, pens, highlighters, markers, erasers, rulers, scissors, staplers, paper, notecards, paper clips, and any other office supplies you think or know you will use.

- **Art Supplies:** These materials include crayons, colored pencils, glue, tape, construction paper, water-based markers, and scissors.
- **Science Equipment:** Science equipment should be purchased as needed, but some items you will eventually need include scales, measuring beakers, measuring tape, a periodic table, lenses, and a hot plate.
- **Math Manipulatives:** Young children will need materials, such as number lines, rulers, and counters, while older children may need calculators, protractors, and scales. As your child progresses in math, they will need more manipulatives or complex devices, such as a graphing calculator. If you use an online math curriculum, it may have digital tools embedded in the program. However, using hands-on materials whenever possible is always a good idea. There may be "gently used" teacher supply stores in your area. These are goldmines for all sorts of materials at discount prices.
- **Computer and Internet Access:** If you have more than one child, consider purchasing equipment that is age-appropriate and suitable for what is needed.
- **Printer and Scanners**
- **Reference Materials:** Materials needed for research and writing include a dictionary, a thesaurus, and an atlases.
- **A Wall Whiteboard or Chalkboard:** Handheld whiteboards or chalkboards can save a lot of paper, too.
- **Musical Instruments:** Purchase if your child wants to learn to play an instrument or consider a rental if your child only wants to explore playing one.
- **Physical Education materials:** Various types of balls—footballs, basketballs, softballs, jump ropes, hula hoops, and other home equipment. The neighborhood park usually has various climbing apparatuses, ball courts, and swings.
- **Library Card:** Almost every library requires each person to have a library card in order to check out books and other materials.
- **Educational Games and Software:** Many sites have built-in learning games that complement that site's philosophy and teaching modalities. Other games to consider are board games, puzzles, and strategy games.
- **Assessment Materials:** This includes practice for the SAT, ACT, various AP classes, and test practice for yearly progress. Study guides and

preparation books can be found online or at big-box bookstores, such as Barnes and Nobles™.

- **Storage and Organization Materials:** These include file cabinets, binders, crates, and caddies.
- **Furniture:** If needed, purchase study desks, chairs, and lighting for study areas.
- **Digital Storage:** These include flash drives or external memory drives.
- **Lists of Places** to go for educational outings and trips.
- **A Support System:** Consider joining homeschooling support groups, and co-ops, and accessing educational experts and consultants.
- **A Record-Keeping System:** You will need portfolios and digital copies of coursework—especially for hours of participation in extracurricular activities, volunteer activities, clubs, and health records for each child.

To ensure a positive, successful term and year in homeschooling you will want to take the time to put these recommendations into place to support you in reaching your homeschooling goals. I have talked a lot about what it will take to support your child, yet here is a list of what you need to support you and your partner in being aligned and focused on your homeschooling goals.

 ## Goals and Objectives

Reason:
- Brief overview of the desire to start homeschooling.
- Goals you want to achieve with each child.
- Reasonable expectations of the whole family.

Legal Considerations:
- Research homeschooling laws and regulations in your state.
- Familiarize yourself with any documentation or reporting requirements.
- Consider joining a local homeschooling association for support and guidance.
- Importance of understanding state homeschooling laws and requirements.

Educational Philosophy and Goals:
- Define your educational philosophy and goals for homeschooling.
- Consider your child's learning style and preferences.
- Establish a flexible curriculum that aligns with your goals and state requirements.

Curriculum Planning:
- Choose a curriculum or educational materials that suit your child's needs.
- Consider a mix of textbooks, workbooks, online resources, and hands-on activities.
- Develop a daily or weekly schedule to provide structure to the learning routine.

Record-Keeping and Documentation:
- Establish a system for tracking your child's progress and achievements.
- Keep records of assignments, assessments, and extracurricular activities.
- Stay organized with a portfolio or digital record-keeping system.

Socialization and Extracurricular Activities:
- Explore local homeschooling groups and co-ops for social interaction.
- Consider involvement in community sports, clubs, or organizations.
- Plan educational field trips and outings to enhance learning experiences.

Support Network:
- Connect with other homeschooling parents for support and advice.
- Attend local homeschooling events, workshops, and conferences.
- Utilize online forums and resources for additional guidance.

Assessment and Adjustments:
- Regularly assess your child's progress and adjust the curriculum as needed.
- Be open to modifying your approach based on your child's feedback and interests.
- Stay informed about educational resources and updates in the home-schooling community.

Know Your Why

Emphasize the ongoing nature of the homeschooling journey.
Encourage flexibility, adaptability, and continuous learning for both parent and child.

A successful year of homeschooling will require a positive mental attitude and a willingness to do whatever it takes to ensure your child is happy and learning to their potential. You should make sure you take time for *yourself* every day to reflect on your teaching techniques and the success of your lessons. Adjust what you feel needs adjusting and apply those tweaks in the following days and lessons. You have the ability to make *your* school unique and tailored to your family. Although I have listed many things here for you to add to your schooling program, the most important aspect is to know that things will shift, new plans will evolve, and you, as a parent, will grow daily as your child's teacher.

You might encounter some days where no one seems to 'get it,' or everyone appears to have gotten up on the wrong side of the bed. On those days you feel your lessons aren't going the way you want them to go, do not get discouraged. Nothing says you have to finish what you planned *today*. Sometimes, everyone just needs a break, so take everyone to the park, take a walk, put on some dance music, or go outside and play a rousing game of stickball! Learning isn't a race, it's a never-ending process just to take another step. You may come to a crossroads. You may have to decide to take the left-hand or right-hand fork in the road of learning. The great news is: *there are no wrong decisions. There are only opportunities to improve and find better ways.* Just remember to breathe and say to yourself, *"There's always tomorrow."*

As we leave this chapter behind, know I am your biggest cheerleader. You will succeed.

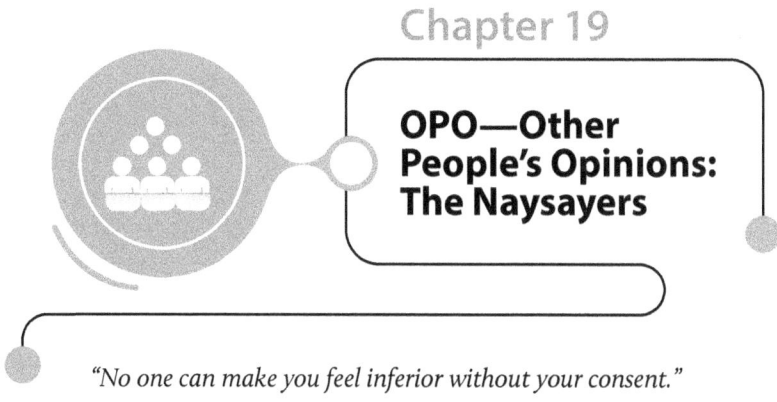

Chapter 19

OPO—Other People's Opinions: The Naysayers

"No one can make you feel inferior without your consent."
—ELEANOR ROOSEVELT

Now that you have decided to homeschool your family, you may run into friends, family, neighbors, in-laws, colleagues, acquaintances, and even the plumber—you name it— who will think you may have 'lost your mind.' They will not only tell you their opinions on homeschooling, but they might also challenge you with comments like, *"You are crazy, you are going to damage your children's future,"* or, *"You are putting your children's futures at risk! They will be so far behind they will never get a good job."*

This chapter is dedicated to supporting you through what others might say and some positive responses you can give to cancel out negative or uninformed opinions.

 ### Supporting Your Decision

When it comes to other people's opinions, you may hear, *"What makes you think you are qualified to teach your child?" "How do you know you can be a good teacher?" "Shouldn't children be in school?"* My thoughts about those kinds of questions are, *"Wow! That's likely them just projecting their insecurities!"* My usual response when I hear comments like these is, *"I am more familiar with my children than anyone else. I know their needs and struggles more intimately than any other adult. I am positive I can educate them effectively."* Whenever I give this answer, I see the wheels turning in their minds, and I immediately know they think the same about their children. Parents know the emotional, mental, and physical capabilities of their children. Parents can make the best teachers for their children with the proper training, support, and skills. They simply need to learn the nuts and bolts of administering information in a learnable way.

When you homeschool, you spend a lot more time with your child and learn how to utilize teaching techniques that help educate them better than a stranger who may only see them forty to sixty minutes a day. If you are already homeschooling, or preparing to homeschool, you are likely motivated to provide an effective educational experience to your children based on their needs. You want what is best for them and are committed to gaining the skills to provide it. Not knowing how important homeschooling is to you or the value it brings your child, some people may disagree with your decision and not be afraid to voice their concerns.

Responding to criticism about homeschooling requires a thoughtful and respectful approach. Here are five responses you can consider:

Share Your Positive Experiences:
- "I appreciate your concern, but homeschooling has been a very positive experience for our family. We've seen significant academic progress and have the flexibility to tailor our curriculum to our child's individual needs."

Emphasize the Personalization of Learning:
- "I understand that homeschooling may not be the traditional path, but it allows us to tailor our child's education to their unique learning style. This personalized approach has proven to be very effective for us."

Highlight Socialization Opportunities:
- "I can see why you might be concerned about socialization. However, home-schooling doesn't mean isolation. Our child can interact with a diverse group of people through various activities, co-ops, and community events."

Discuss the Flexibility of Schedule:
- "One of the reasons we chose homeschooling is its flexibility. It allows us to travel, explore different learning opportunities, and adapt our schedules to our family's needs. It's been a rewarding experience for us."

Express Confidence in Your Decision:
- "I understand that homeschooling isn't the conventional choice for everyone, but we're confident in our decision. We've done thorough research, and our child is thriving academically and socially. If you have any specific concerns, I'd be happy to discuss them further."

Remember to stay calm and open to opinions, focusing on the positive aspects of your homeschooling experience. Every family's situation is unique, and what works for one may not work for another. Your confidence and commitment to your child's education can help alleviate concerns and foster understanding.

 ## Adjusting Timelines

Most teachers have a daily lesson plan that *has* to be taught because, at specific intervals, they have to test their class to see who learned the content and who did not. This is based on the spring testing that every school in the nation has to take. Homeschooling parents don't have to 'stick to that plan.' They have more flexibility in addressing each need independently—if their children are struggling or if their children 'get it' within a few minutes and are ready to move on to something more stimulating. This is why homeschooled children are often accelerated beyond their traditional school peers. Children do not have to wait an hour for everyone else to complete the day's 'lesson plan objectives' when they may be ready to move to more challenging material in a few minutes. As a homeschooling parent, you decide based on your child's abilities.

You may find some people don't understand the benefit of how flexible it is to have your child advance grades and excel in classes they favor. In a world where traditional schooling often follows a one-size-fits-all approach, homeschooling allows *your* child to embrace their strengths and passions. Homeschooling empowers you to tailor *your* child's education to their unique needs and interests. Embracing this flexibility can lead to remarkable academic achievements and personal growth, ultimately helping your child reach their fullest potential. It's important to stay confident in your homeschooling journey and be prepared to address and educate others about the many benefits.

While traditional public schools are required to set a yearly schedule of a one hundred and eighty-day school year for children to attend school, you have three hundred and sixty-five days in a year to educate your children. This extended time frame provides you with the opportunity to create a holistic and well-rounded educational experience that goes beyond just classroom learning. You can take advantage of the natural world as your classroom, explore real-life applications of subjects, and foster a deep love for learning that extends beyond the confines of a traditional school calendar. Your dedication to providing your child with an education tailored to their needs and interests is a testament to your commitment as a homeschooling parent, and it's a path that can lead to academic success and a profound sense of fulfillment for you and your child. Embrace the year-round possibilities of homeschooling with confidence and enthusiasm!

 ## Environmental Teaching

You may encounter people who are surprised at the time they see you are *not* conforming to the traditional teaching timelines and criticize the amount of environmental learning you enjoy. This may include the number of outings you take or field trips you attend. However, it's crucial to remember that these outings are not just recreational but valuable educational experiences. Field trips and outings offer hands-on learning opportunities to enhance your child's understanding of various subjects, promote critical thinking, and foster a deeper connection to the world around them. These excursions are an integral part of your homeschooling journey. While some may question their frequency, they provide unique insights and real-world applications that a classroom alone cannot offer. So, don't be discouraged by such criticism; instead, embrace these enriching experiences as essential components of your child's education. Your dedication to providing a well-rounded education reflects your commitment to holistically nurturing your child's growth and development.

Responding to criticism about taking your homeschooled child on outings and field trips involves emphasizing the educational value and positive experiences. Here are three responses you might consider:

Highlighting Educational Benefits:

- "I understand that it might seem like we're frequently going on outings, but each trip is carefully planned to enhance our curriculum. Whether visiting a museum, historical site, or nature reserve, these experiences provide hands-on learning opportunities beyond what traditional classrooms offer. It's an important part of our educational approach to make learning come alive."

Emphasizing Real-World Learning:

- "We firmly believe in the value of real-world experiences. Field trips are not just a break from routine but an integral part of our homeschooling journey. These outings expose my children to diverse environments, cultures, and practical applications of their learning. It's about fostering a love for learning beyond textbooks."

Encouraging Socialization and Community Engagement:

- "I appreciate your concern, but our outings aren't just about academics. They also play a crucial role in socialization and community engagement. By participating in local events and interacting with people from various backgrounds, my child develops important social skills and a sense of community. It's about creating a well-rounded education."

Use your response to focus on the educational and social benefits of outings and field trips. It helps to convey that these experiences are intentional and contribute significantly to your child's holistic development.

 ## Utilizing Resources

Homeschooling parents have many materials and resources to support their children's learning at every age. They don't have to obtain what a school administration or district approves. Materials to teach with are abundant. You can find materials online for free or at a small charge, go to the library, or ask other homeschooling parents who are generally happy to share and exchange material and ideas about online and hard copy curriculums they have found useful.

Bookstores have study materials and other reference books for purchase. Teaching materials can be found at educational brick-and-mortar stores where all sorts of workbooks, resources, manipulatives, projects, and other materials are available. These stores are also useful if you want to look at certain materials before you purchase them, especially if you find them at a more economical price online. You get to tailor your child's education and take advantage of the latest resources and the most current teaching trends.

Numerous resources are available for purchasing homeschooling materials, catering to various educational philosophies and approaches. I have included several websites that cater to homeschooling families on the resource pages. Look for Rainbow Resource Center, BookShark, and Christianbook under the heading 'Curriculum-Based Sites.'

When purchasing homeschooling materials, it's essential to consider your educational philosophy, your child's learning style, and your family's specific needs. Additionally, exploring reviews, attending homeschooling conferences, and connecting with other homeschooling families can help you make informed decisions about the materials that best suit your goals. I have made sure to supply you with many more resources that you will find at the back of the book. Be sure to visit that section to find a wide range of resources to support you even more.

 ## Socialization

Some people may argue that your children might not be as well-socialized as those who attend traditional school. As a homeschooling family, you can interact with various people in different settings, such as homeschooling co-ops and extracurricular activities that you feel add value to your child's learning. Volunteer activities and clubs, such as Boy Scouts, Girl Guides, Boys and Girls Club of America, and 4-H, to name a few, create socialization and skill-based interactions. Positive socialization is one reason parents homeschool their children because they get to choose who their kids are in contact with, rather than have them in a social setting where the parents can't monitor their children's friends and social interactions.

Positive socialization is crucial for a child's development, helping them build social skills, emotional intelligence, and a sense of belonging. Feeling accepted and connected does not just happen in a school setting. As long as the child receives positive social interactions, the place is not the factor; the experience is. As their parent, you can ensure your child is feeling socially engaged and developing positively by incorporating these five key indicators of positive socialization into their daily routine:

Effective Communication Skills:
- Children engaged in positive socialization demonstrate effective communication skills. This includes expressing themselves clearly, actively listening to others, and engaging in conversations respectfully.

Empathy and Cooperation:
- Positive socialization fosters empathy and cooperation. Children understand and share the feelings of their peers, and they work collaboratively in group activities, demonstrating a sense of teamwork.

Appropriate Social Behavior:
- Children who have experienced positive socialization exhibit appropriate social behavior. This includes understanding and following social norms, sharing, taking turns, and respecting personal boundaries.

Conflict Resolution Skills:
- Positive socialization equips children with effective conflict resolution skills. They learn how to navigate disagreements, negotiate solutions, and handle conflicts constructively and non-aggressively.

Healthy Peer Relationships:
- Positive socialization contributes to the development of healthy peer relationships. Children form friendships, show kindness to others, and experience a sense of belonging within their social groups.

It's important to note that positive socialization is a dynamic and ongoing process. Parents, caregivers, and educators play crucial roles in creating environments that support positive social interactions and provide opportunities for children to develop and practice these key principles.

Addressing concerns about socialization is a common criticism of homeschooling. Here are two responses that emphasize the positive social experiences of homeschooled children:

Highlight Diverse Social Opportunities:
- "Contrary to the perception that homeschoolers lack socialization, our children engage in a wide range of social opportunities. They participate in local homeschooling groups, co-ops, and extracurricular activities where they interact with peers. Additionally, we encourage involvement in community events, sports, and volunteer work, providing them diverse social experiences extending beyond the confines of a traditional classroom."

Emphasize Quality over Quantity:
- "While the number of social interactions in a traditional school setting may be higher, we believe in prioritizing the quality of socialization. Homeschooled children have the opportunity to develop meaningful relationships with peers of different ages, backgrounds, and interests. This often leads to more authentic connections and a supportive social environment that fosters empathy, cooperation, and a sense of community."

These responses aim to address the misconception that homeschooling inherently limits socialization. By emphasizing the variety and depth of social opportunities available to homeschooled children, you can help challenge the notion that homeschoolers lack social experiences.

 ## Diversity and Acceptance

Another viewpoint of non-homeschoolers is that homeschooled children must be exposed to diverse perspectives and ideas. However, homeschooling parents will tell you their children can learn about different cultures and perspectives through reading, field trips, and interactions through their co-ops, extracurricular activities, clubs, religious settings, and other activities such as vacationing in different countries or regions of their own country. Homeschool parents do not have to rely on school initiatives or guest speakers brought into the classroom to present what guests do or information they want to distribute to their child. Addressing concerns about the lack of diversity in homeschooling is important, and there are ways to respond that highlight how homeschooled children can be exposed to diverse experiences. Here are three responses:

Emphasize Diverse Learning Environments:
- "While our children may not be in a traditional school setting, we actively seek diverse learning environments. We participate in community events, cultural festivals, and field trips to museums and places that celebrate diversity. Additionally, we encourage friendships with children from various backgrounds, providing an enriching social environment that reflects the world's diversity."

Highlight Tailored Experiences:
- "One of the advantages of homeschooling is the ability to tailor our curriculum to include diverse perspectives and experiences. We integrate literature, history, and cultural studies that reflect the richness of our global society. This personalized approach ensures that our children are exposed to a broad range of voices, cultures, and ideas, fostering a deep understanding of diversity."

Participation in Homeschooling Groups and Co-ops:
- "Far from being isolated, our homeschooling community is diverse in itself. We actively participate in homeschooling groups and co-ops where families come together for collaborative learning. This exposes our children to different teaching styles, backgrounds, and cultural influences. Additionally, these groups often organize events that celebrate diversity, creating a well-rounded social experience."

In each response, the emphasis is on the intentional efforts made to expose homeschooled children to academically and socially diverse experiences. It's essential to convey that homeschooling can provide a flexible and personalized approach to learning that actively incorporates and celebrates diversity.

 ## Success From Homeschooling

Some people may tell you that your children won't be prepared for college or have documentation to go to college. Not only did we discuss college earlier, but we know that many people have gone on to college and have successful careers who were homeschooled. The following are examples of a few homeschooled individuals who have gone on to have successful careers:

- **Ryan Hurd,** Country Music Singer/Songwriter
- **Lila Rose**, pro-life activist and founder of Live Action
- **Ben Carson,** former neurosurgeon and past US Secretary of Housing and Urban Development
- **Blake Ross**, co-creator of the Mozilla Firefox web browser
- **Rachel DeMille**, founder of DeMille Tutoring
- **Abigail Adams**, former first lady
- **Albert Einstein**, Theoretical Physicist
- **Michael Faraday**, scientist and inventor in the fields of electromagnetism and electrochemistry
- **John D. Rockefeller**, a successful businessperson, and philanthropist
- **Julius Summer Miller**, a renowned physicist and science educator
- **Rachael Field**, bestselling children's author
- **Andrew Carnegie**, a successful businessman, and philanthropist
- **Zac Sunderland,** the youngest person to sail around the world
- **Eliza Lucas Pinckney**, botanist, agriculturalist, and businessperson
- **Thomas Edison**, inventor and businessperson
- **Isaac Newton**, mathematician, and physicist
- **Tim Ferris**, entrepreneur, author, and podcast host

As you can see, although this is just a small list of homeschooled people, some of them are famous and whom we depend upon to this day because of their discoveries and what they've done for the world.

 ## Costing Criticism

The final point naysayers like to point out is that homeschooling is expensive, especially if they have to buy a curriculum or pay for extracurricular activities and classes. However, homeschooling parents quickly will point out that many free and low-cost resources are available for homeschooling, such as online materials and websites and the local library with free resources. Local homeschooling groups usually share resources. They do not have to buy uniforms, pay for extra gasoline to drive their kids to school if busses aren't available, they don't have to purchase multiple sets of school supplies for each child in the family, purchase separate individual meals, or deal with 'keeping up with the joneses' with clothing styles, shoe styles, or hairstyles. Also, many traditionally schooled children participate in similar extracurricular activities they pay for. Remember, though, the homeschooled parent can use it as an elective on a transcript where the traditionally educated child cannot.

What is important to remember is that no two families are the same. That includes those who use traditional public and private schools and homeschooling families. What works for one family may not work for another. People choose to homeschool for many reasons, but people who prefer public school send their children because it fits their family and lifestyle. While it is true that traditional public schools educate the masses, and many public school graduates have gone on to successful careers, the number of homeschooled children is increasing year to year.

It is likely that debate and criticism may continue until homeschooling is more widely recognized and more widely accepted as a viable alternative to traditional education. As a homeschooling parent, you may become the advocate and trailblazer of its continued success and benefits. As you blaze that trail, I will share some valuable topics of interest and helpful ideas to share with those who may be open to learning more and honoring your decision.

Below are positive trends in homeschooling, along with a brief comparison to aspects of traditional public schooling:

Personalized Learning:
- *Homeschooling:* Homeschooling allows for personalized learning experiences tailored to each student's pace, interests, and learning style.
- *Public School:* Public schools often have larger class sizes, making providing individualized attention to each student challenging.

Flexible Schedule:
- *Homeschooling:* Homeschooling provides flexibility in scheduling, allowing families to adapt learning to the rhythms of daily life and explore educational opportunities beyond traditional hours.
- *Public School:* Public schools typically follow fixed schedules, which may limit flexibility for families with unique needs or preferences.

Diverse Learning Environments:
- *Homeschooling:* Homeschooled students have the flexibility to learn in various environments, including at home, on field trips, in nature, and within the community.
- *Public School:* Public schools primarily operate within a traditional classroom setting, limiting the diversity of learning environments.

Customized Curriculum:
- *Homeschooling:* Families can choose or create a curriculum that aligns with their educational philosophy, values, and each child's specific needs.
- *Public School:* Public schools follow a standardized curriculum mandated by educational authorities, allowing less room for customization.

Stronger Family Bonds:
- *Homeschooling:* Homeschooling often fosters stronger family bonds as parents actively engage in their child's education, leading to a collaborative learning experience.
- *Public School:* In public schools, the separation between school and home life can sometimes limit the involvement of parents in the daily educational experience.

Individualized Pace:

- *Homeschooling:* Homeschooled students can progress at their own pace, allowing for mastery of subjects before moving on to more advanced material.
- *Public School:* Public schools may follow a fixed curriculum pace, potentially leading to varying levels of understanding among students in a single class.

Focus on Character Education:

- *Homeschooling:* Homeschooling often provides opportunities for intentional character education, incorporating values, ethics, and social-emotional learning.
- *Public School:* While character education is a component of public schooling, it may not receive the same emphasis as in homeschooling settings.

Experiential Learning:

- *Homeschooling:* Homeschooling often incorporates experiential learning with field trips, hands-on projects, and real-world applications of concepts.
- *Public School:* Due to logistical challenges, public schools may face limitations in organizing frequent experiential learning opportunities.

It's important to note that both homeschooling and public schooling have their strengths, and the choice between them depends on each family's unique needs and preferences. The positive trends in homeschooling highlight this educational approach's flexibility, individualization, and family-centered aspects.

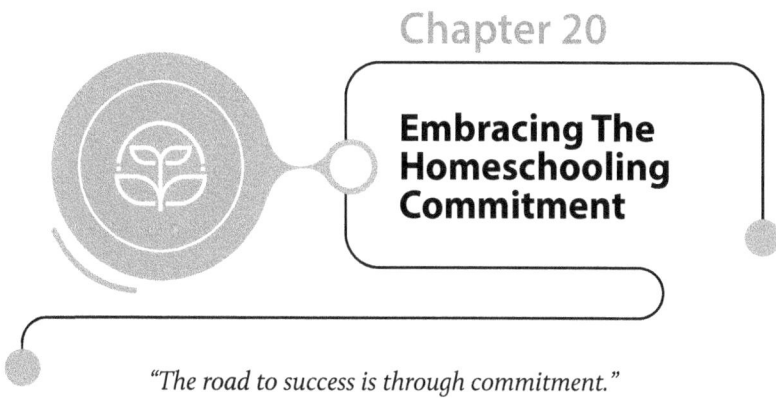

Chapter 20

Embracing The Homeschooling Commitment

"The road to success is through commitment."
—WILL SMITH

Will Smith's quote, *"The road to success is through commitment,"* resonates with me because it highlights the path to achievement. When it comes to homeschooling, *commitment* is key, *but what does commitment mean in this context?* The dictionary defines it as "the state or quality of being dedicated to a cause, activity, etc." and "a pledge or undertaking." That definition perfectly encapsulates homeschooling, as you pledge yourself to the cause of educating your children. It's a significant undertaking! When you choose to homeschool, you commit to giving your children the best education possible down the long road of their schooling years. You're committed to ensuring they acquire fundamental math, reading, grammar, language, science, and history knowledge, and the advanced skills necessary for college and life. It's a considerable challenge, but you cannot afford to fail, given what's at stake: your children's future.

While it may sound daunting, remember that *Rome wasn't built in a day*. Acknowledge that you won't be perfect starting day one of your homeschooling journey. Mistakes will be made, and even the most trained educators make mistakes. Over my forty-plus years of teaching in public and private schools, I made my fair share of them. However, with time, I improved and came to love the challenges I encountered every day. I examined my educational experiences, identifying what I excelled at and what challenged me. I adapted my teaching methods to leverage my strengths and took a different approach to the subjects I struggled with.

I had to understand why I faced difficulties to avoid repeating those mistakes with my students. I want you to do the same. There will be days you need to reflect and then encourage yourself to keep going. There will be times that you want to give in and will need to stop what you're doing, take a walk or go on a drive, and not think about any aspect of homeschooling—focus on *you!* After you return home, sit down and make a side-by-side double list. On the left-hand side, label it "Things I Need to Improve." On the right-hand side, label it "What I Can Do to Improve." This will give you perspective on the things that have you feeling defeated and ways to get you back to the confident and positive teacher you are. I encourage you to take the time to reflect on your strengths and then look at the areas within you that feel uncertain.

Keep improving your strengths and embracing your areas of uncertainty with curiosity, and see them as opportunities for growth. As homeschooling parents, your journey is unique. Be open to exploring new teaching methods and resources that can enrich your homeschooling journey. Collaboration with other homeschooling families, attending workshops, and seeking guidance from educational experts can provide valuable insights and support. Your children rely on you to deliver a high-quality education, so do your best to give them that. Take the time to reinforce your proficiency in subjects you excel in and diligently work on areas where you need improvement. Applying this model to your children's education will make you a more effective teacher and support your commitment to carry on.

Occasionally, you may encounter family issues. Sibling rivalry, for example, can arise when one child feels they're not receiving as much attention as another. In such situations, it's crucial to empathetically listen to your child's concerns and reassure them of your love through compassion and understanding. Homeschooling doesn't eliminate normal family dynamics; kids will still argue just as they always have. It is essential to establish family values and ensure each family member can openly express their concerns. Learning to negotiate peacefully is challenging but worthwhile.

Unexpected events may also occur, such as illnesses, accidents, or family deaths, requiring considerations and negotiations within the family. In these trying times, honesty with your children is essential while maintaining composure in adversity. Children emulate what they see, so be aware that your children will follow your example. How you handle difficulties will set the tone for them. Learn to negotiate while supporting boundaries, and discover the art of brokering peaceful family agreements and heartfelt compromise.

As homeschooling becomes the norm in your family, certain new arrangements, systems, and ingenuities will filter into your lifestyle and daily activities. Homeschooling offers flexibility in how and where learning takes place. Be inventive, creative, and flexible when needed. Ask your children, *"Who says you can't study in your pajamas? Who says you can't snack while working on algebra problems? Who says you can't take your history lesson to the dentist's office or learn about Newton's Laws of motion while skiing?"* These are just a few examples of the countless possibilities in homeschooling that are seldom found in traditional public schooling. Once your children realize that the classroom can be their cozy bed, a tree in the backyard, or even the dog-walking route, they'll likely embrace homeschooling much faster and appreciate the choice you made.

When you commit to homeschooling your children, be sure to familiarize yourself with your local school supervisors and the requirements of homeschooling where you live. This is crucial because, in some places, keeping your children out of public school can result in fines or legal consequences unless they are enrolled in a religious or private institution.

To support your commitment to homeschooling, arm yourself with tools, resources, and support. Explore the websites listed at the end of this book to give you a head start in your process and equip you with the many materials you will need. Investigate the different resources available, find the ones that are suitable for your family, and implement what they offer. Many of these resources give free and valuable, up-to-date information. Those with membership fees are usually more affordable than expensive pre-packaged curricula and can be used month-by-month. You'll likely need supplementary materials to help your children master subjects, especially as they progress in their education, so use what I have listed to research what will work best for you.

When selecting educational materials, prioritize high-quality resources. Some of the websites and organizations mentioned at the end of this book may cater specifically to certain states within the US, addressing local regulations. When searching for materials, prioritize those that encourage critical thinking and open-ended questions, allowing your child to provide answers and justify their thinking. Steer clear of materials that solely rely on yes/no questions or require rote memorization. While these have their place, a well-rounded education demands more. Keep seeking excellent materials, especially if you have multiple children who can benefit from them.

Regarding student laptops, it's advisable to assert each child's specific needs before purchasing individual laptops. Older children might require different features, such as music composition software or graphics, compared to younger children with simpler needs or less memory capacity or processing speed. Assess their requirements before investing in expensive technology.

To support you in learning the latest homeschooling techniques or finding out what others are doing to create success in their families, consider joining social media groups dedicated to homeschooling, like those on Facebook™ or TikTok™. These groups are valuable sources of tips and tricks and build camaraderie with other homeschooling parents. Remember, approximately fifteen million children are homeschooled daily, and parents are always searching for other parents to help them and build support and community. Be willing to learn from those who have been homeschooling longer than you and utilize their winning processes. Online social support can come from children the same age as yours or those with the same innovative learning styles that your child has. Many specific niches on social media cater to many unique aspects of every child.

Inquire within your local homeschooling community to find out if there are any homeschooling groups or co-ops in your area. Attend gatherings and assess whether they align with your family's needs, and be open to starting your own group if none are available or offering what you prefer. Don't hesitate to explore all your options. Remember that these groups often share resources, so having multiple channels for acquiring ideas, information, and materials is advantageous. You may possess knowledge or materials that others could benefit from, and vice versa. Collaborate to exchange expertise through physical meetings or online platforms like Facetime™ or Zoom™. Sharing information and ideas benefits everyone involved.

Documenting your children's schoolwork is vital. Just as professionals maintain records for their resumes, save your children's schoolwork in a portfolio. Begin with preschool and continue throughout their education. These portfolios prove your child's progress and justify the grades you assign them in each subject. Whether you opt for an internet-based homeschool program or a mix of online and traditional coursework, these portfolios can be invaluable, especially if you must demonstrate mastery when moving to another state.

Regarding high school transcripts, creating one is straightforward. However, it's important to be prepared for potential scrutiny of the grading marks you assign to your child's efforts in each subject. Your child's portfolios provide ample evidence of their abilities, reinforcing the effort and achievement you expect from them. Be sure to clearly name your child's transcript, such as "John Alexander Smith's Homeschool High School Transcript" or "Smith Family Official High School Transcript," and keep proficient notes. Develop a daily, weekly, and monthly routine of scheduling field trips, other academic explorations, online learning time, various appointments, and exploratory activities, such as music lessons, writing courses, or club meetings.

When homeschooling your children, there are considerations regarding spaces, equipment, supplies, and other resources. Where you choose to hold classes when you are teaching, some parents use office space. In contrast, others gather around the dining room table for formal teaching, giving kids a comfortable activity space. Some families designate a shelf or file cabinet for materials like pencils, paper, highlighters, and construction paper, making them easily accessible for all learners in your household.

Homeschooling parents must define their expectations regarding family values, standards, interactions, and responsibilities—why they chose this educational path. However, don't assume your children automatically understand these expectations. Hold a family meeting to discuss these values, standards, interactions, and responsibilities. Plan excursions and events that allow your children to put these values into practice with others. Clarity is essential; there should be no doubt about these aspects. Your children should know your beliefs regarding the values of human existence, the importance of supporting each other's interests, working together for mutual success, and always striving to improve.

Mastery of essential subject matter is crucial because unaddressed gaps can lead to problems later. Take math, for instance; concepts build on each other. Understanding the concept of adding zero to any number lays the foundation for more advanced concepts like the zero property of addition in algebra. As your child advances in math, having a solid grasp of fundamental concepts will make it easier for them to navigate more complex topics.

Accentuate your child's innovative learning style and surround them with those who learn like them. Pair your Amazing Adaptive child with a Conscious Creative learner, and watch what they come up with! Bring focus to an Exceptional Ecologist with the insights of the Impressive Independent learner. The geometric mind of the Magical Mathematician and the Super Spatialist will design amazing projects together. At the same time, the Phenomenal Physicalist and the Vivacious Verbalist will bring incredible adventures together in written works of art. And don't forget *your* gifts that are all a part of your personality and learning styles. Ask yourself, *"How can I use how I think and learn to better equip these unique and precious children? What can I do to spark my imagination and creativity to foster learning and continue lifetime learning?"*

In those times when you want even more support, consider utilizing the expertise of a homeschooling coach. A homeschool coach is a professional who offers guidance and support to families educating their children at home. They can assist with curriculum planning, teaching methods, and educational resources, and advise on legal and administrative aspects of homeschooling. Some homeschool coaches offer one-on-one tutoring or small group instruction for specific subjects and work closely with parents to provide assistance and guidance. The ultimate goal of a homeschool coach is to help families ensure that their children not only learn but excel and thrive in their education, nurturing successful lifelong learners and individuals. When embarking on this homeschooling journey or seeking fresh and exciting ideas as your children's teacher, lean on those who specialize in this field. As children grow and advance, stimulating experiences and innovative ideas become essential, and coaches help you expand your thinking and enhance your intrinsic skills. A homeschool coach like myself can help you clarify your expectations and design exceptional activities and lessons for you and your entire family.

Homeschooling is a dynamic process that evolves as your children and family grow. Your approach to homeschooling one child may differ when homeschooling multiple children. Given the diverse components involved, what works best for one family may not work for another. You'll naturally adapt your methods as you gain more knowledge and ideas. However, your core values will remain constant, driven by your unwavering commitment to homeschooling each innovative learner. You know your children best; let your choices always reflect their highest interests and personal growth.

To support you in your commitment, here is a checklist of what you need to start homeschooling. Reviewing and ensuring you have everything you need to homeschool your children effectively is useful.

- ❏ I have made a list of my whys for homeschooling my children.
- ❏ I have researched the requirements for homeschooling my child in the state in which we live.
- ❏ I have administered the survey for The Theory of Multiple Intelligences to my children and explored the meaning of their learning styles.
- ❏ I have explored the following in the area where I live:
- ❏ Access to various academic and extracurricular activities
- ❏ Qualified and certified teachers willing to help me when needed
- ❏ Access to resources such as libraries, technology, and sports facilities
- ❏ Online homeschooling programs that I like or have been recommended
- ❏ Free educational websites and materials
- ❏ Opportunities for socialization and making friends
- ❏ College prep and resources
- ❏ Specialized programs such as language or gifted and talented programs
- ❏ Access to various academic and extracurricular activities
- ❏ Homeschool organizations in the area where we live
- ❏ Social media organizations and groups
- ❏ State standards of learning of the state in which we live for standardized testing purposes
- ❏ Developed a working schedule for school and family chores and activities.
- ❏ Developed a working high school transcript to be filled out as my children progress in their studies.
- ❏ Discussed your intentions of homeschooling with your children and other family members outside the home.
- ❏ I have arranged our home to be the perfect atmosphere for each of my children for their personal learning spaces and where I will be teaching them.
- ❏ I have purchased appropriate materials for the collective learning of my children: pencils, paper, colored pencils, etc.
- ❏ I have purchased appropriate electronic learning materials: laptops, internet access, websites, etc.

Armed with all this information and everything you have learned about home-schooling, I am confident you now have all the tools needed to bring your homeschool to new heights of excellence and fulfillment. While challenges may arise, remember that your unwavering dedication to your children's education will be the cornerstone of their growth and development. As you continue along this path, keep nurturing their curiosity, fostering a love for learning, and creating a nurturing educational environment that celebrates the unique journey of homeschooling. The road may be winding, but with commitment, you are on the right track to achieving educational success and building lasting memories with your family.

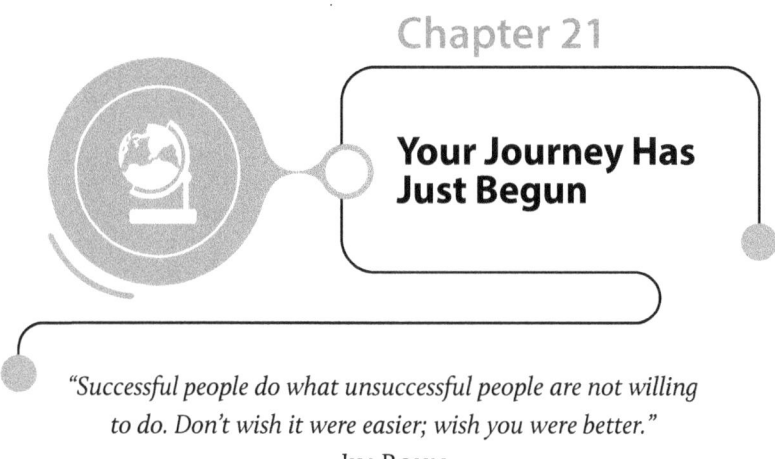

Chapter 21

Your Journey Has Just Begun

"Successful people do what unsuccessful people are not willing to do. Don't wish it were easier; wish you were better."
—JIM ROHN

I hope you have read this book and taken copious notes to support your homeschooling journey. It is now time to take your decisions to the next level and implement them! I am excited for you to make homeschooling a reality and enjoy the unique opportunity to provide your children with an individualized education tailored to their needs, interests, and learning styles. Homeschooling is not without its challenges and demands, yet you now have the tools and understanding to make educated decisions going forward. As a homeschool parent, you get to make that unwavering commitment to ensure a successful homeschooling experience for you, your child, and your entire family.

You'll want to provide your children with a safe and nurturing learning environment to have the outcomes you desire in your homeschooling endeavor. This includes being their parent first and their teacher second. That will require creative maneuvering and tactful times to balance personal and emotional needs with school requirements and your teaching structure. You and your children will have to find your footing for the difference between when you are a parent and when you are their teacher.

Balancing parent and teacher roles when homeschooling can be challenging, but creating clear boundaries can help maintain a healthy parent-child dynamic. Here are four ways parents can separate their roles as teacher and parent:

Establish Clear Daily Routines:
- Create a structured daily routine that includes dedicated time for homeschooling and other times for family activities, meals, and relaxation. Having a clear schedule helps children understand when it's time for learning and when it's time for family.

Designate a Learning Space:
- Set up a specific area in your home for homeschooling activities. When you're in this designated learning space, you take on the role of the teacher. Once the learning session is over, leave the space together to signal the transition back to the parent-child relationship.

Use Visual Cues or Props:
- Introduce visual cues or props to signify when the teaching role is in effect. For example, you might wear a "teacher hat" during learning time and remove it afterward. This simple act can help create a mental shift for you and your child.

Establish Teacher Time and Parent Time:
- Communicate with your child about the different roles you play. Establish clear expectations for when you are the teacher and when you are the parent. For example, during "teacher time," you focus on academic activities, and during "parent time," you are available for emotional support and bonding.

Emphasizing the emotional aspect of the parent-teacher relationship can contribute to a more empathetic and understanding learning environment. Here are four ways parents can navigate the emotional aspect of being both a teacher and a parent:

Establish Emotional Check-ins:
- Begin each learning session with a brief emotional check-in. Ask your child how they're feeling and if there's anything on their mind. This practice encourages open communication about emotions and helps create a positive learning environment.

Create a Safe Emotional Space:
- Emphasize the importance of a safe emotional space during learning. Let your child know it's okay to express their feelings, whether it's frustration with a challenging lesson or excitement about a new concept. Acknowledge and validate their emotions, fostering a sense of emotional security.

Implement "Emotion Breaks":
- Recognize that emotions can play a significant role in the learning process. If your child is feeling overwhelmed or stressed, introduce the concept of "emotion breaks." Take a short break together to discuss their feelings, engage in a calming activity, or simply have a moment of connection.

Separate Emotion-Focused Time:
- Designate specific times for emotion-focused discussions separate from academic lessons. This could involve setting aside a "feelings circle" or incorporating a daily journal where your child can freely express their emotions. Having dedicated emotional check-ins reinforces the importance of both roles—teacher and parent.

Navigating emotions is a shared experience. Acknowledging and addressing feelings first can strengthen your parent-child bond. By integrating emotional well-being into your homeschooling approach, you create an environment where learning becomes both a cognitive experience and an emotionally supportive one.

Remember that flexibility is key, and it's normal for these roles to overlap at times. The goal is to create a balance that works for your family and ensures that your child receives both academic guidance and emotional support. Open communication with your child about these boundaries can also help them understand and adapt to the dual roles you play in their education.

What makes homeschooling so rewarding is that it encompasses not only academic subjects but also life skills, ingenuity, and innovativeness. This enables you to teach your child values such as respect and responsibility, encouraging critical thinking and questioning while fostering individuality and uniqueness. Honoring emotions, addressing feelings, and caring for your child's mental health are integral to the homeschooling experience. It's an opportunity to create a safe and nurturing environment where emotional intelligence is valued and emotional well-being is prioritized. By embracing the holistic approach of homeschooling, you not only impart knowledge but also nurture well-rounded individuals equipped to navigate life's complexities with resilience and empathy. Your dedication to teaching values, fostering curiosity, and caring for your child's mental and emotional health is a testament to the profound impact homeschooling can have on shaping well-adjusted, compassionate, and capable individuals ready to face the world with confidence and integrity.

As your child's teacher, always maintain open communication and seek ways for your child to give honest feedback and supportive suggestions. Make space for them to share their ideas and complaints constructively and helpfully. You are all learning together, so it will take time to get it right for everyone. Your child will need to know it is okay for them to tell you how they are feeling and give suggestions throughout the process.

Be sure to carve out opportunities for yourself to stay refreshed and motivated throughout the homeschooling journey. You must walk this path with your children to ensure they receive a high-quality education and the best possible homeschooling experience. If you are not okay, your kids will not be okay, so avoid burning the candle at both ends or staying up too late. Prioritize self-care, seek support from fellow homeschooling parents or support groups, and remember that taking breaks and nurturing your own well-being is not a sign of weakness but a vital part of being the best parent and educator you can be for your children. In taking care of yourself, you set a powerful example for them, demonstrating the importance of balance and self-care as they grow and learn alongside you.

At each stage of your homeschooling journey, staying connected and seeking support when needed are essential. Your emotional care and well-being are paramount, so be sure to take care of you. Honoring your emotional well-being as a parent is crucial for maintaining a positive homeschooling experience. Here are three things you can do to prioritize your emotional self-care:

Establish Self-Care Rituals:
- Set clear boundaries between your roles as a parent, teacher, and individual. Designate specific times for homeschooling, and make sure to

carve out moments for your own self-care. Create rituals that bring you joy and relaxation, whether it's enjoying a quiet cup of tea, taking a short walk, or engaging in a hobby. Consistently practicing self-care rituals helps recharge your emotional batteries.

Connect with Support Networks:
- Seek out and connect with other homeschooling parents or support groups. Sharing experiences, challenges, and successes with like-minded individuals can provide emotional support and reduce feelings of isolation. These connections can offer valuable insights and a sense of community, whether in-person or online.

Prioritize Communication and Flexibility:
- Communicate openly with your child about your own emotions and challenges. Encourage open dialogue, allowing both you and your child to express feelings and concerns. Additionally, be flexible with your homeschooling schedule and expectations. Recognize that some days may be more challenging, and it's okay to adapt your plans to better accommodate your emotional well-being.

Remember that taking care of yourself emotionally is not selfish but essential for providing a positive and nurturing environment for your child's education. By incorporating these practices into your routine, you can strike a balance between homeschooling responsibilities and your own emotional well-being.

If ever you need a little extra, or I can be of support, please reach out to me directly. I would be happy to help you and your children in your homeschooling endeavors. I love providing personalized guidance, customized educational plans, and regular check-ins to ensure your homeschooling experience remains positive and successful. I also have ways of easing stress and giving new insight into common issues parents often face. My calendar always has room to schedule a face-to-face discussion, as I know the value of helping one-on-one.

You can find me on social media as Melanie Summers, email me at amelliemoment@gmail.com, or book a free consultation on my website, www.innovativehomeschoolsolutions.com—I'd love to hear from you and find out the wonderful things you do while homeschooling your children.

If anything you have read here has helped you, or you want to share how my book *Learning Outside the Line* has made a difference in your child's life, please email me and share your experiences. Your feedback and success stories are valuable to me and can inspire and motivate other homeschooling parents on their own educational journeys. Your insights and achievements serve as a testament to the power of innovative homeschooling, and I look forward to hearing from you and celebrating your educational milestones together.

If you are looking for more ways to grow *your* teaching expertise, my website is filled with useful resources for all your homeschooling needs. You can explore a selection of my international bestselling books, access the Innovative Homeschool Inventory in PDF format, stay updated with informative blog posts, and receive personalized guidance and support tailored to your unique homeschooling goals and challenges. Whether you're just starting or looking to enhance your homeschooling experience, I want to empower you with the tools and knowledge you need for successful and innovative homeschooling.

In writing this book, I aimed to supply you with the information you need to make the appropriate decisions when considering homeschooling your children. I know that with valuable information on how to educate your children concerning how they think, you can address their specific needs and become the game-changer in their homeschooling experience. I want you to feel empowered to teach your amazing specific learners and celebrate their beautiful uniqueness. I also want you to know that it takes a special parent to take on this role, and you are nothing short of incredible. Not every parent has this drive or willingness to homeschool as you do, so please take the time to congratulate yourself on being driven to ensure your children have a successful education that will lead them to a happy and prosperous life.

Children are a gift we give to the planet and preparing them with the skills they need to become conscious citizens, helpful individuals, and supportive parents themselves will add to the fabric of the future, for all people. Your dedication to homeschool is part of that framework and a fundamental ingredient wherein education, schooling, and communication between individuals fosters a better world for everyone.

In closing, I leave you with this: *Embrace the adventure of homeschooling with joy and enthusiasm, and may your homeschooling experiences be filled with happiness and valuable learning moments for both you and your children for many years to come!*

Section 4

Websites And More

Dear Reader,

I want to take the opportunity to thank you for purchasing my book on home-schooling. I truly hope you gained a lot of insight and information that will guide you in your endeavors to teach your children at home. I salute you because it will be the ultimate gift you give your children–their education. For those standing on the edge, ready to jump, but needing that last little bit of encouragement, I say, you are more resourceful and savvy than you think.

As a parting gift, the websites below are all websites I have personally gone to for information and/or use. Some have a small joining fee or monthly usage fee. However, I included all because they all have pertinent information and advice. Most interactive learning sites have a free trial period, so you can try them out before you buy. If you ever need to contact me for advice or want to know more about what I can do for you, I offer a one-time free consultation.

Happy child, happy parent, happy homeschooling!

Melanie Summers

WEBSITES

INTERACTIVE LEARNING SITES:

ABCMouse: Online educational platform for children ages 2-8 providing interactive activities and games. (www.abcmouse.com)

ABCya: Educational platform for children ages K-5 featuring free games, activities and lessons. (www.abcya.com)

Book Adventure: Book Adventure is a website that encourages kids to explore and read books. It offers activities, quizzes, and rewards to help motivate kids to read more. https://www.bookadventure.com/

Bookopolis: Bookopolis is a virtual book club for kids. It provides a safe place for kids to connect with other readers and explore books from around the world. https://www.bookopolis.com/

BrainPOP Online learning platform for students in grades 3-12 featuring educational videos and activities. (www.brainpop.com)

BrainPOP Jr. Online learning platform for students in grades K-3 featuring educational videos and activities. (www.brainpopjr.com)

Discovery Education: An online resource for teaching and learning with digital media. (www.discoveryeducation.com)

Epic!: Epic! is an app that provides access to a library of over 35,000 books, videos, and other educational content for kids. It is a great resource for kids to find books that match their interests and reading level. https://www.getepic.com/

Funbrain: Funbrain is a website that provides educational games, activities, and resources for students in grades K-8. It is a great resource for teachers and parents to help kids explore a variety of topics. (www.funbrain.com)

Kids Discover Online: An online learning platform with interactive activities and videos for grades PreK–8. (www.kids discover.com)

Literactive: a website that provides interactive activities to help young learners practice reading, writing, and other literacy skills. It is a great resource for parents and teachers to help students develop early literacy skills. http://www.literactive.com/

National Geographic Education: An online resource providing educational resources, activities, and videos related to geography and science. (www.natgeoed.org)

PBS Kids: An online learning platform with educational games and activities for kids. (www.pbskids.org)

PBS Learning Media: An online resource providing educational videos and activities for PreK–12th grade. (www.pbslearningmedia.org)

Quizlet: An online study tool with flashcards and learning activities. (www.quizlet.com)

YouTube EDU: An educational platform featuring videos from universities and organizations worldwide. (www.youtube.com/edu)

WORKSHEETS/ACTIVITIES/PRINTABLES/RESOURCES:

Abcteach: An online resource providing teachers and homeschoolers with worksheets, activities, and printables. (www.abcteach.com)

edHelper: An online resource providing worksheets, activities, and lesson plans for teachers and homeschoolers. (www.edhelper.com)

Education World: A comprehensive resource for educators, administrators, and parents. (www.educationworld.com)

Education.com: An online resource providing educational activities, worksheets, and games. (www.education.com)

Edutopia: A website dedicated to promoting innovative practices in K-12 education. (www.edutopia.org)

ERIC: A database of research and resources related to education. https://eric.ed.gov/

Homeschool Classroom: A website with homeschooling tips, resources, and activities. https://www.homeschoolclassroom.com/

Learning Page: A subscription-based service with printable worksheets and activities for homeschoolers. (www.learningpage.com)

Homeschool Helper Online: A website with resources and tools for homeschoolers. https://www.homeschoolhelperonline.com/

Scholastic Teachables: Printables and lesson plans for teaching every subject. https://www.teachables.scholastic.com/

Scholastic Teacher Express: An online resource providing lesson plans, activities, and professional development. (teacherexpress.scholastic.com)

SuperTeachers: An online resource providing lesson plans, worksheets, and activities for teachers. (www.superteachers.com)

Teach Hub: An online resource for teachers providing lesson plans, activities, and professional development. (www.teachhub.com)

Teachers Pay Teachers: An online marketplace for educators to buy and sell educational resources. (www.teacherspayteachers.com)

TeachersFirst: An online resource providing lesson plans and activities for teachers. (www.teachersfirst.com)

TeacherVision: An online resource for teachers providing lesson plans, activities, and professional development. (www.teachervision.com)

Teach-nology: A website with resources, worksheets, and lesson plans for homeschoolers. (www.teach-nology.com)

The Teacher's Corner: The Teacher's Corner is a website that provides resources and activities for teachers in grades K-12. It is a great resource for teachers to find lesson plans, worksheets, and student activities and games. (www.theteacherscorner.net)

CURRICULUM-BASED SITES:

Connections Academy: An online public school program for grades K -12. https://www.connectionsacademy.com/

Core Knowledge: A curriculum-based program that focuses on building knowledge in history, language arts, mathematics, science, and the arts. https://www.coreknowledge.org/

Coursera: A leading online learning platform offering courses from leading universities and companies. (www.coursera.org)

EasyPeasy: An open-source, free online curriculum for all grade levels. https://allinonehomeschool.com/

EdX: leading online learning platform offering courses from top universities worldwide. www.edx.org)

IXL: An online learning platform with math and language arts activities for PreK–12th grade. (www.ixl.com)

Khan Academy: Free online courses and resources for teaching various topics in math, science, history, and more. https://www.khanacademy.org/

Scratch: An educational programming language and online community where people can create interactive stories, games, and animations. (www.scratch.mit.edu)

Splashlearn: An online math and reading platform for PreK–5th grade with interactive activities and games. (www.splashlearn.com)

Starfall: An online interactive learning platform for PreK–2nd grade. (www.starfall.com)

Time4Learning: An online educational system with curriculum-based content for various grade levels. https://time4learning.com/

Rainbow Resource Center: Rainbow Resource Center offers a vast selection of homeschooling materials, including curriculum, books, educational games, and resources for various subjects and grade levels. (www.rainbowresource.com)

BookShark: BookShark provides literature-based homeschooling curriculum packages for a range of grade levels. Their materials include reading books, instructor guides, and hands-on resources. (www.bookshark.com)

Christianbook: provides a variety of homeschooling materials with a focus on Christian-based resources. They offer curriculum, textbooks, educational games, and supplementary materials. (www.christianbook.com)

SUBJECT BASED FOR INSTRUCTION SITES:

PBS LearningMedia : provided by the Public Broadcasting Service (PBS) in the United States. It offers various free digital resources for educators, students, and parents, including videos, lesson plans, interactive activities, and more, covering various subjects such as science, math, history, and the arts. (www.pbslearningmedia.org)

CuriosityStream: a subscription-based streaming platform that focuses on providing high-quality documentaries and non-fiction content. It offers a vast library of documentaries spanning multiple genres, including science, history, technology, nature, and more. CuriosityStream is designed to entertain and educate viewers through engaging and visually appealing documentaries. (www.curiositystream.com)

Art for Kids Hub: Art for Kids Hub is a website that provides art tutorials, activities, and resources for students in grades K-8. It is a great resource for teachers and parents to help kids explore art concepts. https://www.artforkidshub.com/

Bill Nye the Science Guy: a website that provides educational videos, activities, and experiments to help students in grades K-12 learn about science topics. It is a great resource for teachers and parents to help kids explore science. https://billnye.com/

Codecademy: Online educational platform offering programming and coding courses. (www.codecademy.com)

CommonLit: Online literacy platform featuring free reading activities, lessons, and assessments for grades 5-12 students. (www.commonlit.org)

Crayola: Crayola is a website that provides educational activities and resources for students in grades K-8. It is a great resource for teachers and parents to help kids explore geography and social studies topics. https://www.crayola.com/

DreamBox Learning: DreamBox Learning is an online math program for students in grades K-8. It provides interactive lessons and practice activities to help students develop a deep understanding of math concepts. https://www.dreambox.com/

Duolingo: Duolingo is a language-learning platform that provides interactive lessons to help students learn foreign languages. It is a great resource for teachers and parents to help kids learn languages. https://www.duolingo.com/

Geography for Kids: Geography for Kids is a website that provides activities, games, and lessons to help students in grades K-8 learn about geography and social studies topics. It is a great resource for teachers and parents to help kids explore the world. https://www.geography4kids.com/

Homeschool Math: A comprehensive math curriculum for grades K–12. https://www.homeschoolmath.net/

Homeschool Science Lab: Science lab kits and lessons for homeschoolers. https://homeschoolsciencelab.com/

International Children's Digital Library: International Children's Digital Library (ICDL) is a collection of digital books that can be accessed for free online. It contains books from around the world in a variety of languages. https://en.childrenslibrary.org/

Kid World Citizen: Kid World Citizen is a website that provides resources and activities to help students in grades K-8 learn about geography and social studies topics. It is a great resource for teachers and parents to help kids explore the world. https://kidworldcitizen.org/

Lynda.com: An online learning platform with business, technology, and creative skills courses. (www.lynda.com)

Math Mammoth: Math Mammoth is a website that provides math activities, worksheets, and games for grades K-12. It is a great resource for students to practice math and develop critical thinking skills. https://www.mathmammoth.com/

Math Blaster: An educational website with math games and activities for students in grades K–6 students. (www.mathblaster.com)

Math Game Time: Math Game Time is a website that offers math activities, games, and videos for students in grades K-6. It is a great resource for teachers and parents to help kids learn math concepts. https://www.mathgametime.com/

Math Goodies: Math Goodies is a website that provides activities, lessons, and games to help students in grades K-8 learn and practice math. It is a great resource for teachers and parents to help kids learn math concepts. https://www.mathgoodies.com/

Math Is Fun: Math Is Fun is a website that provides math activities, games, and lessons for grades K-12. It is a great resource for students to learn and practice math. https://www.mathsisfun.com/

Math Playground: An online math learning website with math games and activities for grades K–8. (www.mathplayground.com)

Mathwire: Mathwire is a website that provides resources and activities for teachers and students in grades K-12. It is a great resource for students to practice and improve their math skills. http://mathwire.com/

Mr. Nussbaum: Mr. Nussbaum is a website that provides educational resources, activities, and games to help students in grades K-8 learn about geography and social studies topics. It is a great resource for teachers and parents to help kids explore the world. https://mrnussbaum.com/

Music Tech Teacher: Music Tech Teacher is a website that provides resources and activities to help students in grades K-12 learn about music. It is a great resource for teachers and parents to help kids explore music concepts. http://www.musictechteacher.com/

National Council for Social Studies: The National Council for Social Studies website provides resources and activities to help students in grades K-12 learn about geography and social studies topics. It is a great resource for teachers and parents to help kids explore the world. https://www.socialstudies.org/

National Geographic Kids: National Geographic Kids is a website that provides educational resources and activities to help students in grades K-8 learn about science topics. It is a great resource for teachers and parents to help kids explore science. https://kids.nationalgeographic.com/

National Science Digital Library: A nonprofit organization providing access to digital resources in science, technology, engineering, and mathematics. (www.nsdl.org)

PBS LearningMedia: PBS LearningMedia is a website that provides educational videos and activities for students in grades K-12. It is a great resource for teachers and parents to help kids learn about geography and social studies topics. https://www.pbslearningmedia.org/

Reading A-Z: An online PreK–6th-grade reading platform with leveled eBooks and activities. (www.readinga-z.com)

Reading Eggs: An online reading program designed to help children ages 3–13 learn to read. (www.readingeggs.com)

Reading Rockets: Reading Rockets is a website dedicated to helping students in grades K-8 become better readers. It provides activities, articles, and resources designed to help students develop literacy skills, such as comprehension, fluency, and vocabulary. https://www.readingrockets.org/

Science4Us: Science4Us is an online science program for students in grades K-5. It provides interactive lessons and activities to help students understand science topics. https://www.science4us.com/

Science Bob: Science Bob is a website that provides science activities, experiments, and games for students in grades K-12. It is a great resource for teachers and parents to help kids learn and explore science topics. https://sciencebob.com/

Science Buddies: Science Buddies is a website that provides resources to help students in grades K-12 learn and explore science topics. It is a great resource for teachers and parents to help kids develop scientific literacy. https://www.sciencebuddies.org/

Science Kids: Science Kids is a website that provides science activities, experiments, and games for students in grades K-8. It is a great resource for teachers and parents to help kids learn and explore science topics. https://www.sciencekids.co.nz/

Science News for Students: Science News for Students is a website that provides educational articles and activities to help grades K-12 learn about science topics. It is a great resource for teachers and parents to help kids explore science. https://www.sciencenewsforstudents.org/

Sheppard Software: Sheppard Software is a website that provides educational games and activities to help students in grades K-12 learn about geography and social studies topics. It is a great resource for teachers and parents to help kids explore the world. https://www.sheppardsoftware.com/

Smithsonian Education: Smithsonian Education is a website that provides educational resources, activities, and games for students in grades K-12. It is a great resource for teachers and parents to help kids learn about science topics. **https://**education.si.edu/

Scholastic: Scholastic is an educational media and publishing company that offers reading and literature resources for schools. It is a great resource for teachers, providing educational materials and activities for students in preschool through high school students. https://www.scholastic.com/

Social Studies for Kids: Social Studies for Kids is a website that provides activities, games, and lessons for students in grades K-12. It is a great resource for teachers and parents to help kids learn about geography and social studies topics. http://www.socialstudiesforkids.com/

Storyline Online: Storyline Online is a website that streams videos featuring actors reading popular children's books. It is a fantastic way to encourage children to read and to provide a fun and interactive way to explore stories. https://www.storylineonline.net/

ThinkQuest: ThinkQuest is a website that provides educational resources, activities, and games to help students in grades K-12 learn science topics. It is a great resource for teachers and parents to help kids learn science. https://www.thinkquest.org/

Typing.com: Typing.com is an online typing program that provides lessons and activities to help students learn how to type. It is a great resource for teachers and parents to help kids develop typing skills. https://www.typing.com/

Typing Club: Typing Club is an online typing program that provides lessons and activities to help students learn how to type. It is a great resource for teachers and parents to help kids develop typing skills. https://www.typingclub.com/

World Atlas: World Atlas is a website that provides maps and resources to help students in grades K-12 learn about geography and social studies topics. It is a great resource for teachers and parents to help kids explore the world. https://www.worldatlas.com/

Crack the Cursive Code | Learn Cursive Writing: is a website designed to provide you with a systematic way to teach your child how to write in cursive. https://www.crackthecursivecode.com

SUPPORT SITES:

American Homeschool Association: Non-profit organization providing resources, support, and advocacy for homeschooling. https://www.ahaparenting.com/

American Homeschoolers Association: Non-profit organization offering homeschoolers support, community, and resources. https://www.ahamembers.org/

Association of Christian Schools International: Global organization provides resources, support, and accreditation for Christian schools. https://www.acsi.org/

Home Education Magazine: A magazine with articles, tips, and resources about homeschooling. https://www.homeedmag.com/

Home Education Research and Resources: A database of research and resources related to homeschooling. https://www.homeeducationresources.org/

Home School Education Network: Resources and support for homeschoolers. https://www.homeschoolnetwork.org/

Home School Enrichment Magazine: A magazine that offers resources, articles, and tips for homeschooling families. https://www.homeschoolenrichment.com/

Home School Foundation: https://homeschoolfoundation.org/

Home School Legal Defense Association: A nonprofit organization that advocates for homeschoolers' rights. https://hslda.org/

Home Schooling Research Review: A database of research and reviews on homeschooling. https://www.homeschoolingresearchreview.com/

Home Schooling Research: A website with research and resources on the effects of homeschooling on students. https://www.homeschoolingresearch.com/

Home Schooling Resources: A list of national organizations for homeschooling parents in the US. https://www.homeschoolingresources.org/

Homeschool Buyers Co-op: A co-op offering discounts and special offers on homeschooling materials. https://www.homeschoolbuyersco-op.org/

Homeschool Curriculum Reviews: Reviews of the best homeschool curriculum and resources. https://www.homeschoolcurriculumreviews.com/

Homeschool Degrees: A website that offers resources and advice on college admissions for homeschoolers. https://www.homeschooldegrees.com/

Homeschool Research: A website with research and studies related to homeschooling. https://www.homeschoolresearch.com/

Homeschool Tracker: An online homeschool planner and recordkeeping system. https://homeschooltracker.com/

Homeschool World: A website with resources and articles for homeschoolers. https://www.homeschoolworld.com/

Homeschool.com: A comprehensive website with resources and support for homeschooling families. https://www.homeschool.com/

Homeschooling 101: An online course to help new homeschoolers get started. https://www.homeschooling-101.com/

Homeschooling Magazine: An online magazine with articles and resources for homeschoolers. https://www.homeschoolingmagazine.com/

Homeschooling Trends: A website with research and articles about the current trends in homeschooling. https://www.homeschooling-trends.com

International Network of Home Education (INHE): List research websites that homeschooling parents would find useful https://www.inhe.org/

National Catholic Education Association (NCEA): An organization dedicated to promoting excellence in Catholic education. https://ncea.org/

National Center for Education Statistics (NCES): A federal agency that collects and reports U.S. education data (https://nces.ed.gov/).

National Coalition for Home Education (NCHE): An organization dedicated to promoting homeschooling rights and providing resources to homeschooling families (https://nche.com/).

National Home Education Network: A comprehensive information, support, and advocacy resource for homeschooling. https://www.nhen.org/

National Home Education Research Institute (NHERI): A research organization dedicated to studying home education. https://www.nheri.org/

National Home School Association (NHSA): An organization dedicated to promoting homeschooling and providing resources and support to homeschooling families (https://www.nhsa.org/).

National Private Schools Accreditation Alliance: An organization dedicated to accrediting independent and private schools in the United States. https://www.npsaa.org/

PR Homeschoolers: A resource for parents homeschooling special needs children. A resource for parents who are homeschooling special needs children. (www.prhomeschoolers.com)

ProTeacher Community: An online community for teachers providing resources and support. (www.proteacher.com)

The Home School Foundation: A nonprofit organization that provides grants for homeschoolers in need. (https://www.homeschoolfoundation.org/)

The Home School Legal Defense Association (HSLDA): A nonprofit organization that provides legal support and resources for homeschoolers. (https://hslda.org/)

The HomeScholar: A membership-based site dedicated to helping homeschool parents get organized and plan for college. https://thehomescholar.com/

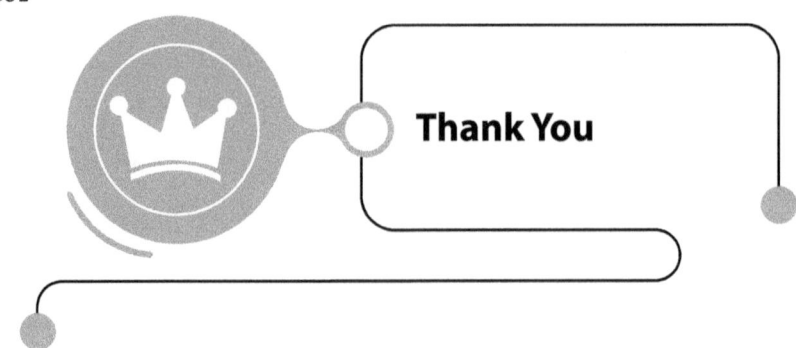

Thank You

As I stand on the cusp of the launch of *Learning Outside the Line,* I find myself overwhelmed with gratitude for the incredible journey that led me to this moment. This book is not just a collection of words on pages; it's the culmination of my life's work and my passion for children's education.

When I reflect on my background, the decision to become a homeschool consultant, and the journey that brought this book to life, I am filled with a profound sense of purpose. It's a journey that wouldn't have been possible without the support and guidance of some remarkable individuals.

I want to thank Serena Brown-Travis for lending her wisdom and eloquence to this book by writing the foreword. Your contribution has added depth and credibility to *Learning Outside the Line.*

I am immensely grateful to Lady JB Owen for being my guiding light throughout this endeavor. Your unwavering support, wisdom, and expertise have transformed this book from mere chapters into the masterpiece it is today. *Learning Outside the Line* is a testament to your mentorship, and I am proud to have worked alongside you.

To the parents who choose to embark on this homeschooling journey with *Learning Outside the Line* in hand, I thank you. Your trust in my forty-two years of expertise and experience is deeply appreciated. I sincerely hope this book will open new horizons for you and your children, fostering a love for learning beyond the conventional classroom.

As I pen these words of thanks, I am reminded that no endeavor is accomplished in isolation. *Learning Outside the Line* is a collective effort, a labor of love that would not have been possible without the support, guidance, and expertise of each person mentioned here and countless others who have touched my life along the way.

Behind the scenes, a dedicated team of editors and production professionals at Ignite Publishing worked tirelessly to bring this book to fruition. Your attention to detail and commitment to excellence shines through every page, and I am grateful for your hard work. A special thank you goes to Ignite Publishing Co-Founder Peter Giesin, Lead Editor Mimi Safiyah, Proofreader Zoe Wong, Typesetter Kristine Magno, Graphic Designer Katie Smetherman, and Chief Administrator Carolina Gold.

As *Learning Outside the Line* finds its way into the hands of eager parents and educators, I can't help but feel a sense of pride and accomplishment. This book represents not just my journey but also the journeys of all those who have been a part of it and those who will benefit from it in years to come.

Thank you for being a part of this incredible adventure. May *Learning Outside the Line* inspire a new generation of homeschoolers and ignite a love for learning that knows no bounds.

With heartfelt gratitude,
Melanie Summers

Author Bio

Melanie Summers is a Homeschool Coach and Consultant with over forty years of experience as an educator. Her love for educating children is a lifelong passion. After a career that took her across four states as a teacher, lead teacher, and Inclusion specialist, Melanie retired in 2017 and founded *Innovative Homeschool Solutions*. Her company brings together Melanie's extensive knowledge of homeschooling, alternative learning, and curriculum development, offering services that teach parents how to teach their children.

Melanie holds a Masters in Curriculum and Instruction and was part of her RESA's team that developed guidelines and strategies for including special needs students in the classroom. She then went on to train other teachers on how to use these guidelines.

Since retiring, Melanie has found incredible success beyond her career as an educator. She is a two-time internationally bestselling author for her chapters in *Ignite Your Wisdom and Ignite Forgiveness*. Melanie is also a certified Health and Wellness Coach through the *American Sports and Fitness Association* and coaches others on how to implement a healthy lifestyle. Through her extensive dedication to Natural remedies and alternative health care she and her husband have lost 180 pounds collectively.

Outside of Melanie's decades of educational excellence, she is the mother of three children, her sons Ryan and Chad, and her stepdaughter, Brandi. She also is a proud grandmother to five grandchildren. She lives in Mesa, Arizona, with her husband, Rick, two cats, Bugsie and Mickey, and her pup, Ollie.